The Soviet Union and Disarmament

PRAEGER SPECIAL STUDIES IN
INTERNATIONAL POLITICS AND ADMINISTRATION

The Soviet Union and Disarmament

AN APPRAISAL OF SOVIET ATTITUDES AND INTENTIONS

by

ALEXANDER DALLIN and others

Published for the

School of International Affairs
Columbia University
by

FREDERICK A. PRAEGER, Publishers
New York · Washington · London

THE PURPOSE of the Praeger Special Studies is to make specialized research monographs in international economics and politics available to the academic, business, and government communities. For further information, write to the Special Projects Division, Frederick A. Praeger, Publishers, 111 Fourth Avenue, New York, N.Y. 10003.

This Report was prepared under contract with the United States Arms Control and Disarmament Agency. The judgments are those of the authors and do not necessarily reflect the views of the United States Arms Control and Disarmament Agency or any other department or agency of the United States Government, or of Columbia University.

FREDERICK A. PRAEGER, *Publishers*
111 Fourth Avenue, New York 3, N.Y., U.S.A.
77-79 Charlotte Street, London W.1, England

Published in the United States of America in 1964
for the School of International Affairs, Columbia University
by Frederick A. Praeger, Inc., Publishers

PREFACE

In the spring of 1963, the United States Arms Control and Disarmament Agency (ACDA) invited a group of scholars to undertake a study of Soviet attitudes toward arms control and disarmament. The importance of the subject, it was apparent to us, was matched by the striking absence of authoritative studies or indeed of specialists prepared to deal with the many facets of the disarmament conundrum.

As a result of this approach, a Study of Soviet Attitudes Toward Arms Control and Disarmament was initiated at Columbia University. A contract with ACDA made possible the organization of a summer seminar, which in turn was to provide the basis for a report to ACDA on those "basic factors ... which are of the greatest relevance to an understanding of Soviet attitudes toward arms control and disarmament." The two-week seminar, held on July 8-20, 1963, at Airlie House, Warrenton, Virginia, amounted to an intensive immersion of a group of leading specialists from the United States and from abroad into a wide pool of problems, ranging from "kremlinology" to future trends in weapons systems. A smaller group met for a weekend session at Arden House, Harriman, New York, on November 22-24, 1963, to give further consideration to some of the key problems discussed. Both before and after each meeting, the staff engaged in the preparation of reports and compilations in support of the Study.

The meetings soon confirmed the belief that there were indeed very few experts fully conversant with Soviet affairs and with the intricacies of the "arms-control" field.[1] Thus, one immediate and by no means negligible effect of the summer seminar was the exposure of a group of specialists in Soviet studies to some of the best thinking in the United States on arms and arms control. In return, military and disarmament experts attending the meetings found themselves exposed to a consideration of the special problems pertaining to the study of Soviet developments. Both groups indicated, then and later, an aware-

i

ness of the beneficial effects of this learning process for their own understanding of these complex fields.

By the same token, the "sovietologists" have been obliged to rely on experts in other fields for judgments or opinions on matters beyond their ken—for instance, on the balance of strategic capabilities among the major powers, the likelihood of a unilateral breakthrough in military technology in the next decade, or the gravity of security implications if the U.S.S.R. were to violate a given international arms-control agreement.

This point is made here not to divest the group of responsibility for its findings but to indicate the highly fragmented character of the expert community and to underscore the need to encourage the training of at least a small number of top specialists capable of scanning and understanding the entire horizon of the sciences and social sciences.

This Study touches only briefly on some of the problems as this group sees them. Much remains unsaid and unexplored. Moreover, a great deal in the actual conduct of policy turns out to be contingent and unforeseen. There is, therefore, in this Report little detailed examination of individual steps and measures, regarding which policy decisions may indeed be unpredictable. But reference to the contingent and unknown is not intended as an excuse for the failure of this volume to chart the future. This, it neither can nor is expected to do. It does try to suggest ways of approaching the problem and to outline some elements in the Soviet consideration of it which may be helpful in an assessment of Soviet intentions and techniques, and thereby perhaps in the reconsideration of American policy.

The following roster lists all participants and guests at our meetings.* It is a proud pleasure to be able to express our genuine gratitude to this group for its splendid contribution, which often led to animated discussions until well into the night, and to the pursuit of new insight and truth at the sacrifice of rest and leisure.

PRINCIPAL PARTICIPANTS

*Professor Raymond A. Bauer
Graduate School of Business
    Administration
Harvard University

Mr. Seweryn Bialer
Russian Institute
Columbia University

Dr. Walter C. Clemens, Jr.
Center for International Studies
Massachusetts Institute of
    Technology

*Professor Alexander Dallin
Russian Institute
Columbia University

*Dr. Herbert S. Dinerstein
The RAND Corporation
Santa Monica, California

*Mr. Peter C. Dobell
Canadian Mission to the
    United Nations

*Professor George Fischer
Department of Government
Cornell University

Mr. Max Frankel
The New York Times
Washington Bureau

Mr. Franklyn J. C. Griffiths
Center for International
    Studies
Massachusetts Institute of
    Technology

Professor Gregory Grossman
Department of Economics
University of California, Berkeley

Professor Andrew Gyorgy
Department of Political Science
Boston University

Mr. Wolfgang Leonhard
Russian Institute
Columbia University

*Mr. J. Malcolm Mackintosh
Institute for Strategic Studies
London, England

*Mr. Constantine Menges
Institute of War and Peace Studies
Columbia University

Professor Alfred G. Meyer
Department of Political Science
Michigan State University

Professor Alec Nove
Department of International
    Economic Studies
University of Glasgow

*Professor Marshall D. Shulman
Fletcher School of Law and
    Diplomacy
Tufts University

*Professor Robert C. Tucker
Department of Politics
Princeton University

*All the participants listed in this roster attended the Airlie House
meeting. Those whose name is preceded by an asterisk also attended
the follow-up Arden House conference.

Bryant Wedge, M.D.
Institute for the Study of
   National Behavior
Princeton, New Jersey

Mr. Christopher Wright
Council for Atomic Age Studies
Columbia University

*Dr. Thomas W. Wolfe
The RAND Corporation
Washington, D.C.

INTERIM PARTICIPANTS

Dr. Donald G. Brennan
Hudson Institute
Harmon, New York

Professor Amitai Etzioni
Department of Sociology
Columbia University

Professor Paul M. Doty
Department of Chemistry
Harvard University

Professor Ithiel de Sola Pool
Department of Social Science
Massachusetts Institute of
   Technology

GUESTS

Mr. Paul K. Cook
Department of State

Dr. George W. Rathjens
U.S. Arms Control and
   Disarmament Agency

Dr. Raymond L. Garthoff
Department of State

Mr. Vincent P. Rock
Institute for Defense Analyses

Mr. Robert E. Matteson
U.S. Arms Control and
   Disarmament Agency

Mr. Helmut Sonnenfeldt
Department of State

Professor Matthew Meselson
Department of Biology
Harvard University

Ambassador Charles C. Stelle
Department of State

Mr. John T. Whitman
Washington, D.C.

Colonel Kent K. Parrot
U.S. Arms Control and
   Disarmament Agency

This Report makes extensive use of the working papers drafted at the close of the Airlie House meetings by the various subcommittees to which all participants were assigned. We are indebted to Professor George Fischer for his painstaking efforts in assembling and editing, with refreshing good sense, the various conference materials and reports, which proved to be extremely useful in the preparation of this Report, and in eliciting comments from participants and observers. In addition, the chairman had the privilege of having the advice of an informal committee consisting of Herbert S. Dinerstein, George Fischer, and Marshall D. Shulman.

The Report itself also benefited and, in varying degrees, borrowed from contributions by Herbert S. Dinerstein, J. Malcolm Mackintosh, Constantine Menges, and Thomas W. Wolfe, particularly to the chapters on military affairs and arms-control policy. Professor Shulman made a central "input" by authoring a paper on which much of the discussion at Arden House centered, stimulating the staff to explore additional avenues, generously offering the chairman his wise counsel, and providing drafts for parts of several chapters of this Report. Grey Hodnett supplied very helpful drafts, marked by thoughtfulness and precision, for two other sections. The undersigned was compelled to produce the present Report, using what he could and adding what he must, and profiting greatly from comments received from his colleagues on the basis of an earlier draft. Thanks are due, in particular, to Gregory Grossman and Helmut Sonnenfeldt for their valuable comments and their help in rescuing the chairman from multiple errors.

By its very nature, then, this volume represents the views of no single person. The judgments expressed are those of the participants and authors, and do not necessarily reflect the views of the United States Arms Control and Disarmament Agency, or any other department or agency of the United States Government, or of Columbia University. The deliberations inevitably, and healthily, revealed some significant disagreements among the participants. In fact, it is perhaps surprising that there was not a greater measure of fundamental dissent. While a single manuscript cannot reflect the views of each participant on every issue, we have striven to take account responsibly of the diversity of views and, where appropriate, to indicate (primarily in footnotes) the significant differences as they became apparent from remarks made during the conferences or from comments received afterwards.

The chairman of the Study had the benefit of an excellent and devoted staff. Harris L. Coulter served as executive officer from May through July, 1963. Constantine Menges was a dedicated and stimulating staff associate for the same period. For the transcripts of the conference sessions themselves, the Study is indebted to the conscientious and informed services of the rapporteurs, Grey Hodnett, Thomas P. Raynor, and William Zimmerman IV. Knowledgeable research in support of the project was conducted by James E. Morrison and Julie B. Martin. Miss Martin contributed in a variety of ways to all phases of the Study, including the compilation and analysis of materials on which the Appendix is based. We would also like to express our gratitude to Elizabeth A. Pond for her wise comments and expert substantive and stylistic help, and to Nora B. Beeson for editorial assistance. Theodore Dutko kindly permitted us to use some information contained in an unpublished seminar paper on the political role of the Soviet military.

We gratefully acknowledge permission of The RAND Corporation, of Santa Monica, California, to cite several passages from research memoranda produced by its staff. Similarly we appreciate permission to use excerpts from translations which originally appeared in The Current Digest of the Soviet Press, published weekly at Columbia University by the Joint Committee on Slavic Studies, appointed by the American Council of Learned Societies and the Social Science Research Council.

These prefatory comments would be strikingly incomplete if they failed to single out Constance A. Bezer, Administrative Assistant of the Study. Without her skillful and dedicated help this Report would scarcely have been produced; indeed, the conferences themselves would not have come about nor business transacted, without her attending to innumerable matters, large and small, with cheer and dispatch. Finally, it is a pleasure to acknowledge with real appreciation the expert and understanding assistance of the liaison officers from ACDA, Robert E. Matteson and Kent K. Parrot.

It should be added that the general approach and argument presented below were formulated, for the most part, in the summer of 1963. The intervening year has clarified rather than confused the outlook, though not so much as one would have wished. If some notions tentatively put forth a year ago have meanwhile become commonplaces, it is hoped that this Study has also been strengthened by recent evidence and perspectives.

Alexander Dallin
Chairman, Study of Soviet Attitudes Toward
Arms Control and Disarmament, Columbia University

August, 1964

POSTSCRIPT

This volume was already completed and set when word came of the ouster of Nikita Khrushchev and the first nuclear explosion in China. I have chosen not to make any last minute attempt to take cognizance of these events in the body of the Report. Their full impact, generally on world affairs and specifically in the arms-control and disarmament field, may not become clear for some time. Meanwhile I believe the Report still retains its relevance. The Chinese events were, after all, anticipated for some time. And the change in Soviet leadership in no sense alters the basic options and constraints, the general outlook and the experience of the Soviet authorities.

A.D.

October, 1964

TABLE OF CONTENTS

Part III — THE OUTLOOK

Part I

THE PROBLEM

Chapter 1

ASSUMPTIONS AND CONCLUSIONS

What is the attitude of the Soviet leadership toward disarmament? In 1957, when the U.S. Senate Subcommittee on Disarmament solicited statements on this question, a number of American scholars and observers either refused to commit themselves or else failed to see solid grounds for crediting the Soviet Union with honorable intentions in this field. While today a consensus would be harder to reach, there has meanwhile taken place a significant "qualitative" change in the assessment of the Soviet scene—a change frankly recognized by most participants of the conferences which provided the foundation for the present Report.[1]

This awareness of change and a concomitant sense of modest hopefulness were present even before the nuclear test-ban treaty was negotiated and before the Sino-Soviet conflict reached a new peak of intensity in the summer of 1963. The cautious optimism reflected in these pages stems not from the past Soviet record on disarmament but rather from our assessment of present trends and prospects in Soviet politics and society as a whole. At the same time, the dominant mood of our meetings and deliberations was one of tentativeness, both because of the changes going on inside the Soviet Union, and because of the difficulties of interpreting them.

APPROACHES AND ASSUMPTIONS

The pronounced fluidity and ambiguity present in the Soviet scene recommends an open-ended perspective for the years ahead—a prospect rather unfamiliar to veteran students of Soviet affairs. Perhaps the most striking feature of our meetings was the extent to which specialists on the Soviet Union agreed that all static conceptions of the Soviet system, ideology, and policies are inadequate.

The balance between elements of change and continuity requires constant re-examination of the information at our disposal. To weigh the continuing changes in the Soviet situation—real and apparent, deliberate and unintended, lasting and

3

transient—the observer must reach judgments based on uncertain data and frequently contradictory impressions.

In addition to registering the contradictory nature of the evidence on Soviet disarmament policies and the conflicting stresses in Soviet politics and society, we must try to strike a new balance in our perception of the Soviet position. We must recognize the significance of changes in Soviet outlook and attitude, but also the limits of these changes. We must acknowledge the continued gravity of the Soviet challenge, but also be aware of the real easing of grievances and tensions in recent years.

What has already been said reflects the conviction that, in order to understand Soviet attitudes on disarmament or on other issues, it is imperative to look at a broader context, ask general questions, avoid hard-and-fast answers and oversimplifications. It is not helpful, for instance, to inquire in blanket fashion whether "the Soviets really want disarmament" or whether they "can be trusted to keep any treaty." It is more realistic to ask such questions in terms of alternatives, priorities, benefits, costs, and risks. Thus, one may fruitfully inquire at what price or under what conditions Soviet leaders are interested in a given arms-control agreement. A treaty once refused may, in a package or in another setting, become negotiable. The same arrangement may be rejected in 1961 but be accepted in 1963.

It is futile, moreover, to expect clear-cut or consistent Soviet positions at all times. Despite the general continuity of the Bolshevik outlook, there are issues—and disarmament is manifestly one of them—over which uncertainty and serious disagreements have existed within the leadership itself. Indeed, one reason for the inability of our conferences to come up with an integrated schema that would account for all, or even most, of the known evidence regarding Soviet attitudes on disarmament, may be precisely the fact that different and unreconciled approaches in the U.S.S.R. continue to exist. The crux of the matter, it would seem, is the fact that—depending on one's interpretation—the body of ideological doctrine makes it possible to present an entirely defensible "Marxist-Leninist" argument on behalf of any one of several disparate approaches to arms control and disarmament. Four such, easily identifiable, positions are:

1. The view that disarmament is a good issue to advocate

but an impossible one to reach hard-and-fast agreements on, given the ultimate irreconcilability of the Communist and non-Communist worlds.

2. The view that in the thermonuclear age a minimum of arms-control and disarmament agreements, especially with regard to war prevention and perhaps non-proliferation of weapons, is an essential prerequisite for survival.

3. The view that an emerging but limited community of interests among the powers makes possible the negotiation of certain arms-control and disarmament agreements which are of distinct and probably asymmetrical benefit to the Soviet Union and its allies.

4. The view that, regardless of the prospects of its realization, substantial moves in the direction of and including general and complete disarmament (GCD) would ultimately redound to the benefit of the Socialist camp.

While these major positions may resemble familiar American postures, it should be said from the outset that the assumptions and syllogisms leading to the Soviet choices may differ drastically from their American equivalents.

The complex of arms control must not be narrowly considered in isolation from other facets of a nation's (or the world's) search for security.[2] A state may seek to enhance its security by a variety of means—including armaments, alliances, and disarmament. Arms control, then, describes only one of several types of moves which may be adopted in the pursuit of greater security. The integral relationship of arms-control policies and over-all military and political policies should be self-evident.

If we seek to understand how Soviet policy-makers assess arms restraints and limitations it is important to remind ourselves that they, too, view the problem not as a technical question but as a political matter with certain technical aspects and overtones. Ultimately, Soviet decisions require political choices, whatever the weight of military and scientific considerations. There is, in other words, no independent Soviet arms-control policy, but only what in the U.S. would be called the arms-control component of national policy—an organic part of Soviet world policy.

It has become a commonplace in Western thinking about war and disarmament that in the nuclear age there is not and cannot be any absolute security. International security is

...a state of affairs in which the inhibitions and disin-
centives to making war are stronger than the incentives
and operate with equal force on all important parties to the
manifold disputes which conflicting ambitions and ideologies
create between nation states. More than that, it is a state
of affairs in which the alternatives to a forceful solution
to any conflict are as numerous, as sparing of national
pride, as readily available as human wit can devise,
whether they be political, diplomatic, or judicial.... The
collapse of any concept of victory in a great-power war has
stimulated our interest in the security of our adversaries
as well as in our own.[3]

American and British thought on this challenge has advanced
in recent years to a far more "possibilist" position than heretofore and to ingenious assessments of odds since no foolproof solution, no certainty, is to be had. Soviet writing and,
it appears, thinking have not explicitly recognized this type of
approach, which—like any variant of an uncertainty principle—
flies in the face of orthodox Leninist axioms. In fact, however,
Soviet decision-makers have resorted to quite similar modes of
reasoning both in the military and in the political realms. Thus,
the Soviet position on the adequacy of a given number of permissible inspections implies the acceptance, at least "in
principle," of sampling and probability.

While at one time the Soviet approach to the entire field of
arms control (a term still vigorously rejected by the U.S.S.R.)
was woefully primitive, most Western observers at present
detect a considerable increment in Soviet sophistication and
flexibility. At any rate, genuine failure or inability to understand the argumentation of Western specialists is not a major
stumbling-block in negotiations if a disposition to seek reasonable agreement exists on other grounds. The speed and ease
with which it was possible to agree to outlaw weapons in outer
space is a case in point. Indeed, Soviet specialists may privately agree with the formula that "the risks one is willing to
assume in the direction of disarmament are a direct function
of the risks one believes to be inherent in the race for armament supremacy."[4]

Much of the thought devoted to the reduction of the danger
of thermonuclear war has ended in frustration because it has
failed to recognize the depth of the conflict of purposes between
the Soviet and American systems. Abstract models, universal

formulae, and theoretical solutions—however clever—are of little use if they are based only on "hardware," on numbers of weapons, on reaction time or capabilities, but ignore the intentions, objectives, and perceptions of one or the other set of leaders. At the other extreme, a preoccupation with the conflict—the Cold War—has tended to intensify the spiral of insecurity and suspicion which seems to be generated by modern arms technology.

To move beyond the simple polarities of "toughness" and "softness," of "Cold War" and "peaceful coexistence," requires fresh habits of thought and, as part of them, a fresh look at Soviet attitudes as well as at the whole complex of arms control. Indeed, a widespread predisposition to seek a new approach is indicated in the quest for solutions permitting one to emerge neither "red" nor "dead." Such a new outlook means, first of all, a recognition of the changing circumstances before us. It means, further, running the risk of being misunderstood by those who have grown to feel at home amidst the simple extremes. The present situation is not one in which the international conflict exists merely "in the mind" or is fed only, or primarily, by our characterization of it. Nor, on the other hand, is it the case that any optimism about changes in Soviet attitudes or behavior permits a weakening of our resistance to Communism. Moscow, too, insists on the ideological incompatibility of the "two world systems." Yet, even while taking continued enmity for granted—whatever its scope or intensity, its source or its expression—one may and one must search for areas of common, coincident, or parallel interest, beginning with the recognition of the catastrophically destructive nature of thermonuclear war and the shared commitment to avoid it.

To identify such areas of coincident interests, and to negotiate agreements intended to cement or augment them, must not be considered a sign of "softness" toward Communism or toward the Soviet Union. It must be viewed instead as an index of growing sophistication in the search for measures which are realistic and valuable, despite their limited scope.

Any attempt to explain Soviet behavior in the field of arms control and disarmament—marked as it is by such perplexing contrasts between verbal claims and actual performance— must take account of different levels of analysis and, one may assume, a variety of purposes which disarmament gestures and postures are intended to serve. No doubt, many relevant facts remain unknown to the foreign observer. We are nonetheless persuaded that much of Soviet policy in this field can be interpreted as a composite of several strata of different objectives and strategic and tactical lines. A systematic review of the record of shifting Soviet policy over the years, explained in terms of several such variables, remains to be attempted. It is well worth making, but it cannot be made here. Suffice it to suggest that different Soviet moves in the arms-control field may well pursue different purposes, and one challenge to the outsider consists precisely in identifying each of the major layers of motives and attitudes: the underlying, long-range assessment; the estimate of a given strategic phase; a specific proposal made only for purposes of negotiation, or propaganda, or in the pursuit of unilateral military advantage.

Most observers seem agreed that, until 1954-55, the basic Soviet motivation with regard to any arms-control or disarmament proposals cannot be considered to have been "sincere." Some Soviet statements have, in fact, recognized that until at least 1953 Moscow did not believe disarmament to be possible or desirable for the U.S.S.R.[5] Probably a fundamental change in outlook did occur. It was first adumbrated in the Soviet proposals of September 30, 1954—at the very time when the Khrushchev group had successfully challenged the incumbents and begun to assert itself on other foreign-policy issues (such as relations with Communist China and Yugoslavia) as well. The reorientation is more strikingly identified with the Soviet disarmament proposals of May 10, 1955; circumstantial evidence regarding other Soviet moves in foreign affairs in the same period again provides a plausible context of significant political reappraisals and new departures in the first months of the Bulganin-Khrushchev regime.

Since 1960 Soviet documents of relatively high esoteric sanctity, such as the new Communist Party of the Soviet Union (CPSU) Program, have in their references to disarmament provided evidence of Soviet "seriousness of purpose." So have the Soviet-Albanian and Soviet-Chinese exchanges, including those not intended for outside eyes and ears.[6]

To recognize this earnest interest is not to say just what priority disarmament holds, nor what, in the view of the Soviet leaders, possible forms, costs, conditions, or timing might be. There exist also formidable impediments to the conclusion and implementation of meaningful agreements on disarmament. In the past, they have included such ideological restraints as a permanent commitment to change in accordance with the Communist image of the future, a suspicion of all agreements with "hostile" and "alien" forces, the time-honored Soviet proclivity to use military force for political gains, and the concept of the "objective" difficulties of arms-control and disarmament deals.

In the minds of some Communists, difficulties persist in reconciling a genuine commitment to arms-control measures with a genuine commitment to Marxism-Leninism and all it implies. As was pointed out, the doctrine does in fact permit different and, in part, mutually incompatible approaches. Operationally, the difficulty is, of course, the impossibility of telling at any given time which of the attitudes toward arms control a given proposal expresses or a given individual has chosen to adopt. Neither public pronouncements nor the record of negotiations can, after all, be accepted as an adequate guide to Soviet intentions.

One may argue that the ups and downs in Soviet disarmament policy since 1955 are explicable only as the product of various (and conflicting) pressures and priorities. One might identify several separate lines of development in the following manner:

1. The phases of major international political effort in the disarmament field—1955, 1959-60, 1963-64—can be related to broader Soviet political endeavors in the direction of a détente with the West.

2. Changing Soviet views of the strategic balance and military opportunities dictated certain Soviet changes in disarmament policy—most demonstrably in 1957, on the eve of the successful Soviet launching of the first ICBM and the first sputnik; and probably in the aftermath of the Cuban crisis of October, 1962.

3. Given the interconnection of domestic, Bloc - wide, and foreign policies, a variety of domestic and Bloc problems have impinged on disarmament policy; suffice it to mention the general "de-Stalinization," the debates over resource allocation, the succession struggle, and the October, 1956, crisis in Eastern Europe.

4. Certain Soviet shifts in attitude may be explained as responses to American positions or behavior.

5. Soviet arms-control efforts have repeatedly been linked

with other proposals of a transient or predictably unacceptable nature—proposals whose rejection has led in turn to the
failure of the arms-control proposals. When this technique has
been used, it has, of course, revealed the relatively subordinate
place which the disarmament scheme has occupied on the
priority scale of Soviet negotiators.

6. Disarmament issues have often served the pursuit of
international political opportunities, such as the attempted
blocking of the European Defense Community, the formation
of NATO, and West German rearmament in earlier years;
the ending of détente probes in 1961 (with the breaking off of
test-ban negotiations); the dueling with China in recent years
(with the proposal on non-proliferation of nuclear weapons);
and opposition to the Multilateral Nuclear Force in 1963-64.

7. Undoubtedly some disarmament proposals have served,
at home and abroad, primarily as vehicles for propaganda in
the broadest sense of the term.

8. In at least a few instances, one may surmise, changes
of Soviet policy have been due to reconsideration in Moscow,
perhaps as a result of transferring a problem to a higher level
of decision-making or as a result of support secured from
additional individuals or organs in Moscow. An example of this
is probably the ill-fated "war propaganda" ban, which was
brought to the verge of agreement but suddenly withdrawn at
the last minute.

9. Some proposals have been made in the hope of "putting something over," i.e., securing a unilateral military or
political advantage if the other side accepts. Others have sought
a Western quid pro quo for Soviet troop reductions or other
measures already decided upon unilaterally as a matter of
military reorganization or economy.

10. Finally, some Soviet proposals are advanced purely as
a negotiating gambit—either without any expectation of reaching agreement, or else in the knowledge that the proposal will
have to be abandoned or significantly modified if agreement
is ever to result.

While the relative importance of these, and other, strands
has varied over the years and at times has defied analysis
altogether, only a combination of these can provide an adequate
explanation of the record of Soviet behavior and help us to
anticipate, albeit with humility and hesitation, Soviet behavior
in the years ahead.

SOME CONCLUSIONS: A SUMMARY

It is our conclusion, in essence, that as of 1964 continuing changes in the Soviet system have not yet significantly diminished the underlying causes of international conflict; nor have they removed the fundamental obstacles to substantial disarmament agreements. However, the effect of changes both in military technology and in various areas of Soviet life on the dominant Soviet outlook may make possible a more productive approach to reducing the chances of general war and perhaps the scope of war, should it come. Unlike the more distant goal of disarmament (in its traditional meaning), this approach would be based on the recognition that even adversary systems share a common interest in dampening down the danger of thermonuclear war, even while lower-scale military clashes and especially non-violent forms of political, ideological, and economic conflict persist.

The reasoning which leads to this conclusion rests in the first instance upon a re-evaluation of changes in Soviet policy, Soviet society, and Soviet system. The chapters which follow summarize the findings on these points.

On the domestic scene, one principal determinant of the shifting Soviet outlook has been the state of the economy.[7] Economic changes have not operated continuously in the same direction. In the years following the Twentieth Congress of the CPSU in 1956, the Soviet leadership evinced a mood of buoyant optimism based in large measure on the expectation that a rapidly-growing Soviet economy would provide one essential weight to help tip the world balance of power in Soviet favor, and thereby ultimately validate the entire policy of "peaceful co-existence."

Since about 1960, however, increased military expenditures, inadequacies in planning and administration, and low agricultural productivity have contributed to a darker mood of anxious preoccupation with economic shortcomings. These problems have promoted reorganizations within the Communist Party and state administration, and the planning machinery, and a substantial deflation of the mood of rising expectations.

When it looked abroad, the Soviet leadership similarly found the evidence for political gains strangely wanting. Its recognition that the prospects for an early relief from strategic inferiority were dim (barring some unlikely technological innovation or unexpected Western weakness), evidently induced two contradictory policy reactions—one, a search for short cuts to an improved power position, as in the Cuban adventure; the other, acceptance of restraint and détente, or at least an atmosphere of détente. Whether the latter policy is bound to endure, or whether domestic needs will lower the threshold of resistance to the acceptance of conditions necessary to implement arms-reduction programs, is still a matter of speculation. Some see economic pressures as an element contributing to restraints on the freedom of action of the Soviet leadership; others argue that the policy-makers are shifting their compass as a matter of choice, not necessity. At any rate, the U.S.S.R. may be expected to be increasingly disposed to give consideration to measures which will reduce the hazard of war without significantly jeopardizing Soviet political objectives.

Other domestic changes which may be relevant to arms-control policies—and perhaps to arms limitations specifically—might be attributed, most broadly, to the requirements of a complex developing society. In the experience of recent years, some limited "liberalization" and "rationalization" have been reflected, for instance, in the increasing use of positive incentives in the economy, intermittent experimentation with loosened controls over cultural and intellectual life, and increased contacts with the outside world.

In this realm it is particularly difficult to distinguish what is apparent from what is real, what is transient from what is irreversible. The increase of travel and cultural contacts with the non-Communist world, for example, might be thought to involve a diminution of secrecy and perhaps a change of attitude with regard to some forms of international inspection. But thus far the tight limits within which these contacts are allowed to operate do not afford much encouragement for the expectation that the Soviet Union is about to take a large step toward becoming an "open society."

In the changing relations between the U.S.S.R. and other Communist states, the collapse of the unitary Bloc has some bearing on the Soviet approach to arms control. The Soviet leadership has been increasingly preoccupied with the process of fragmentation within its camp, and the process itself imposes restraints on Soviet action. On the one hand, this appears to strengthen Soviet interest in moves intended to produce some relaxation of tensions with the United States. On the other hand, it is bound to increase concern about the centrifugal potential of autonomous Rumanian, Polish, and other contacts with the

non-Communist world. Whether the trend will stimulate or inhibit a more positive attitude toward regional arrangements
for the limitation of armaments is certainly far from clear. At
any rate, Soviet relations with other Communist Parties and
states are far from a stable equilibrium.

The open and vigorous Chinese challenge to Soviet leadership of the Communist world not only compounds Soviet difficulties in negotiating arms limitations; it also adds to the
restraints on Soviet freedom of action, and raises questions
regarding the fundamental orientation of Soviet political strategy
in relation to the West.

The exacerbation of the Sino-Soviet dispute has also obliged
the Soviet leadership to articulate and defend the fundamental
assumptions upon which its strategy of "peaceful coexistence"
is based. The Chinese Communists have not only explicitly
challenged Soviet disarmament "deals" with the West and, more
privately, expressed fear that Khrushchev is in earnest about
disarmament; they have also called into question the assumption that there can be any area of binding or lasting agreement
with the major Western non-Communist states. In turn, "peaceful coexistence," originally a temporary and fluctuating tactic,
has been evolving into the long-range strategy of a Soviet elite
increasingly preoccupied with international power and politics
rather than with social revolution. Since the Twentieth CPSU
Congress the "coexistence line" has been acquiring a theoretical underpinning from the reformulation of related doctrines,
such as the possibility of a peaceful transition to socialism
and the non-inevitability of war.

This process marks but another stage in the step-by-step
adaptation of the Soviet leadership to reality: to the radical
changes that have been taking place in the character of international politics since 1945; to the technological revolution
which has changed the nature of war and its anticipation; to
the seeming upsurge of national consciousness in countries
where "proletarian" bonds have proved to be weak or non-
existent; to the many strains and stresses within the U.S.S.R.
itself.

It would be naive to assume that the modest evolution taking
place must continue in a unilinear course. While one's response
to this question is bound to be largely intuitive, there is some
supporting evidence for the prevalent view that a return to
Stalinism, such as the Soviet Union knew it some fifteen years
ago, is now impossible. Yet in a modest way most of the recent

policies, both domestic and foreign, are reversible. They might be especially prone to be revoked under a new leadership—or indeed in the critical moments of a succession crisis. As the subsequent discussion will show, not all changes are equally relevant, of course, to Soviet disarmament policy.

Other trends of recent years are, by contrast, irreversible. These are the products of "objective" change. Social stratification, generational change, and the implications of weapons technology are but some of the obvious cases in point. Another, real but still hard to define, is the emergence of interest groups within the Soviet elite—potentially a most important development.

On the immediate political plane, of course, such mildly reassuring long-term perspectives are hardly of help. After all, the commitment of the Soviet leadership to the current foreign-policy line—including a modus vivendi with the United States and a variety of small-scale arms-control agreements, beginning with the "hot line" and the test-ban treaty of 1963— is still best characterized as tentative and tenuous. Especially under conditions of further Soviet setbacks—at home, in the Communist world, and in foreign affairs—pressures for a drastic change in policy might well increase. Yet the balance of considerations that made the present efforts seem preferable to all alternatives, is more likely than not to remain at least as persuasive as it originally was. By the same token, the relative weight of American and other foreign behavior in influencing Soviet action may be greater at such relatively fluid and uncertain times as the past year.

Although changes in Soviet policies result largely from forces over which the West has little control, they are also in part a Soviet reaction to Western policies. There has been a substantial amount of interaction between Soviet and American attitudes. The external condition which has most favored the evolution of Soviet policy in the direction of restraint has been a firm resistance to Soviet probes—as in Berlin and in Cuba—combined with demonstrated political and economic vitality on the part of the non-Communist world. Yet, at certain critical junctures Western flexibility, receptivity to Soviet proposals, or even unilateral gestures of good will seem to have been required to tip Soviet decisions one way rather than the other.

While the changes alluded to above may be of considerable importance in the future, they have not yet produced any significant reduction in Soviet reliance on secrecy or in the commitment to the eventual replacement of non-Communist regimes by ones which would be responsive to the U.S.S.R. The underlying causes of conflict do not yet appear to have been substantially modified; nor do those obstacles to major disarmament agreements which inhere in the Soviet system itself appear to have been "qualitatively" diminished.

One may take for granted Moscow's strong and continuing resistance to any effort to limit its freedom of choice or action, be it in the form of inspection or a veto-free international police force. The same determination to keep its hands untied—and to cultivate an image of untied hands, of acting from strength and not from weakness, whatever the truth of the situation—is likely to make the Soviet leadership opt for a tit-for-tat approach over more formal arms-control agreements. In a peculiar form of not-so-esoteric communication between Moscow and Washington, a series of unilateral moves—each reciprocated by the other side—has provided some assurance of voluntary compliance and immunity from "contamination" and "betrayal," while obviating the complications of treaty negotiation and ratification. There is, of course, a threshold beyond which "agreement by ping-pong" cannot be carried and a simultaneous bilaterally-binding commitment must be secured instead. It is likely that, in the judgment of Soviet policy-makers, this threshold is still quite far away. We, too, tend toward this view.

There is then some reason for hoping that the Soviet leadership can be increasingly brought to perceive a self-interest in some limited agreements regarding the arms race. The optimists among foreign observers can take some comfort in the fact that, since about the time of the Cuban crisis of 1962, Soviet journals have featured substantially more discussion of arms control, or rather, what the Russians call "partial measures" of disarmament. A growing number of Soviet specialists are demonstrating familiarity with Western arms-control literature and competence in its concepts. Indeed, Soviet leaders may at last come to share the view that their own interest recommends not "general and complete disarmament" but far more modest and attainable measures intended to introduce some stability and moderation into the military part of Soviet-American confrontation without requiring millenial changes in either system. Such measures would seem to be most feasible in the field of war prevention or arms restraints (where some of the obvious possibilities have already been exhausted).

They might be possible in the field of war control (though doctrinal and manipulative obstacles are substantially greater here). They would be more difficult to agree on, though prospects are not hopeless, in the remaining area of "partial measures," including a limited arms reduction and non-proliferation of nuclear weapons.

As both sides acquire a better grasp of alternatives and a better recognition of the consequences of their actions, the great confrontation may move into a new phase. At that stage the adversary powers may be prepared to introduce safeguards on military power and its use, to identify areas of overlapping or parallel interests, and to explore limited understandings through reciprocal or common action.

Chapter 2

THE UNCERTAIN BALANCE

The evidence on Soviet motives and attitudes is thoroughly contradictory. It militates partly for and partly against a belief in Soviet interest in realistic arms-control and disarmament agreements. To survey the salient considerations rapidly, before examining some of them further, it is helpful to draw up something of a balance, entering "pro" and "con" arguments on opposite sides of the ledger.

This accounting must, of course, be assayed against the background of almost half a century of Bolshevik pronouncements and actions relating to disarmament. That historical record, available in other studies, cannot be retold here.[1] Suffice it to say that initially the Communists considered negotiated disarmament impossible in a world dominated by capitalist powers and unnecessary in a world dominated by Communists. As the journal of the Communist Academy in Moscow put it, "the road to true disarmament is to be seen not in diplomatic agreements but in the proletarian revolution."[2]

If, then, the Soviet government, from 1922 on, advocated various forms of disarmament and soon came to advance sweeping proposals with gusto, eloquence, and seeming conviction, the Sixth Comintern Congress, meeting in Moscow in 1928, explained that "the aim of the Soviet proposals is not to spread pacifist illusions, but to destroy them; . . . disarmament and the abolition of war are possible only with the fall of capitalism." And it went on to declare with remarkable candor, "it goes without saying, that not a single Communist thought for a moment that the imperialists would accept the Soviet disarmament proposals."[3] Again, after World War II (as even friends of the Soviet Union agree in retrospect), Stalin was committed to avoiding agreements.

Time and again Soviet negotiators were patently stalling and preventing even limited accords, whether on conventional weapons or on the international control of fissionable materials.

Against this background, the hypothesis that a break with past assumptions underlying Soviet disarmament policy may have occurred in the years since 1953 might seem less credible—precisely because Moscow today invokes, in arguing the legitimacy of its present policy, instances of earlier Soviet disarmament proposals which were obviously not calculated to lead to agreements.

The counter-argument would dismiss these doubts in the following manner:

1. Given the strong compulsion in Bolshevik rhetoric to invoke precedents to sanction and sanctify all its actions, it was predictable that the present Soviet leadership would seek to find authoritative examples in the past, whether or not they fitted properly.

2. Moreover, a drastic shift in Soviet policy on arms control and disarmament need not be surprising. In this as in other areas, policy is commonly derived from broader political decisions "at the top"; once a change in general political strategy is approved, a corresponding shift in arms-control and disarmament attitudes may be expected to follow suit.

3. Finally, Soviet pronouncements readily grant, these days, that one's position on this or that aspect of disarmament policy must not remain rigidly "principled" and hence constant but, on the contrary, must vary in manipulative fashion according to changing circumstances—depending, e.g., on whether or not the U.S. has the monopoly of nuclear weapons, or whether or not the U.S.S.R. leads in space travel.

In defense of its record, the Soviet government replied with refreshing candor to the Chinese charges of opportunism and surrender:

In the early years after the United States developed nuclear weapons, when the U.S. had a nuclear monopoly and the security of the socialist countries was thus endangered, the Soviet government proceeded from the consideration that the main thing was to deprive the U.S. of this advantage. That could be achieved either through a complete ban on nuclear weapons, which would have been tantamount to taking them away from the only nuclear power of the day, the United States; or through developing nuclear weapons of our own which would serve to protect the security of all the socialist countries.

Since the West had rejected the Soviet proposal to ban and destroy all nuclear weapons, the Soviet note continued,

> Naturally, the banning of nuclear tests without simultaneous destruction of the nuclear weapons which America possessed would not in those years have been in the interests of the socialist states: it would have brought to a halt the work of developing nuclear weapons in the Soviet Union and perpetuated the American nuclear monopoly.

But once the Soviet Union acquired nuclear weapons, the situation changed:

> Now the continuation of nuclear testing could only push the nuclear arms-race spiral higher and higher, in which the socialist countries—and all peaceable states—are not interested. At the same time, with the new balance of strength, a nuclear test ban would now perpetuate not the American nuclear monopoly but the fact of its liquidation, not a unilateral advantage of the imperialist camp but the new balance of strength in the sphere of nuclear weapons.[4]

"PRO" FACTORS

The public record of Soviet pronouncements leaves no doubt that one purpose of disarmament advocacy and proposals is "political warfare" or, more sweepingly, political mobilization of "broad masses" throughout the world to whom disarmament appeals as a drastic way of preventing wars and making possible a more productive use of resources. In line with the Moscow formulation of a community of interests between various strata of society with regard to "peace" and other issues, Khrushchev has recognized that "a primary condition for progress in disarmament is the mobilization of the people, their growing pressure on the imperialist governments."[5] Not agreement but agitation here seems to be the goal.

The "agitational" and propaganda uses of disarmament are scarcely in doubt or dispute. Somewhat more of an interest in substantive results has been displayed in those instances in which Moscow has put forth proposals in order to extract a quid pro quo from other powers for steps which the U.S.S.R. intends to take unilaterally anyway. Examples of such endeavors can be adduced from 1922 to the present—most obviously, the reduction of the number of men under arms or of military budgets, or (between 1957 and 1960) the temporary suspension of nuclear testing, presumably for technological reasons. These, however, are special circumstances hardly indicative of a general Soviet willingness to carry out arms-control or disarmament agreements.

What can be said about Soviet attitudes with regard to such general commitments? A distinction must be made, first of all, between the traditional Communist argument to the effect that disarmament is desirable but impossible (because the West will not consent to it, or cannot afford it, or does not want it), and the current Soviet insistence that agreements are both desirable and possible, even before "imperialism" vanishes from the face of the earth. The key to Soviet perceptions, here as elsewhere, is to be found <u>outside</u> the arms-control field, in more general Soviet political assessments.

The most important new element affecting Soviet attitudes, is doubtlessly the advent of atomic weapons and, more specifically, the leadership's awareness of the destructive nature of thermonuclear war. Soviet statements, since about 1956, abundantly reflect this knowledge. Khrushchev has argued, publicly and privately, that the cost of victory in a showdown between nuclear super-powers would be such as to make the meaning of "victory" ludicrous. To be sure, Moscow has also maintained (largely, one suspects, as a mild deterrent argument against Western "aggressiveness" and as a demonstration of old-fashioned Leninist optimism) that the U.S. is bound to suffer greater damage than the U.S.S.R., and that another world war would witness the total collapse of capitalism. But it has warned the Chinese Communists and their followers that, as a consequence of such a "victory," the Socialist camp would be thrown back so far into conditions of primitive survival that the ascent to Communism would be immeasurably harder even if no capitalist powers survived.[6] There are no grounds for questioning the reality of this fundamental insight on the part of the Soviet leadership.

The nuclear revolution has tended to undermine orthodox Communist doctrine on the link between war and revolution. War can no longer safely fulfill the socio-political function of enhancing the conditions for, and triggering, socialist revolution, which (in the Soviet reading) the experience of two world wars seemed to confirm. Besides calling into doubt the role of war as the "midwife of revolution," a nuclear environment tends

to put a brake on other forms of controlled revolutionary behavior, for even small conflicts may jeopardize the survival
of the Soviet system, since they always threaten to escalate
into a big nuclear war.

These considerations are at the core of the strategy of
"peaceful coexistence" as it has evolved in recent years. Indeed, in its major reply to Peking, on the eve of the nuclear
test-ban agreement Moscow pilloried the Chinese Communists'
indifference to the fate of "hundreds of millions of people who
are doomed to death in the event of a thermonuclear war" and
the ensuing "destruction of the values of human civilization."
It went on to declare what critics of Marxism had argued for
years: technological change could override ideological categories and could indeed arrest historical laws hitherto deemed
universal and ineluctable. As the CPSU's "Open Letter" of
July 14, 1963, succintly phrased it, "the atomic bomb does not
adhere to the class principle."

These insights—even if not unanimously shared within the
Soviet elite—have logically led to a determination to avoid nuclear conflict. They have encouraged Soviet leaders to shrink
back from a showdown with the United States—be it in Berlin,
in Cuba, or the Congo, or Laos, even though the frequency of
Soviet miscalculation of what constitutes a dangerous challenge
to the United States permits scant comfort with regard to the
future. They have further led to a desire to reduce the chances
of the outbreak of nuclear war through accident, miscalculation, failure of communication among the principal parties, or
any related misunderstanding. Even though Soviet arguments on
these contingencies have been generally more primitive than
corresponding American analyses, the basic Soviet understanding of the prospects is confirmed by a variety of statements
and gestures, including the establishment of the so-called "hot
line." Further moves calculated to prevent "unintended" war
may thus be one of the areas in which the U.S.S.R. is most
likely to seek agreement on acceptable terms.[7]

Another trend which the Soviet Union may be unable to
control is the proliferation of nuclear weapons to additional
powers. Such an attitude marks an obvious reversal from that
earlier espoused in Moscow when Soviet aid, was, it seems,
essential in getting China started down the nuclear path. Given
the Soviet argument (consistent with other facets of its modern-
ized military doctrine) that limited wars tend to escalate into
nuclear conflicts involving the super-powers, one may accept

as real the Soviet fear of having other states—in particular, West Germany and Communist China—produce or secure nuclear weapons. (The prospect of agreements slowing or barring the diffusion of nuclear weapons may be attractive to Moscow also because of the tension they would generate between the United States and some of its allies, such as France and West Germany.) A related danger, as Moscow seems to see it, is the involvement of the great powers in a war precipitated, or even provoked, by powers not now possessing nuclear weapons; Soviet refusal since 1958-59, to give blanket support to Communist China's operations and aspirations is a case in point.

In all these variants, what the Soviet leadership seeks is to increase its security by avoiding nuclear war. It is setting up, in effect, survive as a prerequisite for all else. That is indeed one of the Chinese accusations against Moscow. As Liu Shao-ch'i put it,

> In the eyes of the modern revisionists, the main contradiction of our time is between mankind and nuclear weapons, between life and death. All class and national contradictions must now be subordinated to this contradiction. To survive is everything. The philosophy of survival has replaced the revolutionary theories of Marxism-Leninism.[8]

Such a general outlook, reflecting a fundamental change in the real world, has required an ideological redefinition by the U.S.S.R. It presupposes—so long as long-range Soviet objectives remain substantially unchanged—confidence that these objectives can be attained without war. Such confidence did and probably still does exist among the key Soviet leaders. At the very least, it reflects a belief that the risks of a "forward" policy, coupled with an arms race, are greater than the price of postponement of such Communist victories as would require Soviet involvement abroad or could precipitate such involvement.

Furthermore, these days the Soviet leaders' conviction that they can "win without war" is the obverse of the realization that they cannot win by war. If indeed the Soviet Union has no effective war-winning strategy against its principal adversary, now or in the foreseeable future, its military posture must strive to achieve the greatest possible deterrent and the greatest possible political effect abroad. Both of these goals of maximizing security and support can be promoted by arms-control agreements.

There is another cluster of considerations that rationally leads the Soviet Union away from an all-out arms race with the United States and hence in the direction of measures—tacit or explicit, unilateral or multilateral—which will permit the reduction of military forces, weapons, or budgets. We have no certain evidence to tell us how the Soviet leaders, political or military, see the consequences of an intensified build-up of forces on both sides. One may surmise (with, for instance, the experience of the "missile gap" at hand) that many among them would be dubious as to whether such an arms race would relatively improve Soviet security or strategic capabilities vis-à-vis the United States. And they are likely to have concluded that the Soviet Union would find it harder to keep up with further rounds of the arms spiral than would the United States.[9]

Besides seeking to avoid counter-effective responses abroad, Soviet leaders are certain to take into account domestic implications of alternative arms policies. It is an axiom that there is an organic interconnection between Soviet domestic, foreign, and military (and hence arms-control) policies. Politically, a positive posture on disarmament is bound to find a resonance and evoke a measure of support in the Soviet population which the present (and presumably any future) leadership seeks to nurture and promote. Ideologically, the regime's commitment to "build a Communist society" in the next generation is widely interpreted among the Soviet population as a promise of rising standards of living. Such a welfare orientation presupposes the maintenance of peace—a condition equated in wide circles, perhaps somewhat naively, with the advent of partial or full disarmament. It is in the economy that the internal effects of any disarmament arrangement appear in their most clear-cut form.

It may well be that some observers have oversimplified the Soviet dilemma and exaggerated the extent to which economic imperatives drive the U.S.S.R. to seek a reduction in military spending. The fact remains that "resource allocation" is the central decision-making process which determines the relative share of the various branches—investments in civil and military sectors, heavy and light industries, present and future returns and benefits. Even official Soviet data reveal

a real need for substantial capital investment in such criticial
non-military areas as agriculture and housing if just the most
modest plans of the welfare program dangled before Soviet con-
sumers' eyes are to be implemented. The relative failure of
the present leadership to provide substantial, lasting relief
in these non-military fields is only likely to increase the internal pressure for greater attention—and hence allocations—
to them.

In fact, specialists predicted that the test-ban treaty would
be used by Khrushchev to give greater allocations to "soft"
sectors of the economy; the commitment in December, 1963, to
a forced development of the fertilizer industry in order to re-
lieve agricultural needs was indeed accompanied by a reduction of the Soviet military budget. To some extent, there is
thus a reciprocal relationship between "guns and butter." True,
this relationship needs to be qualified, for the statesman must
responsibly provide for security even if—in quest of popularity,
out of a sense of mission, or for other reasons—he would prefer
to shift more resources to more visible, more "popular," or
more consumable products and services. Khrushchev himself
has evidently vacillated between the possible and the desirable.
Time and again—as in mid-1960 and again in early 1963—he ad-
mitted that consumer welfare must take second place to defense needs. Yet there continues to be considerable pressure
in the opposite direction, too.

A sense of proportion is required in assessing the economic
components of Soviet motivation. While undoubtedly the military
establishment and related research and development systems,
along with the space program, heavily tax certain resources
in short supply, including skilled labor, economic constraints
are likely to be of a reinforcing rather than a compelling sort.
Not only are Soviet decisions political par excellence; but a
growing gross national product (GNP) will enable Moscow to
commit greater resources for military purposes—should it so
desire—without thereby increasing their relative strain on the
GNP.

One should, finally, not discount totally the nurturing of
expectations and the reinforcement of values among the Soviet
population by the intensive outpouring of Soviet statements and
writings on disarmament. One of the more effective arguments of this propaganda campaign has called for the translation of any savings effected as a consequence of disarming into
other, more basic, more enjoyable, more civilized, or more

productive uses. While much of this type of writing is addressed to the "new countries," the Soviet population itself is also a target of such statements. Khrushchev remarked on his return from Camp David in the fall of 1959, "If these [Soviet disarmament] proposals were adopted by all countries and we could reach an agreement on universal disarmament, our country would be able to start the change-over to a six-hour working day much sooner. . . ."[10] The same pleasant results, he made clear on other occasions, could also accrue in areas of even more urgent economic needs. The line between serious argument and cheap propaganda in all this is at times hard to draw.[11] Inversely, Moscow has also blamed its inability to improve living conditions on Western "refusal" to accept its disarmament proposals.

There is, finally, another significant cluster of considerations militating in favor of disarmament or arms-control negotiations. This is the expectation that negotiations and accords will improve the relative Soviet position vis-à-vis the West (or other adversaries). In its minimal form, the very process of negotiating—whether culminating in agreement or not—bears political dividends by strengthening an image of the Soviet Union as the champion of peace and disarmament, and by "engaging" official and unofficial groups in the opposite camp in a peculiar dialogue. (Even inconclusive negotiations may lead to technical and strategic advantages, such as those which the Soviet Union obtained by preparing—during a drawn-out period of test-ban negotiations—for resumption of nuclear testing in the fall of 1961.)

Some types of limited disarmament arrangements, particularly regional measures affecting Europe (nuclear-free zone, non-aggression pact, etc.), probably hold a definite appeal for the Soviet leaders as means of opening the way to political gains—such as dividing NATO, putting the seal of acceptance on Soviet-dominated regimes in Eastern Europe, and neutralizing West Germany's future military-political potential.

For the Soviet Union one of the most important political, as well as military, prospects in this attractive series of measures, is the removal of United States presence, or at least some retraction of Western military force (and concomitant political influence), from along the perimeter of the Soviet Union or its allies. Various disengagement, nuclear-free zone, and other arms-control agreements would place inhibitions on the location and the use of military force by the West and—

Moscow reasons—on anti-Soviet initiatives abroad.

Similarly, even partial disarmament or regional disengagement in non-Western areas may be interpreted in Moscow as providing a boost to "national-liberation movements." While some of the Soviet arguments on this score have been patently disingenuous rationalizations (intended to offset Chinese Communist charges of cowardice and betrayal in opting for peaceful or gradual change in collusion with the American archenemy), Soviet analysts did probably conclude that real opportunities may arise for accelerating "national-liberation movements" in various countries without fear of effective Western intervention and Soviet involvement. Moreover, Soviet leaders may hope that "partial measures," such as the scrapping of nuclear delivery systems and withdrawal from overseas military bases, could bring about the demoralization and crisis of the Western alliance system.

All these Soviet calculations presuppose, of course, a continued "rightist" strategy of moderation. They assume that a neutral belt around the Soviet Union would be preferable to a Western-oriented one. They posit that national-liberation movements, even when nationalist-controlled, must eventually benefit the Communists and not their enemies. They believe that something useful will derive from "engaging" the maximum number of groups and individuals abroad in common causes (or at least in common meetings and institutions) with the U.S.S.R. and its allies. In brief, they require faith that time is on the side of the Communists. Until now—or, more precisely, until recently—there has been little to lead the men in Moscow to question this assumption. Paradoxically, only the total failure of either side is likely to scatter this cluster of assumptions; even proof of logical fallacy might not shake this commitment to the faith. The appearance of new and dramatic opportunities which could be adequately exploited only by means of a more vigorous but dangerous policy, could operationally cast doubt on these expectations and beliefs.

In fact, from the American perspective it may be salutary for Soviet policy-makers to believe (provided they are wrong) that the effects of disarmament or arms-control measures would be asymmetrical in benefitting the Soviet camp more than the West. Viewed in this light, disarmament—like peaceful coexistence itself—becomes just another "form of struggle" between the two systems, and arms-control agreements become instruments in the global conflict. Disarmament and arms control thus become easier for "good Communists" to justify in doctrinal terms.[12]

Such a view of disarmament as a vehicle to victory may be but is not necessarily in conflict with the earlier hypothesis that disarmament appears to the Soviet leaders as a means of survival. While some may stop at the latter elementary argument, others no doubt are prepared to accept both. There is a characteristic Bolshevik tendency to identify minimum and maximum benefits to be derived from a given policy. The entire concept of "peaceful coexistence" builds on a dialectical formula of "unity and struggle," which sees no problem in maintaining that both cooperative and competitive elements are inherent in it.[13]

All the arguments advanced thus far concern policy options on the part of Soviet leaders, implying "subjective" judgments on their part. A different line of argument points to "objective" trends in the Soviet system—or at least plausible speculation about "objective" trends. While the considerations heretofore enumerated are presumably acceptable to at least some "committed" Communists and spell no abandonment of long-term visions or objectives, the same policies could, with equal or greater cogency, be supported by others for whom the revolutionary, international aspects of Communism occupy a subsidiary or operationally insignificant place. The sentiments of the latter group may be expected to gain in acceptance in the Soviet Union as time goes on.

While in a few cases—against Poland in 1920, for instance—the Soviet leadership was prepared to use its force and resources to establish a Communist regime at a cost to itself, Moscow has usually shrunk back from committing itself to the defense or promotion of revolutions elsewhere—be it in Spain in the 1930's, or in China in 1946-49, or in Kerala or Guatemala in the 1950's.

With the breakup of the Bloc as an organic unit, the Soviet Communist Party could scarcely keep up the Stalinist argument that what was good for the Soviet state was also—and always—good for the international Communist movement as a whole. Now Moscow is constrained to recognize that at times the interests of the rest of the movement can be a serious burden to the Soviet Union; junior partners can present the U.S.S.R. with dilemmas between unpopular "sell-outs" and risky adventures; claimants from vast backward areas can require resources and aid far beyond the scope of Moscow's own desires.[14]

There is, then, some cogency to the expectation that there will grow a self-centered approach (among Soviet Communists and non-Communists alike) and the conviction that Soviet Russia need not make substantial sacrifices or take undue risks for the benefit of others.

A related phenomenon which might make for far-reaching changes in the Soviet outlook is the trend variously described as liberalization or embourgeoisement of Soviet society. The Chinese Communists, among others, seem to feel that this trend increasingly disqualifies the Soviet Union from leadership of the world Communist movement and renders it susceptible to revisionist apostasy and ultimate accommodation with the enemy camp.

Another consideration bearing on prospects of change in the Soviet outlook concerns the possibly habit-forming effects of pursuing a policy that observes at least the form, if not the content, of peaceful coexistence. Now that the forms of peaceful coexistence are very much in vogue, there may be some possibility that in the course of time the content will be subtly transformed into something closer to the Western notion of what the phrase should mean.

The extent to which and the speed with which the Soviet system and Soviet society can be expected to evolve or change will remain a matter of dispute among specialists. All change need not be relevant or helpful. But the fact that changes are taking place makes it necessary to relate their impact to arms-control negotiations.

"CON" FACTORS

The ideological obstacles to Soviet acceptance of arms-control and disarmament agreements seem to fall into two major categories. Both rise out of many years of deeply-engrained attitudes which, we may assume, are impossible to shed at will and which are often not even perceived as explicit impediments.

There are, first, the doctrinal difficulties in acknowledging the utility of agreements with the "enemy" which deprive the Soviet as well as the other side of at least some elements of its physical forces or freedom of action. While such doctrines have often been perceived and reiterated by anti-Communists in extreme and unwarrantedly primitive form, there is after all among Communists an ideological commitment to a world view that sees change as a perennial process—change throughout the era of "class society"—in the form of violence, not because violence is good or desirable but because of the inherent and ineradicable conflict of interest between exploiting and exploited classes. With more or less sophistication and reiteration, this argument can become second nature. It leads to a corollary expectation of conflict and of secular irreconcilability among opposing classes and among opposing "world systems" (which are seen to stand for opposite classes or class symbols). It assumes an organic duality underlying the dialectical process—good and evil, new and old, exploiter and exploited, winner and loser.

It would be superfluous to restate these verities in such elementary fashion were there not a widespread tendency to dismiss such categories of thought and perception as hardly unique or as irrelevant. Experience shows that it is possible to overcome the distorting, constricting consequences of this dialectical perspective. A number of ex-Communists and men who continue to consider themselves Communists (Yugoslavs and Poles, for instance) provide examples that changes can take place. But this emancipation does not come easily or rapidly to those who have been exposed and inured to Communist concepts and categories, to agitation and indoctrination for years without comparable exposure to other systems.

Seemingly, the commitment to total change, which is basic to the whole Communist image of the future and of the historical process, argues against conditions of stability, which, in the Western view, are a necessary adjunct of arms control. Without such total change, after all, how can the transition from the present to a Communist society be accomplished? Conditions of disarmament, or conditions of security, are likely to be significantly different for the two sides: while the standard American formula provides for the maintenance of the status quo, the Soviet formula provides for change—whether as a consequence of or in spite of disarmament or arms-control measures.

One problem thus emerging is the need to stabilize the balance of deterrence without also freezing the political process which, Soviet analysts insist, must continue to work itself out. Thus Moscow will in all likelihood continue to insist on the legitimacy of "national-liberation wars" and other "sub-conventional" types of conflict. It is likely to continue being suspicious of all proposals which would circumscribe or limit the sovereign prerogatives of any state, including the international police forces and tribunals promoted in some Western plans. And it is likely to respond with hostility to attempts at "penetrations" into its domain under the "guise" of inspection for disarmament.

Such are some of the ideological imperatives which continue to have an important bearing on Soviet willingness to engage in meaningful measures in this field.

Other negative considerations stem from the lesson Moscow has learned, namely, that its own international position and influence have been enhanced by its military power and by the evidence of Soviet scientific and technological progress. Indeed, one might say that the Soviet Union's status as a "super-power" was not confirmed in the world's eyes until the Soviet Union became a full-fledged member of the "nuclear club." Modern arms have thus given the present leadership a capability for influencing events on a global scale which no previous generation of Soviet leaders enjoyed. This heady sense of power will not be easy to part with, the more so since it is linked with a conviction, in some quarters, that the Soviet armed forces are an indispensable safeguard of Soviet security against the hostile designs of the capitalist world.

This outlook is perhaps not even so important in military as in political terms, for it places a heavy premium on preserving the image of a militarily powerful state. Indeed, for a few years before the Sino-Soviet split and the Cuban crisis of October, 1962, the Soviet Union asserted that a fundamental change in the "correlation of forces" on the international plane was taking place or was about to take place. Even if this extreme claim is dropped, there remain both a manipulative Soviet interest in creating a presumption that the Soviet Union is prepared to use force as part of its international conduct, and a profound commitment to the political use of military power. For the present, at least, it appears to be a far more ambitious commitment than merely a protective "containment" of the enemy camp or a pledge to assist friends and allies against "counter-revolutionary" efforts from abroad. Indeed, the Soviet variant of the Churchillian dictum that they seek not war but merely the fruits of war has permitted a dangerous and in many respects uncharacteristic kind of "brinkmanship" (as in Cuba). One must assume, finally, that Soviet policy-

makers are aware of the fact that some of their successes have been due to the fear of other nations that the U.S.S.R. will not hesitate to use force. Under such conditions, Moscow would experience considerable difficulty in relinquishing the use of, or at least the access to, force.

In other words, Soviet military power backs up political moves and deters Western or other countermoves. And while in the nuclear age war no longer serves as a deliberate instrument of rational policy (most Soviet leaders would agree), precisely because of the nature of nuclear war the potential political benefits from the possession of modern military power have increased. So of course have the risks, and one may suspect that at least some members of the Soviet elite have concluded that the political dividends reaped from military power have been rather slim, considering the resources involved.

Some benefit, Moscow may feel, can also be derived from merely championing the cause of disarmament and the "peace" struggle—a benefit which would be denied by the very fulfillment of purpose. While opinions abroad may differ concerning the importance to Moscow of "keeping the disarmament pot boiling," this objective is evidently not a major one in any case.

Another, more rational and more weighty consideration is the fact that Soviet authority in the Communist world—especially in Eastern Europe—is closely related to Soviet military might and to Moscow's ability to provide a military or nuclear umbrella for its allies (or, alternatively, to defeat them). Even "partial" or "regional" arms-control measures would be apt to weaken Soviet authority even further if they involved the diminution of Soviet military presence or a reduction of the threat of Soviet intervention. To what extent Moscow may be willing or obliged to tolerate the autonomy of other Communist states under any circumstances is another question, which the Soviet leadership may not yet have decided itself.

It may be well to remind ourselves that the basic Soviet commitment to "peaceful coexistence" as a strategy presupposes sufficient Soviet strategic power to deter any challenge from the West. Soviet military force thus has—as always in the Communist mind—both offensive and defensive potentialities and implications. The whole weight of past assumptions and experience militates against the Soviet leadership's trading this

powerful military machinery for a scrap of paper. Moscow has
made it clear that it is disposed to entrust its security to its
own forces, under its own control and command, rather than
to an international accord, whatever its form or instrumentalities. Some sense of this attitude is also conveyed in a re-
mark made by Khrushchev in February, 1963:

> If we stop paying attention to our defensive capabilities, then
> the balance of forces can change to our disadvantage. . . .
> We do not suppose, of course, that our policy of peace and
> peaceful coexistence will of itself find such acceptance
> among the imperialists that they will come and say, "Yes,
> you are right and we have been wrong. Let it be your
> way." No, our calculations are not built on such an unstable
> ground. The foreign policy of the Soviet Union relies on
> the firm foundation of our economic and military might. . . . [15]

To be sure, the Soviet leadership has come to realize that at
present any effort to achieve parity with the United States is
certain to fail. In fact, as will be elaborated in another chapter, the most plausible explanation of the events of October,
1962, is to see the Cuban strike as a desperate effort to shift
the balance, once Soviet leaders had come to realize their continued military inferiority. Recognition of actual inferiority does
not by any means imply acceptance of its permanence, however. Moreover, not all Soviet commanders seem to see eye
to eye on this score. Military specialists in the West have felt
that the large body of Soviet writings insisting on the necessity
of securing military superiority over the United States—at
the very time when serious literature in the West is debating
the desirability of seeking to maintain a superior military posture—suggests a conceptual hiatus which is not altogether promising for Soviet interest in bringing a technological arms race
to an end.

There is, finally, an obvious Soviet concern about charges of
reformism, pacifism, cowardice, and flabbiness raised by Communist China, Albania, and other quarters from within the
Communist world. Concern about the effect of such charges on
others in the Communist world, has at times slowed down Soviet
exploration of common ground with the West. No doubt it
still exercises some restraint. Yet, in the last analysis, Moscow made a choice, at the cost of further alienating Peking, in

favor of the nuclear test-ban treaty and other arms-control moves.

THE BALANCE

What all these—and other—considerations add up to remains a matter of speculation. There was and is an ambivalence in Communist thinking which has permitted several mutually exclusive perspectives, or "truths," to be developed by "good Communists." Khrushchev himself has at times hesitated between his own radical proposals for general and complete disarmament and the use of the image of the mighty U.S.S.R. for his own political ends. He and other Soviet leaders have acknowledged both the logic of the disarmament argument and the impulse toward continued reliance on one's own forces. Perhaps in significantly differing proportions, they have espoused arms-control measures and also feared them. There is here a certain similarity between Soviet and American attitudes.

Yet the similarity stops here. What is, after all, wrong with the listing of "pro" and "con" considerations such as have been enumerated in the pages above? For one thing, it is a typically "American" device to cumulate "factors" without indicating any hierarchy of Soviet values and objectives, without exploring which are determinant and which ancillary. For another, whatever the economic or military or sociological arguments, in the case of the Soviet Union we are dealing with fundamentally political decision-making. This centrality of politics will be a recurring theme, as will be two corollary questions: (1) Given the Soviet compulsion toward consistency and interrelatedness of responses to an entire set of problems, what determines the total "mix"? (2) Given the contradictory evidence—largely orthodox Communist formulae and attitudes on the one hand, and a more realistic, "up-to-date," revisionist approach on the other—it behooves us to inquire time and again into the extent and significance of the changes that have set in during the post-Stalin decade and to ask how far they have carried or may carry the U.S.S.R.

Even a cursory examination of the evidence will show a shift in the past decade in the direction of the advocates, rather than the opponents, of arms control. Thus, the Soviet articulation of the belief that war is no longer inevitable and Soviet awareness of the destructive power of nuclear weapons have affected the balance. To some extent, the disappearance of

Communist belief in the imminent crisis of capitalism and some general reconsideration of the nature of contemporary capitalism have made the Soviet posture more credible. Furthermore, Communist China is no longer the major effective restraint on Soviet action in this field. The test-ban treaty of 1963 has provided an object lesson on this score. Even the Soviet commitment to the use of military power for political purposes is now somewhat balanced by the Soviet interest in using disarmament for political ends. While the test-ban treaty may have been desirable in itself, Moscow may also have seen it as an instrument to promote the political détente with the United States which it has wished to achieve. Finally, if it is true (as will be discussed later on) that the Soviet leadership has accepted the fact that it is at present unable to gain military superiority, the ensuing espousal of arms-control proposals as an equalizer adds further credibility to the reality— though not to the unselfishness—of Soviet interest in some forms of arms control and disarmament.

Part II

THE CONTEXT

Chapter 3

IDEOLOGY AND BEHAVIOR

The nature of the Soviet system is too well-known to require restatement here. At least in its "classical" garb, it had all the attributes of a tightly-controlled totalitarianism, with a vast apparatus of compulsion and wanton arbitrariness, a single-Party elite, a highly-developed pseudo-scientific ideology, a centrally planned economy, a combination of elemental intolerance with tactical flexibility, along with a measure of true idealism and rational adaptation.

Whereas, some years back, it might have seemed adequate to refer to this system or to any of its key aspects, in order to explain Soviet attitudes or behavior, such facile or peremptory reference appears decreasingly satisfactory, now that we know the system to be capable of far greater malleability and variability than most observers would have foreseen. One of the central issues in any analysis of the post-Stalin era is precisely the extent and meaning of the diversity so strikingly apparent throughout the Communist world. No pretense is made here to cover the whole field of relevant problems with equal adequacy or depth.

IDEOLOGY: ITS ROLE IN SOVIET OBJECTIVES
AND OPERATIONS

The role of ideology in Soviet policy is one of the perennial objects of debate and disagreement among "sovietologists." Is the guiding force ideology or power, or both, or something else altogether? Are we dealing with an empire or a church? Are the Soviet leaders presiding over a cause or a country? And in their perceptions and options, are they impelled by a pragmatism or by preconceptions?

While opinions on this issue differ sharply, observers tend to agree on the inadequacy of any simple, single answer. There is a need, for instance, to probe for changing contents of old and familiar formulae.

It is almost meaningless, then, to speak of the Soviet Union as being committed to a single, unchanging objective such as

37

"world revolution" or "world domination." How, where, when, and at what price are these to be achieved? While the goal of world Communism is envisaged as lying at the end of an historical process, it is not a single objective to be achieved in a simple unilinear development; indeed, it requires the attainment of many intermediate goals, which often are in competition with each other. Thus, it might be more useful to view the formation of actual Soviet policy objectives as a process itself constantly undergoing adjustment and modification. One may, moreover, usefully distinguish between the purely doctrinal and the operationally significant or useful elements in the ideology, which are in turn distinct from actual or putative objectives pursued by the regime at a given time.

Uncertainty and disagreement pertain largely to the question whether Communist theory is (as it claims to be) a "guide to action" or whether (in the recent retort of one skeptic) action is not "a guide to theory." It has characteristics both of great flexibility and of great rigidity.[1] It is most realistic to see ideology as an essential part of the framework but only rarely as a guide to specific action—if only because action relates to circumstances not envisaged by the "classics of Marxism-Leninism"—or to specifics not predetermined by the "general line." In the words of one scholar, ideology thus becomes a guide to perception.

Here it is important to distinguish between the formal doctrine and the world view of individual Soviet leaders. Closer examination of pronouncements and actions would suggest that one must allow for real doubts and ambiguities—and contradictions—in the Soviet leaders' own assumptions and thinking. Ideology, as "the language of politics," serves as a frame of reference and provides a set of concepts and categories for perceiving the world and its problems. Indeed, some of the most durable elements of "Marxism-Leninism" in the Soviet mind are likely to be broad conceptual categories, such as a self-identification with the course of history, a "goal-oriented" optimistic outlook, a sense of destiny and inevitability, and a perception of nature and society in terms of pairs of opposites (good and evil, rich and poor, old and new).

In the Soviet Union, ideology has become a code of communications more intelligible to some specialists than to the population at large. Its specific contents invite distortions (e.g., they make it difficult for those initiated in the ideology to understand American political life), but may at times also provide special insights (e.g., the socio-economic basis of political alignments or the nature of anti-colonialism).

Finally, ideology serves as a long-range goal or vision for the Soviet decision-maker. The awareness of a common, clearly-stated, and presumably inevitable goal toward which humanity—or its "progressive" part—tends, helps to inject a dose of self-confidence despite setbacks, an identification with progress and history, and a flexibility in the choice of means, so long as the ends are constant. Even when specific doctrinal planks are rejected or amended, the general intellectual atmosphere which unwittingly breeds the acceptance of vague but attractive images of the Communist utopia may be assumed to be far more ubiquitous than "Anglo-Saxon pragmatists" have been prepared to see.

For the purposes of the present Report, it seems most useful to differentiate between those doctrines which are likely to hinder or delay decisions in favor of arms-control agreements and those which may assist or speed them. The potentially constructive elements are few in number but, since they are often overlooked, they deserve particular mention. These include an optimistic view of the course of human history; a sense of being in step with the times, whatever the given strategy; and faith in the inevitability of the historical process. Taken together, these generate an ability to postpone possible contests, with confidence in the future.

Hence, if the Soviet leadership is committed to avoiding nuclear war (so long as it is not itself threatened), it can comfort itself with the assumption that time will eventually run its way; history will "dialectically" compensate the Soviet Union for its present inferiority of status or power. (Whether or not this assumption is accurate, is immaterial for the purposes of this discussion.)

It follows—as was suggested at an earlier point—that the opportunities to agree on specific arms-control (or other) accords tend to be greatest when the two sides have diametrically opposite expectations about the asymmetrical consequences of the anticipated deal (but similar expectations about those consequences in which the two partners have coinciding or overlapping interests). The risk, to be sure, is the correspondingly higher probability of destabilizing disappointment of at least one of the signatories at a later date.

The question remains, as one analyst aptly puts it, "whether the Kremlin's faith in the inevitability of ultimate Soviet success

is now great enough to permit it to accept the kind of restraints on its international conduct that a system of effective controls over comprehensive disarmament would require." [2]

On the other side of the ledger, ideological impediments to
disarmament are in large part self-evident. They include, in
addition to the over-all commitment to revolutionary beliefs
and purposes (and consequent lack of interest in an international equilibrium), the deeply-engrained sense of antagonistic
confrontation with its concomitant "either-or" (or "two-camp")
perspective (and hence, a prejudice against "trafficking with the
enemy"); and the theory of the class struggle, with its projection into international affairs. Other impediments have been the
traditional Leninist assumption that meaningful change comes
only through violence and revolution; the closely-related doctrine of the inevitability of wars; the belief that history moves
inexorably through certain well-defined stages, of which Communism will be the last; the sense of affinity for Communist
Parties everywhere, militating against major agreements with
the "bourgeois" governments which many of these Communist
Parties are fighting.

To these might be added some elements in the private "world
view" of the Soviet leaders, elements which have no direct
legitimation in Marx. They include a proclivity to resist agreements circumscribing freedom of action and to resist irreversible steps in politics. They also include a strong sensitivity to "sovereignty" and to actual or even symbolic viola-
tions thereof. It was this kind of consideration which for many
years led "good Communists" to insist that disarmament between Communist and "capitalist" states was impossible.

A real challenge to these various anti-disarmament tendencies has come with the reconsiderations of ideology—a revisionism inspired, most frequently, by setbacks and failures. The
elements of doctrinal change here involved have become familiar
terms in the present Soviet political jargon. The major ideological "revisionism" since 1956 has included a rejection of the
concept of inevitable wars; an extension or reformulation of
the meaning of "peaceful coexistence" as no longer limited
in time but rather as the sole alternative to a nuclear showdown;
the ideological stress on and explanation of the dangers of
thermonuclear war; the abandonment of the doctrine of capitalist encirclement; and the reassessment of the capitalist world,
where, instead of seeing the "ruling circles" as a unified
group of warmongers, Khrushchev-line Communists now see

"reasonable men" winning out over "madmen." All of these have obvious implications for possible arms-control agreements and understandings.

The ideological reformulations have specifically provided sanction for conclusion of disarmament agreements by the U.S.S.R. While revisions of the creed tell us nothing about the motives of Soviet actions, they may be accepted as indicators of Soviet "seriousness of purpose." At the same time, a characteristic poverty of thought and an inherent difficulty in reconciling far-reaching commitments and agreements with elements of Leninist orthodoxy have thus far prevented a fusion of the new Soviet programs for disarmament—for instance, Khrushchev's 1959 proposals in favor of general and complete disarmament—with the Marxist-Leninist doctrine. Interest therefore attaches to the fact that, for the first time since 1922, an effort is now being made to reconcile the possibility of GCD with Marxist ideology; that statements, letters, and speeches by Lenin and other former leaders are now "unearthed" to demonstrate the legitimacy of and the precedents for current innovations, including the recent Soviet disarmament proposals.[3]

To assimilate the advocacy of disarmament and belief in its realizability under "capitalist" conditions, with the rest of orthodox Marxist-Leninist doctrine, is to square the circle. On the other hand, the ideology has so often been invoked for so many unforeseen trends and events and for the legitimation of all Soviet policy, that Soviet ideologists do find it possible to buttress further disarmament agreements with appropriate statements and authoritative quotations from the "classics." This of course tells us nothing about the underlying motivation or the over-all calculus of the signatories.

The ideologically-determined long-range vision has a distinct relation to Soviet calculations on general and complete disarmament. Even if GCD cannot be seen as a practicable proposal (as will be discussed in another chapter), it need not be dismissed as "mere propaganda." It does indeed fit into the Communist image of the emergence of a world-wide Communist society. GCD is, as it were, a functional utopia, an orienting device for a Soviet policy that looks with interest on the possibility of shifting the struggle for world predominance to non-military means. GCD, in other words, is to disarmament policy what full Communism is to Soviet domestic policy.[4]

While the rationality of this vision may be left in doubt, there is a logic here which has both realistic and ideological components. No doubt a denuclearized and even partly disarmed world—and surely a world totally and rapidly disarmed—would provide a fertile environment for the seizure of power by organized revolutionary movements backed by tightly-organized and disciplined Communist societies. Moscow would presumably welcome the destabilizing effects abroad of the dismantling of military machinery and establishments, once this dismantling had proceeded downward past the threshold of minimum deterrence. But Soviet interest in this regard may extend beyond the goal of painless neutralization of any forces opposed to revolution. Thus, it is still the apparently unquestioned Soviet view that, if all variables or multipliers can be canceled out on both sides of the international power equation, "history" will advance unimpeded. Given this belief, "a prolonged state of mutual deterrence can be acceptable to the U.S.S.R. only if [it believes that] its political effects are less than perfectly symmetrical." [5] In the Soviet mind, a stabilization of deterrence must not lead to a stabilization, or freezing, of the "relationship of forces," which (Khrushchev has argued ad nauseam) [6] will continue relentlessly to tilt the balance further in the direction of the Communist camp.

AN EROSION OF IDEOLOGY?

It is the prevalent—though by no means unanimous—view among specialists on Soviet affairs that ideological factors are playing, or are beginning to play, a decreasing role in circumscribing or dictating Soviet perception and policy. At the same time, it would be grossly and perhaps dangerously misleading to argue that Russia has already seen an "end of ideology," that Khrushchev is a "pragmatist," or that Communism is a "veneer" or a "propaganda device" for the "power-mad" men in the Kremlin. More specifically, the revolution in weapons systems, and the Sino-Soviet dispute, have probably contributed to a further reconsideration or a revision of the Soviet world view; but thus far the impact of this revision has fallen overwhelmingly on means rather than on ends. The destructiveness of future general wars impressed itself on Soviet opinion-makers at a time when, for internal reasons, they were more receptive to arguments which justified shrinking back from a policy of widespread violence and high risk-

taking for what seemed to be uncertain and unessential returns.

The process, often labeled the "erosion" of ideology—con-
ceiving of ideology not as a post factum justification of Soviet
conduct but as an impelling motive or compass—has been evident in the years since Stalin's death. It manifests itself (1) in
the adaptation or adjustment of ideological statements to reality,
and (2) in the "relativization" of ideology—that is, its decreasing intensity, fervor, scope, or operational impact.[7]

So far as arms control and disarmament are concerned,
ideological erosion is most readily apparent precisely in the
Soviet perception of nuclear weaponry. However injurious to
the belief in Marxist infallibility, to the unity of the Communist
camp (since Communist China, among others, refuses to accept the Soviet view), or to the maintenance of doctrinal consistency, the post-Stalin leadership has been coldly realistic
in its estimate of thermonuclear weapons. As one American
political scientist has put it:

> Probably the most important aspect of international affairs
> that could promote the erosion of ideology pertains to the
> weapons systems. . . . Under the impact of a concrete factor
> of admittedly decisive importance—the problem of survival—
> the Soviet ideology had gradually to adjust again, modifying
> a hitherto important ideological assumption.

Combined with other forces which make for erosion, this change
opens up the prospect of further change:

> The ideological syndrome, containing an oversimplified con-
> ception of an antagonistic confrontation between two social
> systems and of historical change in general, the commitment
> to conflict, the universality of goals, the sense of self-
> righteousness, and the belief in the imminence of victory—all
> could be threatened by the combined impact of domestic
> change, the emergence of ideological relativism due to the
> spread of Communism, and the stark threat of nuclear ex-
> tinction. A growing willingness to accept some common and
> overt rules of behavior could follow, buttressing the existing
> informal and undefined restraints on violence that both sides
> have tacitly recognized.[8]

Such "erosion" may also occur as a result of increasing, unprofitable discrepancies between ideology and reality in:

   1. Internal Soviet problems of reconciling old dogmas with the demands of a modern industrial society.

   2. The explosive diversity manifested in the international Communist movement and the Soviet Bloc.

   3. The appearance of "revolutionary situations" under circumstances at variance with ideology and with Soviet experience, and beyond Soviet control.

   These changes <u>may</u> have the effect of reinforcing the gradual development of a Soviet willingness to seek "business-like arrangements" with any power prepared to enter into them, and perhaps also of a more explicit "Russia first" orientation. Neither of these tendencies is entirely novel. Both have roots and convenient precedents in Lenin's and Stalin's policies. Even if the process goes a good deal further, one cannot readily foresee an early evanescence of underlying hostilities—for instance, the deeply-engrained animus toward the so-called "imperialist powers."

   The Soviet attitude toward the support of wars and revolutions waged by cognate forces in areas remote from Russia's borders has always been marked by Moscow's reluctance to commit Soviet forces, even in cases where they were needed to save the "just" cause. Despite obvious exceptions, this disinclination to take significant risks at considerable distances away from home has, more recently, been reinforced by the thermonuclear environment and by the assessment of domestic demands as more urgent, more legitimate, and perhaps more important than ever before.

   In the rather informal image evoked by one political scientist, the Soviet leadership may thus be said to resemble an aging Lothario who has difficulty resisting the call to action when enticing opportunities beckon, but who has really more than enough to do at home, is growing increasingly weary, and would rather not have his reputation put to a test over and over again. Revolutionary situations abroad, moreover, have proved to be difficult for Moscow to control and often costly to sustain. Hard as it may be to reconcile this with a wide-spread stereotype, there is some evidence that the Soviet leadership has repeatedly endeavored to restrain its followers abroad—most recently in Cuba and Southeast Asia—from starting trouble which would permit a Communist tail to wag the Soviet dog. Despite all professions of "proletarian internationalism," Soviet self-interest is likely to be asserted in the future even more frankly and conceived even more selfishly than in the past.

INTENTIONS AND OBJECTIVES

Are Soviet policies offensive or defensive? For arms-control negotiations the most significant fact is that the Soviet Union continues to be unwilling to settle for the present world. Its leadership is, and must be expected to remain, wedded to profound and sweeping change—at home as much as abroad.

On one level, Soviet political intentions may thus be regarded as offensive, so long as the commitment to an inevitable worldwide process of change in the direction of Communism remains a fundamental tenet of Soviet outlook and policy. Notwithstanding the changes in policy, outlook, and leadership, it appears that this identification with the march of time is likely to be among the most durable aspects of the Soviet outlook. It should be accepted as such by the outside world. This commitment remains the same even if in practice its relevance and impact have already begun to shrink.

It may be no less correct, however, to suggest an interdependence of defensive and offensive postures in a "two-camp world" which, to the Communist observer, makes the first issue irrelevant (or, at best, reduces responsibility for offense and initiative to a "technical" question). To use a military analogy, the Red Army defending itself (in 1920 against Poland, in 1941 against Germany) at first staged a defensive operation which, gaining in success, then became offensive and not only recouped all lost territory but advanced beyond it. Inevitably, a step forward taken by the Communist world means a step back for the non-Communist world, and vice versa, since nature abhors a vacuum (as Lenin was fond of repeating). Thus the question whether Soviet political intentions are offensive or defensive may be unanswerable or even meaningless. It is certainly true that the Soviet Union would have no moral inhibitions to embark on "forward" action, no more than it has had in the past.

One should, however, distinguish between a commitment to an outlook (with a goodly dose of faith in the operation of "history") and a commitment of one's own forces and resources to attain the end perceived. If indeed the goal of world-wide transformation were to recede or erode to the level of long-range hopes and beliefs without operational import, Soviet attention—inside the country and outside—would correspondingly shift to means and techniques, such as the role of violence, the adequacy of political methods, or the efficacy of economic competition. Some observers maintain that this has already taken place.

While there is room to argue about Soviet political intentions, Soviet military intentions can be considered defensive. Soviet military dispositions seem to be consistent with a doctrine of limited deterrence, and Soviet strategic power appears still to serve the leadership primarily as a warrant of political advantage. There is no evidence of contemplated military aggressions by the U.S.S.R.

Many analysts of the Soviet scene find great difficulty in assigning precise rank-order or weights to specific Soviet objectives. One may argue, in fact, that above all one must understand the interplay of such goals if one wishes to develop some empathy with Soviet decision-making. The problem is complicated by the fact that the considerations that determine the ranking are certain to vary from one member or section of the Soviet elite to another, or from one day to the next. (Hence, also, short-term predictions of events or trends are impossible.)

The security of the Soviet Union—and within it, the stability of the domestic order, including the present leadership—may be considered first in the hierarchy of Soviet objectives. At present, this is largely a problem of maintaining military forces at the size and at the level of technological perfection required by the international situation (as appraised by the leadership). The objective of assuring the physical security of the U.S.S.R. has been largely attained. True, some argument might be had on the meaning of security and of the alternative concept of invulnerability. But for Soviet decision-makers, the operational question is: what policies must be pursued and what expenditures incurred to maintain the present level of security?

While the fulfillment of this first task is a prerequisite for all others, the priority of domestic goals suggests those often subsumed under the term, "building Communism in the Soviet Union," as the next highest cluster of objectives. This includes the promotion of economic growth, the solution of critical problems such as agricultural output, a gradual transformation of the political and cultural tone of the society, and greater satisfaction of demands for consumer goods, welfare needs, and other services. Unlike the quest for security, this task is, of course, very far from completed.

A third group of objectives pertains to the world beyond the borders of the U.S.S.R. In the narrowest sense, the security of the Communist Bloc has ranked as a high-priority goal. It was essentially attained, insofar as Western or foreign intervention or internal disintegration have been identified as impermissible alternatives to the status quo. The situation is far more bothersome, however, in view of the disintegration of the organizational and ideological unity of the Socialist camp and of the international Communist movement. The experience of 1963-64 suggests the possibility of a slippage of Soviet control and authority well beyond the limits heretofore imaginable, as well as unmistakable indications that the U.S.S.R. will not necessarily fight on the side of every other Communist regime.

The complementary problem is, of course, Soviet interest in the further advance of Communism. In its minimal form, this amounts to the erosion of "capitalist" dominance throughout the non-Communist world. In its more vigorous form, it also aims at the promotion of Communism everywhere. The earlier discussion of this problem suggested a possible attrition in the operational force of this aspiration.

Even a cursory consideration of these objectives shows to what extent the interdependence of the various elements, the fluidity of priorities, and the competition among objectives and their requirements are all part of the Soviet scene. In some instances, the pursuit of several goals produces competition for scant resources; in others, the attainment of one objective makes the pursuit of other goals easier. For instance, Soviet military victory in Cuba in 1962 would have improved the prospects for Communism in the Caribbean area, would have enhanced the strategic posture of the Soviet Union vis-à-vis the United States, and would perhaps even have advanced Soviet political aims in Berlin.

Some comfort—as the record of recent years indicates— may be derived from the fact that none of the goals whose attainment would require the most violent and dangerous courses of action ranks near the top of our list of current Soviet objectives. It is only fair to add that neither the rationality of all Soviet decisions nor the permanence of this rank-order can be assumed.

Chapter 4

POLICIES AND POLITICS

THE NATURE OF SOVIET POLITICS

How deep and how far-reaching have been the changes wrought since Stalin's death? This question is particularly pertinent to our assessment of the Soviet elite and of Soviet politics.

For four or five years after 1953, some of the conflicts within the Soviet leadership were visible and subject to scrutiny from the outside. They involved a multiplicity of arguments over genuine policy issues, and clashes among competitors for power and contending personalities. Virtually all the rivals agreed on the cessation of terror as an instrument of rule and, with the obvious exception of the victims of this decision, on the destruction of the secret police empire hitherto ruled by Lavrenti Beria. But the end of the terror also brought in its wake an upsurge of non-conformity inside and outside the remaining "pillars" of government—the state machine, the Communist Party, the military establishment, and the economic apparatus. Within narrow limits, greater diversity of views than had been permitted under Stalin was tolerated or encouraged; within somewhat broader limits, such diversity became a reality as groups and individuals—especially intellectuals but also others—took advantage of the "thaw" to maximize their own "elbow-room."

The realities of post-Stalin Russia made necessary a form of "collective leadership." But before long the conflicts within it strained relations to the point where confrontations resulted in the successive elimination of the anti-Khrushchev elements within the top stratum. Opportunities for disagreements arose more frequently than usual, perhaps because of the continuing search for a new formula of governance, as the leadership found itself, on the one hand, determined to abandon the "excesses" of the Stalin era, yet, on the other, afraid to do so; desiring to innovate and adapt, yet uncertain in what direction, how far, and how fast to move.[1]

48

Unmistakably, the post-Stalin decade heard diverse voices, saw a variety of views, and witnessed the crystallization of different interests close to the apex of power as well as below it. For its part, the new leadership proved to be prepared to listen; in fact, it went out of its way to consult "specialists"— regardless of their formal status in the Soviet hierarchy— before making certain key policy decisions.

In vivid contrast to the practices of the Stalin era, disagreements within the leadership now did not necessarily lead to the dropping of losers from power. A member of the Party Presidium, for instance, might be on the losing side in a given policy argument, without thereby jeopardizing his personal position. By the same token, influences other than those of a single master made themselves felt more readily. A plurality of voices has been heard on the Soviet stage.

But who has the last word in Moscow? On this, there is no full agreement among observers. Khrushchev's position has not been so powerful as that of Stalin during his years of command, but, on the other hand, certainly not as precarious as that of the early post-Stalin "collective leadership." Others within the Soviet elite, and especially on the Presidium, most analysts feel, can make themselves heard—to their colleagues and at times to the outside—but cannot normally impose their will.[2]

It is important to recognize that Western, and especially American, observers have overwhelmingly underestimated the extent, the reality, or the speed of the changes taking place in the U.S.S.R.—whereas Khrushchev, on the contrary, has invariably erred in exaggerating the odds and opportunities for change in his favor. After all, the most dramatic events of the past decade have all been developments not only unforeseen but inconceivable in terms of prior assumptions; suffice it to cite the Polish and Hungarian crises of 1956, de-Stalinization, and the Sino-Soviet rift.

However, even if we conclude that the present Soviet policy orientation cannot easily be reversed—at least to anything resembling Stalinism—it does not follow that there could not take place, under another leader, a retreat from the current flexibility to a mood of greater caution, greater militancy, great xenophobia, or greater isolationism.

More clearly than ever before, the post-Stalin years have crystallized the two contrasting and conflicting political tempers in modern Communism. Both can claim some "legitimate" roots in Marxism-Leninism. Indeed, one of the sources of the Communist appeal thus far has been precisely the ability "dialectically" to combine seemingly conflicting impulses and visions. The contrary pulls of struggle and harmony, of voluntarism and determinism, "left" and "right," necessary stages and "great leaps," initiative and discipline, optimism and gloom, centralism and autonomy—all these have inhered in the Communist outlook from the start. They have formed the content of successive strategies, dictating alternating policies as conditions changed. But only recently have these contradictions been laid bare so dramatically and permitted to polarize. The Soviet leadership has not, after all, been able to square the circle; it is not able to reconcile a commitment to struggle with non-violence, nor the fetish of "unity" with a tolerance of diversity, nor its insistence on obedience with a recognition of independence among comrades abroad. While Khrushchev and other individual leaders may be shown to have vacillated or shifted in their own choices between permissiveness and controls, the two basic clusters of attitudes and tempers have become increasingly clear. The recognition and articulation of views reflecting these distinct positions have been among the most pregnant developments of recent years.

THE SUBSTANCE OF THE KHRUSHCHEV LINE

Allowing for exceptions and individual variations, there is one single paramount phenomenon that identifies many of the alignments in Soviet politics since Stalin's death. Yet the labels used to describe it have been peculiarly inadequate. In essence all of the following pairs of opposites have pointed to this phenomenon—a dichotomy in the Communist world view and in Communist policies: "extremists" versus "moderates"; "hard" versus "soft" Communism; left versus right; Stalinists versus anti-Stalinists; traditionalists versus modernists; "warfare Communism" versus "welfare Communism"; and (to use the terminology employed in the Communists' own charges against their rivals) "sectarians" (or "dogmatists") versus "revisionists" (or "opportunists"). Whatever the transitory and seemingly inconsistent alignment of individuals over specific policy issues, the continuity of the major ideological postures themselves has been impressive.[3]

As the scope of terms such as "revisionism" indicates, each posture has, with considerable consistency, encompassed domestic as well as foreign policies. Summarily, the "modernist" position includes a partiality to "coexistence" and détente abroad; an assumption that wars are no longer inevitable; a keen perception of the nature of thermonuclear war; a preference for gradual, indirect advances with the avoidance of showdowns, but with economic, political, and other "soft" victories in the process of relatively painless revolutions, especially in the underdeveloped areas; a willingness to believe that the "enemy" camp is not plotting aggression and indeed may be in the hands of "men of reason"; the determination that—with adequate deterrence assured—progress can and must be made at home in such areas as consumer goods; a conviction that terror must be avoided, that flexibility of means must be maintained and creative originality encouraged so as to try alternative means where previous approaches have failed.

By and large, the mood and temper produced by this complex of attitudes have made Soviet proposals on disarmament somewhat more credible than the prior spirit and outlook which, in effect, opted for the opposite on each of the above criteria.[4] The importance of the background thinking behind specific proposals has been indicated time and again by Soviet commentators who have observed that whether or not a given move was possible could not be judged without first determining the general environment. "It all depends on the circumstances" becomes, in the context of Communist decision-making, not an evasion of reply but a realization that specific policies are derivative of broader orientations in political strategy.

Despite strong indications of certain "modernist" attitudes, however, an inner ambivalence is characteristic of the contemporary Soviet orientation. Not only do the public pronouncements of individual leaders reveal striking vacillations and inconsistencies on some of the tell-tale issues in dispute, but the actual policy has been characterized by a pattern of zigzags, sharp turns, and seeming improvisations. Insofar as one can perceive, it has been possible and perhaps usual for a single individual to promote policies on different issues—agriculture, Berlin, or Party democracy, for instance—which place him at different points on the left-right spectrum at different times.

Still, the general dichotomy earlier suggested has been marked by a certain consistency, with the "modernist" or moderate orientation likely to prevail.

THE KHRUSHCHEV LINE IN FOREIGN AFFAIRS

Chairman Khrushchev would undoubtedly like to concentrate his energies on domestic affairs. This desire presupposes, and reinforces his preference for, a certain détente in his relations with the major antagonists abroad. At the same time, the success of his foreign policy prescription requires the effective development of the Soviet economy.

The concept of peaceful coexistence has not, of course, been a novelty of the present leadership.[5] Indeed, Khrushchev and others have attempted to impress their policies with the seal of Leninist orthodoxy; Stalin, too (others have argued), did after all pursue a policy of "peaceful coexistence." Soviet leaders have generally preferred political to military means of struggle and advance. Given the belief in the inevitable accretion of Communist forces in the future, it has usually seemed wise to await a more favorable "relationship of forces" at a later date. Coexistence—either in its 1921 or 1951 variety, or in its contemporary garb—required and permitted no surrender of Communist objectives or outlook. While no group of specialists is likely to agree on any precise description of the present-day meaning and implications of "peaceful coexistence," the impression prevails that the phrase has come to stand for something more fundamental and less transient—in practice, if not so explicitly in theory—than it did a generation ago.[6]

In its most widely accepted sense, "coexistence" has in effect been elevated into a permanent prerequisite for survival. The belief in its possibility has been facilitated by the parallel argument of the shifting balance of power and the growing might of the Socialist camp.

In theory, "coexistence" has come to be defined as a form of struggle (just as earlier Bolshevik formulations had labeled peace a special form of war). It did not and does not mean "live and let live." To Soviet analysts, it connotes a dynamic process, with elements of both cooperation and conflict. In its minimum formulation, it amounts to the avoidance of nuclear war; it is thus a peace-keeping formula to defuse situations which threaten to ignite a major conflict.[7] In its more ambitious and extensive meaning, it amounts to an alternative strategy for Communist victories without war. In this sense, it sanctions the use of any means short of general war (and of policies likely to precipitate the latter) in pursuance of the contest between the "two world systems." According to Soviet formulations, that contest remains unaltered, as does the postulate of ultimate future victory of the Communist system on a world-wide scale.

At any rate, the more sweeping content of "coexistence" calls for cooperative peace-keeping arrangements among the major powers concurrent with continued political, ideological, and economic competition in the struggle for world predominance. The two processes of cooperation and conflict are thus viewed as interpenetrating, dialectically compatible phenomena, save in the ideological field where no compromise or collaboration is permissible. To give but one sample formulation of this Soviet view, an authoritative lead article in the monthly journal, International Affairs, declares that "the field of activity for the peaceful coexistence policy, its possibilities and content have changed in the last fifteen years" [italics supplied]. Previously, it goes on to say, peaceful coexistence was "used above all for consolidating the Soviet state, for gaining at least a temporary respite before the next inevitable attack by imperialism. . . ." At present, it serves three major ends: it avoids thermonuclear war; it permits the Communist states to push ahead with their internal development; and it creates throughout the world "a favorable atmosphere for the growth of revolutionary and national-liberation movements."

Reiterating that under peaceful coexistence international relations are marked not only by the absence of war "but also by the continuation of a specific, non-military form of class struggle," the statement continues:

The class struggle embraces all spheres of international relations: politics, economics, and ideology. On all these sectors the socialist [i.e., Communist] states are waging an offensive against the imperialists and their agents. In the course of the political struggle the forces of socialism are exposing the aggressive policy of imperialism, putting up a front of socialist and neutralist states in opposition to it, and are extensively supporting the revolutionary and national-liberation movements. Through economic struggle in the form of peaceful economic competition between the two systems, socialism is demonstrating its advantages over capitalism and is giving economic and technical assistance to young states, which accelerates the advance of national-liberation revolutions. By extending the ideological struggle, the forces of socialism paralyze the corrupting

influence of imperialist propaganda on the national-liberation
movement and equip it with a mighty ideological weapon of
struggle until complete victory over imperialism and colonialism is attained . . .[8]

A similar point of view presumably molds the dominant
Soviet attitude toward arms-control agreements. As Soviet
commentators would argue, arms control on the one hand requires cooperation between adversaries for a common purpose—
for instance, reducing the danger of general war. On the other
hand, it is also an area of competition, leading to agreements
arrived at with due regard by both sides for the ultimately conflicting political interests of the two blocs and (they might add
without the benefit of publicity) contested by parties each of
which tries to secure a unilateral advantage from its reading
of the terms of agreement.[9]

The process of adapting Soviet policy to a more indirect
mode of advancing Soviet interests abroad has been causally
related to a specific sequence of experiences. In 1955, when he
assumed responsibility for the formulation of Soviet world
strategy, Khrushchev in effect argued for a "freeze" in Soviet
and Communist "forward" policies in Europe; in return, he
stressed the great opportunities opening in the non-Western
areas, due above all to the impending "collapse of the colonial
system." Khrushchev's image of the next few years amounted
to a new, "third round" between East and West, in which the
Communist Bloc was bound to grow in strength and probably
in size while a direct showdown was eschewed; the West was
rent by internal "contradictions"; and the colonies, whether
struggling for independence or formally emancipated, would
naturally gravitate toward (or into) the Communist camp. The
prospect was compelling in its attractiveness and seeming
simplicity, and also in the sanction it provided the Soviet
leadership to give primary attention to domestic problems.

Recent years have seen a sequence of severe disappointments
for the Soviet leadership. While there have been undoubted and
considerable successes to report as well, the setbacks have
been more striking because of the great expectations of the
Soviet policy-makers and because of the challenge they implied for Soviet infallibility.

Abroad, the evidence has not sustained Soviet expectations
of imminent crises and the weakening of Western society; nor
is there any sign that the "proletariat" in the advanced countries

is acquiring a revolutionary spirit. The new nations of Africa and Asia, despite substantial Soviet investment of resources and personnel, have not proved to be easy to manipulate in international politics; nor have they been strikingly responsive to the Soviet model of socialism. Instead, the national leaders of the new states have frequently used Soviet aid to bargain or to strengthen their own positions, without thereby trading their new sovereignty for a dependence upon the U.S.S.R. (The sole Soviet "success"—Cuba—was delivered by a non-Communist revolutionary movement. Its success obliged Soviet theorists to devise doctrinal amendments that would take account of the novel "precedent.")

Within the Bloc, the rift with China and the increasing autonomy in East Europe, including successful and at times brazen defiance of Soviet wishes, have provided dramatic and surprising evidence of Moscow's failures. And within the U.S.S.R. the leadership has been concerned with shortcomings in the economy—especially in agriculture—and difficulties in increasing the efficiency of administration and planning; with extensive reshuffling in the Communist Party; with stresses between the regime and the Soviet intelligentsia and probably other strata as well. While the growth rate of the economy was substantial until about 1958, evidence (as discussed at a later point) now suggests a serious decline ever since. When the well-publicized goal of "overtaking the United States" became hopelessly unrealistic, it hurt foreign policy, too; the very strategy of victory without war has been based in large measure on the expectation of a continued or even accelerated growth of the Soviet economy.

The result, it would appear, has been a growth of skepticism and moderation, an increased awareness of complexities and delays,[10] but not a perceptible abandonment of purpose. The prospects of both Communist victory and the avoidance of war remain. As a recent Soviet booklet on disarmament puts it, the central problem is, in essence, "to assure the transition from capitalism to socialism, from colonialism to freedom and progress, under conditions precluding the outbreak of thermo-nuclear war."[11]

The Soviet leadership is no doubt capable of accepting the conclusion that force and violence, especially in the form of nuclear warfare, may be unprofitable or even suicidal, according to a rational calculation of gain and loss. Nonetheless, as is argued elsewhere in this Report, the maintenance of Soviet

armed might has been considered essential to the success of
the Soviet "peace" strategy. Indeed, the claimed shift in the
balance of power is attributed largely to the growth in Soviet
power. Khrushchev has reiterated that he cannot rely on the
enemies of Communism to respect any gestures other than
demonstrations of strength. In his words, "if we underestimate
the significance of the army and of first-class arms, we may
have to pay for it.[12]

Central to Soviet ambivalence on disarmament matters is
a seemingly insuperable obstacle which requires reconsideration. Soviet leaders are not content to accept the international
environment of today as the basis of a lasting status quo. They
cannot—yet?—conceive of a world arrested in its historical
transformations at its present stage of division between two
ultimately incompatible systems. They cannot, in theoretical
terms, conceive of transformations in directions other than
unilinear progress along the lines charted by orthodox Marxism
and later "refined" on the basis of further experience (or
hindsight). Given their endemic optimism, despite failures
and setbacks, and their expectation of the inevitable completion of the "transition from capitalism to Communism," Communist "idealists" are likely to justify disarmament measures,
if they favor them, as eliminating artificial impediments in
the path of change. By contrast, the best assurance of avoiding
nuclear war, Western experts and statesmen have argued, lies
in a system of mutual deterrence, which tends to work toward
a gross equilibrium on the international plane. Such a stabilization is bound to be seen as a freezing of the status quo and an
impediment to change. The question remains whether it is
possible to assuage Soviet fears by stabilizing the balance of
deterrence without "stabilizing" the political status quo; and
whether any mechanism can be devised that permits an adjustment in arms-control formulae acceptable to all concerned as
political conditions change.

The long record of failure in the disarmament talks since
1945 hardly lends encouragement to the belief that delicate,
complex, and potentially fatal agreements can be arrived at
at an early date. On another plane, however, the prospects
have seemed to brighten. By 1963-64, both failures and
successes appeared to Moscow in a clearer light and a more
realistic perspective. As it turned out, elements present
for some time happened to combine fortuitously so as to invite limited agreements on arms control, as well as on trade,

outer space, radio jamming, and the hesitant exploration of other areas of limited but coincident interests between the two camps.

THE PLACE OF INTERNATIONAL COMMUNISM

The world Communist movement is only one of several concerns of the Soviet policy-makers as they view the world beyond Russia's own frontiers. A review of Soviet behavior shows that the interests of the international movement or of its national components abroad have uniformly been subordinated to the needs of Soviet policy. International Communism is thus unlikely to have a direct influence on Soviet arms-control policies. What effect it may have is inherently ambiguous.

In Soviet eyes—though not necessarily in the eyes of other Communists—the objectives of international Communism have been identical with those of the U.S.S.R. For Moscow, therefore, problems have not arisen in the form of policy options involving the subordination of international loyalties to Soviet state purposes. Now that the myth of identical interests can no longer be maintained in the face of the split in the world movement, Moscow proves to be most reluctant to make sacrifices for Communists abroad who may fail to recognize its authority.

For several years, one of the consequences of the Sino-Soviet dispute was Moscow's involvement in ideological two-front warfare: it led Moscow to argue both that it was as "tough" as Peking and that Peking was wrong. It strove to show that it was not "betraying" the cause or "surrendering" to its enemies; and it sought to make clear—to friends and rivals alike—that the "sectarian" and "adventurist" left (as supported by the Chinese and others) is naive, blind, bookish, or else vicious, selfish, and finally, by its own choice, beyond the pale. These conflicting needs made it difficult to pursue a simple and consistent line on arms control.

In this respect the escalation of the Sino-Soviet conflict has eased Moscow's options; indeed, perhaps the desire to ease them contributed significantly to the Soviet decision to sign the test-ban treaty. According to the dominant Soviet view, international Communism would profit from a Soviet-American détente and probably also from a lasting shift of the East-West conflict away from the military arena. This outlook and the policies taken in harmony with it have of course provided

fuel for Chinese Communist counterblasts. Thus, even when
determined not to be inhibited by Peking's views, Moscow
found itself obliged to counteract Chinese Communist efforts
to depict the Soviet commitment to "peaceful coexistence" and
disarmament agreements as detrimental to "national-liberation" movements. The U.S.S.R. has argued with some awk-
wardness that, on the contrary, under conditions of disarmament the colonial powers would be deprived of the means by which
they keep their native subjects in subjection. While the argument has not been uniformly persuasive, Moscow has clearly
concluded that disarmament proposals make good propaganda.
This has certainly been true with regard to most European
Communist Parties. The prospect of arms control, moreover,
is bound to appeal to a wide range of Communists—Tito as
well as the Italian Party, the largest in the West; the Polish
as well as the Scandinavian comrades.

If this part of the Soviet-oriented movement is interested
in stability for the immediate future rather than risky initiatives of "direct action," some other Communist Parties (in
Latin America, North Africa, and the Near East, for instance)
have little use for the strategy pursued by Khrushchev, including limited agreements with the United States. Most disturbing
to the more militant among the world's Communist Parties is
the potential blurring of differences between the Soviet Union
and the United States—a development that would severely test
the loyalty of the Parties' own following and undermine the
Parties' traditional and essential anti-imperialist, anti-Ameri-
can appeals.

Disengagement and elimination of foreign bases would also
be double-edged swords. While on the one hand they would
reduce the network of American and allied positions around
the U.S.S.R., they would significantly weaken Soviet threats
and, therefore, effective Soviet controls in Eastern Europe and
perhaps bar Soviet access to some areas (e.g., Yemen or
Zanzibar) altogether.[13] Finally, agreements providing for inspection and physical verification could (by Soviet definition)
harm Communist security and stability in the U.S.S.R. and
Eastern Europe.

The dispute with Communist China heightens Soviet interest
in certain arms-control measures. It makes—or should make—
serious consideration of GCD impossible so long as the prospect
of a Soviet-Chinese military showdown is not a ludicrous impossibility. Border incidents with China might further stimulate

Soviet interest in the maintenance of strong military power as insurance against Chinese pressures or incursions; this, of course, would reduce Soviet interest in substantial arms-control measures. However, current Soviet interest in agreements providing for the non-proliferation of nuclear weapons is bound to persist even though it cannot actually block Chinese nuclear development.

If the Soviet leadership should decide to mend its relations with others in the Communist world—China above all—rather than preside over the piecemeal liquidation of the international movement, it could probably do so only at a very heavy price. In addition to the blow to Soviet prestige which evidence of such a recognition of failure on the part of Moscow would imply, the Soviet leadership would probably have to scrap its disarmament policy—something which, in turn, would cost it heavily in credibility and standing in the non-Communist world.

The effects of Soviet disarmament policy on Eastern Europe also must be viewed as ambiguous. The Western prediction that the Sino-Soviet rift would further undermine effective Soviet control in this area has been borne out. While the U.S.S.R. may at one time have considered the CMEA [Council for Mutual Economic Assistance, sometimes known as "Comecon"] a possible substitute for more forcible means of control, it must have become aware in the past few years of the low probability of such a development. The withdrawal of Soviet troops behind the Soviet border would probably raise serious political problems for the Soviet Union in Eastern Europe. [14]

It is too early to predict what the effect of regional arms-control agreements would be on the ability of the states involved to pursue a more autonomous policy. [15]

Finally, special mention must be made of the German question. In the Soviet assessment, East Germany would probably be the most exposed and vulnerable bastion in case of a disengagement, neutralization, or stage-by-stage disarmament agreement. And nervousness over East Germany is only compounded by Soviet alarm at the build-up in West Germany. Even if one allows for extensive propaganda use and contrived exaggerations of the Bonn government's plans and purposes, one must recognize that there is here a genuine cause of Soviet concern (be it rational or not) which makes Germany defensively and offensively a formidable stumbling block to various types of disarmament agreement.

A NOTE ON SOVIET POLICY-MAKING ON ARMS
CONTROL AND DISARMAMENT

We know little of the organization and procedures in Moscow by which research is produced, proposals are formulated, recommendations are cleared with interested agencies, and problems and policies in the field of arms control and disarmament are submitted for ultimate decision. The following is therefore put down with an awareness of a greater-than-usual chance of error.

Soviet staff work on disarmament problems, including policy formulation, appears to be less diffuse than its American equivalent. Soviet personnel directly concerned with disarmament number perhaps one tenth of their American counterparts (though in the last two or three years the number of officials involved appears to be increasing). If this makes for some efficiency, it also contributes to what one seasoned observer called a "massive slowness" in Soviet decision-making—in part, because of the shortage of personnel, in part, because of the greater isolation of different bureaucracies at the lower level. There is clearly less flow of information within the Soviet government and Party machinery in Moscow than there is in Washington, because of the virtual absence both of special machinery for this purpose and of informal social occasions at which "shop talk" supplements regular channels of communication.

The isolation of small working staffs may be equally detrimental on a vertical plane. According to one qualified participant, "these people probably never can really get the Soviet leaders to approach the questions of disarmament and arms control in a spirit which seeks an answer acceptable to both sides. There is no policy background against which this process might occur, and until its occurrence the prospects of disarmament are remote."

The shortage of staff on the policy side seems to contrast with what one Soviet official candidly described as a proliferation of arms-control research—in the broadest sense. In fact, every agency with a "legitimate" interest in the subject now appears to be conducting some work of its own.

The most obvious and visible of Soviet agencies is the disarmament section of the Soviet Foreign Ministry. While there is almost nothing about it in the available literature, it is easy to gather some information about it at international meetings and from specialists in this field. Evidently a disarmament staff of some ten men has been working in the Ministry of Foreign Affairs, responsible to I. G. Usachev and indirectly to S. K. Tsarapkin, who heads the ministry's International Organizations Division. While this staff has the authority to initiate proposals, it seems clear that it has little decision-making authority. Its ability to speak for the various interests involved is seriously handicapped by the absence of military or scientific contingents attached to it.

Apart from the secret work of Soviet security and intelligence agencies, the least-known role in disarmament policy formulation is played by the military. The Soviet Ministry of Defense is a closed circle—not only to foreigners but evidently to opposite numbers in the Soviet diplomatic service as well. In fact, the isolation of Soviet civilian specialists from military problems has a direct bearing on the competence of these specialists. One American veteran of the so-called Pugwash conferences believes that Soviet disarmament specialists are more familiar with Western literature on the subject than with the thinking of their own military men. There is evidently little or no contact between the specialists in the Soviet Academy of Sciences and the military establishment. As a result, an American scientist finds, "one never encounters anyone who is well-informed on problems of defense analysis. Thus few Soviet analysts [at international conferences] can make the elementary calculations about rocket circular error probability, which any beginning operations analyst in the United States can do." Even if this judgment should prove to be overstated (thus, military officers are included in Soviet delegations to disarmament conferences), other reports confirm that the basic problem exists.

A good deal of research originates in the Soviet Academy of Sciences. Here, the Institute of World Economy and International Relations (IMEMO) has been engaged in a number of studies, including the first major volume on Soviet disarmament policy between the two World Wars[16] and some work on relevant economic problems. It sponsors the so-called Scientific Group for Disarmament, with Igor Glagolev at its head and Yulian Sheinin as vice-chairman.[17] In addition, other parts of the Academy, such as the Institutes of Law, Military History, and History, carry on rival work relating to disarmament, as undoubtedly do scholars in the pure sciences. Soviet research planners are aware of some of the present shortcomings. A comprehensive discussion of research needs on international relations recently pointed to disarmament as the first field requiring further monographic work. However, with the proper Bolshevik spirit, the author (Academician V. M. Khvostov, a prominent diplomatic historian), demanded such books to "rebutt the tremendous and ever-growing bourgeois literature which distorts the position of the Soviet Union. In the U.S.A. tens of research organizations concern themselves with the disarmament problem; we have work carried on in the Institute of International Relations [IMO]. There have now also been established special sectors [on this subject] in two institutes of the Academy of Sciences of the U.S.S.R."[18] Whether they are to pursue policy-related studies is not clear.

A few leading scientists—one senior American observer guessed that it might be as few as three men—are available to the policy-makers as individual consultants. It was reported that one of the senior Soviet scientists about once a month made a visit to the Party's Central Committee staff or to the Secretariat. In general even the top scientists advising the Soviet leaders—indirectly having some influence on decisions—are used as "resources," invited to comment and express judgments or opinions regarding problems in their own fields of competence. They are, it appears, neither expected nor entitled to argue a case or to voice political judgments.[19]

The staff of the Central Committee and of the Secretariat of the CPSU clearly still plays a crucial part in preparing policy recommendations for the leaders. The normal process appears to consist in their submitting careful presentations to the Party Presidium. Just how important the staff work is, remains in doubt. It is likely that at present the Secretariat and Central Committee sections no longer constitute a bottleneck to communication between outsiders and members of the Presidium; others—senior military commanders or scientists, for instance—can secure access either in an individual or especially in a bureaucratic capacity. Even in such instances, of course, the Secretariat might normally prepare a comment on a report or statement submitted by other institutions. Yet it is known that the Presidium itself has called in specialists in various fields for consultation (regardless of their Party status) before arriving at policy decisions.

It has been impossible to ascertain any details regarding a State Committee on Questions of Disarmament, which was ostensibly established (but evidently not officially announced) a few years ago. It appears possible that such a coordinating agency has been called into existence, but it is almost certain that, if it exists (and is not identical with the research-oriented Glagolev group discussed above) it can neither overcome the different institutional pulls and rivalries nor decisively expand the horizon of Soviet policy advisers, who by and large continue to be characterized by a lack of breadth and detachment.

While we remain ill-informed about internal disagreements on arms control and disarmament, there are numerous indications that policy differences have arisen even since the elimination of the so-called "anti-Party" (i.e., anti-Khrushchev) group in 1957. While some of these may relate to tactical or secondary matters only, it is probable that more fundamental differences remain. In the case of the ban on "war propaganda," which the Soviet negotiators had submitted and pressed, the Party Presidium in Moscow appears to have overruled the Soviet Foreign Ministry after agreement was reached in Geneva. Similarly, there were indications that members of the Soviet delegation at Geneva (and perhaps their diplomatic superiors) regretted or objected to the instructions to break off negotiations on June 27, 1960. Soviet scientists and scholars have privately alluded to divisions in official Soviet circles between pro-disarmament and anti-disarmament positions. Indeed, our conclusions as stated in other parts of this volume lead one to expect such divisions. One can only speculate whether or not some of the charges leveled in 1960-64 at the Chinese Communists as well as at ex-Foreign Minister Molotov were also aimed at some element in the Soviet state bureaucracy, the Party, or the military, who oppose arms-control measures as illusory, dangerous, or naive.

However basic or widespread disagreements among Soviet officialdom may be—and in the past we have tended to underestimate them—ultimately it is the Presidium or a comparable body that makes decisions. If it wishes, it can cut across the deliberate slowness of Soviet bureaucracy; it can unfreeze issues kept on ice for months or years. The possibility of swift decision and action was illustrated when the long drawn-out McCloy-Zorin talks in 1961 suddenly produced agreement on a statement of principles. It was illustrated more recently in the agreement on the banning of nuclear weapons in space. One problem for the Western negotiator is to deal with the U.S.S.R. at a level high enough to encounter a Soviet official who is capable of initiative and fresh thought.

Once the Presidium makes a decision—whatever it is—
the scientists, the military, the bureaucrats, and the rest can
be counted upon to go along regardless of earlier (and continuing) differences of view. There is no evidence that the next
lower echelon of political authority, the Party's Central Committee, is seriously divided. When Khrushchev chose to conclude a test-ban agreement in three environments in July, 1963,
he was evidently able to negotiate without reference to divergent points of view; and the Central Committee, which for the
first time was called upon to take a stand on the matter beginning with its "Open Letter" of July 14, did so without any
evidence of hesitation or division.[20]

Thus it is the members of the Party Presidium—perhaps
meeting in the presence of a few additional specialists invited
for the occasion or, more probably, after hearing their views
and dismissing them—who cast the crucial votes.[21]

Chapter 5

THE SOVIET ECONOMY

To the Soviet regime, the economy has always been an object of special concern. The Bolsheviks were always predisposed to stress material factors in their world view. Their accomplishments in economic development provided the Soviet leaders with objects of genuine pride; and inadequacies of performance or output proved to be areas of particular sensitivity for them. Broadly speaking, the economic goals which the regime set itself, the scarcity of available resources, and the political framework within which the economy developed have all served to circumscribe the Soviet leadership's freedom of choice (including foreign policy choices).

Inevitably, different goals and different interests have competed for the allocation of available but limited resources. Inevitably, the system's inability to satisfy all the demands and claims translates into a measure of constraint on policymakers and into a need for distinct priorities, especially in a system as highly planned and centralized as the Soviet.

STRAINS AND STRESSES

The Soviet regime is solemnly committed to a program of spectacular economic growth, "overtaking America," building the "material-technical base of Communism," rapidly raising the level of consumption at home, and helping less-developed countries abroad. The substantial success of this program is crucial for the validation of the Khrushchev strategy of victory without war. At the same time, the maintenance and perfection of a powerful strategic force has, quite naturally, been regarded as a priority objective vital for the security of the Soviet Union and its allies.

Even if the Soviet defense budget were to remain constant, the simultaneous pursuit of these divergent aims would give rise to serious strains and stresses. Indeed, the economic burdens imposed by the combination of objectives, including the present level of military spending, have of late been underscored by various phenomena. The agricultural crisis—high-

65

lighted in 1963 by the purchase of wheat abroad, the diversion of funds to a "crash" fertilizer program, the uncertain future of the "virgin lands," and the reappearance of food queues in the Soviet capital—illustrates how painful and how contested are the options regarding resource allocation. The rising pressure on Soviet resources has been due in part to below-plan performance in some sectors of the economy (for instance, in construction, agriculture, and economic integration of the Bloc); and in part to growing economic demands (increased defense expenditures in 1961-63, unexpectedly rapid urbanization, assistance to Cuba and Eastern Europe).[1]

The consequences of these pressures have manifested themselves in various ways, such as declines in the investment programs, retardation in the rise of consumption levels, postponement of the scheduled income-tax reductions, and the suspension or postponement of some hydro-electric projects. At the same time, and closely related to the above processes, there has been a "creeping recentralization" and a further complication of the economic-organizational structure.

Clearly, the large resources now devoted to military ends— the armed forces and weapons themselves, as well as related scientific research and development—are a serious burden for the Soviet economy, which operates on a very narrow margin. The leaders would doubtlessly prefer to devote at least a part of these resources to other important goals. It emphatically does not follow, however, that the U.S.S.R. is in any purely economic sense compelled to reduce defense outlays and must, therefore, come to explicit or tacit arms-control agreements with the United States.

After all, in a general atmosphere of (at least ideological and political) conflict with the outside world, the Soviet Union has for some two thirds of the years since 1917 devoted a large share of its annual budget and resources to military ends. The Soviet economy has almost invariably been more highly centralized and mobilized for the prosecution of national goals than was the case with the United States and the United Kingdom even at the height of World War II. In the estimation of the Soviet leaders, the present defense burden can scarcely seem intolerable, since only a relatively few years ago the Soviet Union bore a much heavier burden if measured in proportion to its total annual product. Some expert opinion holds, furthermore, that the recent decline in the Soviet economy's growth rate, in the years since 1958 has not been entirely or even primarily due to military expenditures (nor to the space program).[2] Moreover, one must assume that under appropriate circumstances the Soviet leadership is able and willing to pay the price necessary for continued high defense levels.

It is true, nonetheless, that Khrushchev would much prefer (1) to get "more defense for the ruble," and (2) to follow a policy which, once this is achieved, will permit the reallocation of resources to other sectors. Such economic benefits or savings as may come from a limited understanding with the United States will certainly be welcome, even if the primary motivation behind it is political. On the other hand, economic pressures would, understandably, grow more acute if substantially increased military outlays were contemplated, such as would be required by the development and deployment of an anti-ballistic missile system and perhaps some aspects of space technology. Moreover, the character of military-technology developments makes it likely that arms budgets will require increasing quantities of scarce, high-quality resources.

If this reasoning is correct or is at least shared by Soviet policy-makers, it contributes to the pull toward a Soviet defense establishment of limited but adequate deterrence, not to a commitment to secure strategic parity with the United States. As will be discussed, such a view has some evidence to support it insofar as the post-Cuba phase is concerned. However, it is clearly in conflict with traditional Soviet military doctrine.[3]

POSSIBLE EFFECTS ON THE SOVIET ECONOMY

It is exceedingly difficult to generalize about the likely effects of arms-control agreements on the Soviet economy. First, the resource-releasing effects of various types of arms-control agreements would be very different. Some such agreements would involve only minor resource savings for the U.S.S.R. or none at all. Other agreements might, on the contrary, entail a significant reduction in defense outlay. Others yet might call for appreciable resource commitments for the implementation and verification of arms control. In any event, large reductions in military outlay are likely to be strung out over a number of years, so that the additional resources thus released in any one year are likely to be quite small in

relation to the total volume of resources under the control of
the Soviet authorities.

It is true, nonetheless, that any substantial release of resources as a result of cuts in production (including disarmament) would tend to have a beneficial effect on other parts of
the economy. This much is fairly clear. The more specific
effects of reallocation are conjectural. In the short run, most
of the released resources would probably be directed into investment and probably, to a considerable extent, into investment in consumer-goods industries. This would tend to raise
both the rate of growth of the entire economy and eventually
the level of consumption. How much they would be raised would
depend, among other things, on the pattern of such investment
and on its bottleneck-breaking potential. This last factor is
hard to calculate, for many important bottlenecks derive not
only from scarcities of resources but also from complex
institutional and subjective factors, such as poor planning,
inadequate incentives, and bureaucratic rigidity.[4]

Despite an extensive Soviet propaganda campaign about
the specific construction projects which would become possible if military budgets were reallocated to foreign aid,
Soviet economic and technical assistance (even if substantially increased) would remain of an order of magnitude
markedly smaller than the present military budget.

What has been discussed so far might be called the realloca-
tive effects of a reduction in defense outlays. These may be
significant in the event of a large cut in defense spending, but
their "objective" impact should not be overestimated. Potentially perhaps more important and fundamental are the institutional effects—that is, the effects of a changed economic and
political atmosphere brought about by a significant improvement of relations with the U.S. (as manifested by arms-control
agreements) on the organizational and institutional pattern of
the Soviet economy. In particular, it might provide the impetus
to a drive for a thorough decentralization, which could greatly
improve the efficiency of the Soviet economy, especially with
regard to the extent that consumer needs are effectively met.
Although some recent reforms have pointed the other way, there
is no doubt that even now there are strong forces (both "objective" and "subjective") pushing the Soviet economy in the
direction of decentralization, just as there are powerful vested
interests opposing them.

A détente with the West and a simultaneous reduction in the pressure on resources would be likely to embolden the "decentralizers," while rendering central enforcement of priorities and allocation of funds and materials less urgent. The mechanism of transition from a highly centralized to a largely decentralized economic system would be quite complicated, however; and its completion might still be contingent on several successive changes of leadership.

This is not a prediction of a thorough decentralization of the Soviet economy as a consequence of a détente and of arms-control agreements. Rather, it is to point to one distinct possibility and to stress that such an eventuality might possibly trigger other, far-reaching economic, social, and political changes on the Soviet scene.

At the same time, it should be recognized that, just as there is no real evidence concerning the resource-releasing implications of alternative arms-control arrangements, there is no information about the critical minimum reduction in pressure on resources that might suffice to trigger major institutional changes in the U.S.S.R.

Politically, it was earlier suggested, one effect of a détente coupled with arms-control agreements would be to strengthen centrifugal forces in Eastern Europe. Political steps toward the economic integration of the Soviet Bloc would then be even more difficult to carry out than they are today. Closer trade relations with the West would become even more attractive to the East European states. The U.S.S.R. would be likely to find itself in a weak position to resist the ensuing changes in an atmosphere of general relaxation of tensions. As the example of Rumania shows, the U.S.S.R. already finds it difficult to enforce its wishes, or, rather, is unwilling to pay the price. But it might attempt partially to offset East European moves toward greater economic independence from the U.S.S.R. by other moves, such as a more attractive trade and credit policy toward its allies.

An appreciable measure of arms-reduction arrangements would probably have two contradictory effects on East-West economic relations. On the one hand, the freeing of resources now tied up in arms would increase exportable surpluses, which would facilitate expansion of foreign trade and of economic aid to developing countries. On the other hand, some Soviet import needs have arisen because of the defense program. Hence resources now devoted to military production could

be shifted to the production of equipment now imported. Foreign trade might seem to become a less urgent matter under
such circumstances.

The most likely development would seem to be a moderate
increase in trade—since there would still be a very high demand for imports—with some shift toward the greater import
of consumer goods or related items. (Western fears of large-
scale Soviet exports of surpluses seem unfounded. All signs
point in the direction of a continuing Soviet priority of internal
goals. Moreover, the planning system has a built-in tendency
toward autarky, in the sense of planning to cover the bulk of
domestic needs by domestic production. It is implausible to
assume that the effect of arms reductions on world trade plays
a significant role in Soviet calculations.) [5]

ECONOMIC CONSIDERATIONS IN SOVIET ATTITUDES

How do these economic considerations affect the willingness
of the Soviet leadership to arrive at some forms of arms-control
or disarmament understandings? A simple and "pure" economic
calculus would suggest that (1) unless Soviet policy-makers find
themselves confronted with a choice between intolerable military inferiority and large new outlays well above current spending levels, economic constraints alone will not force them into
arms-control or arms-reduction agreements; and (2) the economic impact of resources released as a consequence of realistically feasible arms-control measures in the next few years
would not be so compellingly attractive as to dictate acceptance
of arms accords unless desired for other reasons as well.

Soviet policy decisions tend to be political decisions. Political (and military) considerations are apt to come first, even
if the policies adopted spell economic burdens and sacrifices.
While it may be entirely true that (according to some Western
economists) realistic disarmament would not have any dramatic
effect on the Soviet economy's growth rate, [6] Soviet leaders and
economists may or may not care to see it this way; the economic
consequences of the peace campaign may look more rosy than
the facts allow.

Soviet budgetary decisions are less likely to be based on
economic imperatives than on economic alternatives. Decisions
involve choices which hinge on the relative value of other uses
of the same capital or resources. It does not follow that a con-

cern for security dictates an increase in Soviet military expenditures. Some might even argue that Moscow strives to take
advantage of the "cover" of nuclear deterrence to effect the
release of resources to other than military purposes, so as
to promote those sectors of the economy whose growth is
deemed essential for the "coexistence" policy to succeed at
all. The official view of the transition to full Communism (as
spelled out since 1959) makes abundance a key prerequisite
of such qualitative progress. Finally, Chairman Khrushchev
and others around him appear to consider certain token moves
significant, either because of their symbolic nature or else
because they could be the first links in a long chain. At any
rate, they have often tended to be overly optimistic in their
assessments of their own (or their Party's, or their country's)
prospects.

On the question of just how much such economic factors weigh
in current Soviet attitudes toward arms control, opinions are
divided: many economists, ironically, tend to minimize their
role, while other specialists tend to give them greater weight.[7]
It is unlikely, of course, that Khrushchev and his associates
can themselves estimate with any precision what the resource-
releasing effects of various disarmament measures might be.
A keen awareness of a multitude of demands for additional investment funds might lead them to overestimate the beneficial
effects of small accords. Furthermore, there need be no direct
correlation between economic savings (or reallocation) and
political effects.

Another important perspective which tends to inflate the
desirability, as seen in some Soviet quarters, of concluding
arms-reduction agreements is the continuing controversy over
priorities in resource allocation. As will be reiterated at
another point, that argument must not be seen merely in terms
of "guns versus butter," or military versus civilian sectors,
or heavy versus light industry. One important axis, among
others, is the choice of present might versus greater future
power. Thus, the assurance that it possesses adequate nuclear
retaliatory capabilities might lead the Soviet Union to shift
some funds to research and development—with possible future
pay-offs—as well as toward branches connected with the consumer world (agricultural machinery, fertilizer, housing, etc.).
The urgency of these choices must be apparent to Soviet leaders,
at a time when their arms-control policy must be based in part

upon an estimate of future costs of space-age weapons systems. That these costs would rise steeply from present levels,
and that they tend to involve particularly scarce materials and
highly trained manpower, are facts which the Soviet leadership
cannot ignore.

Finally, the battles over the level of military spending (discussed in a later chapter) reveal that an important segment of
the Soviet elite is quite sensitive to the pressure of military
expenditures on available resources. The announcement of a
cut in Soviet armed forces in January, 1960, at the height of
one attempted détente (soon after Khrushchev's first visit to
President Eisenhower), evidently precipitated strong fears and
objections in military quarters. Similarly, the announcement
of a 600-million-ruble cut in the stated military budget (from
13.9 to 13.3 billion rubles for 1964), made at the December,
1963, session of the Supreme Soviet—the first after the test-
ban treaty—provides another indication of the direction in which
decisions may go if the détente gains in reality.

The political calculus of the Soviet leadership, based on a
reading of economic factors, seems to point in the direction
of serious interest in arms-control and disarmament measures. However, this inference is certainly not unanimously
accepted in Moscow, and it is at least partly offset by a variety
of other considerations. Among the latter are the possible
effects—economic, strategic, political, and psychological—of
alternative Western policies.

Chapter 6

SOVIET SOCIETY AND PUBLIC OPINION

Stratification and differentiation in Soviet society are among the least studied and least "researchable" phenomena in the U.S.S.R. today. Yet potentially they hold considerable promise for benign changes on the Soviet scene. Studies of Soviet society are severely handicapped by the impossibility of systematic, empirical, on-the-spot research and by the lack of acknowledged Soviet interest in or recognition of some of the problems. In addition, there is considerable theoretical confusion. Neither the Soviet model of a classless society (or at any rate, of the present Soviet society in which—we are told—there are only non-antagonistic strata, cooperating in an "all-peoples' state"), nor the standard Western image of totalitarianism recognizes the existence of diverse groups with potentially or actually conflicting interests. Recent evidence and study suggest that there were such groups even during the most effective atomization of society in the Stalin era. All the more have identifiable groups crystallized during the post-Stalin decade.[1]

There are a variety of reasons for this development. Social and economic change in the U.S.S.R. has helped establish functional and generational loyalties not previously present; by political choice, the regime—both in the "collective leadership" phase and later—has solicited expert opinion, has provided channels of communication for such experts, and has given them an opportunity to be heard; the personal style of the present leaders has helped to identify elite groups and causes. If the personal elements are transient, the social and to some extent the political changes cannot be revoked. Indeed, there is an organic logic in the broad transformation which all modernizing, industrializing, urbanizing societies must undergo, if only for the sake of greater efficiency and specialization. This remains true even if these uniformities are suppressed, delayed, or perverted for a time.

In the present ambiguous state of Soviet society, significant recent modifications of the system exist side by side with "Stalinist" and even earlier patterns of behavior. The significant reduction in the use (and the felt omnipresence) of terror, along with a greater reliance on persuasion and incentives, has been a central feature of post-Stalin "liberalization." To be sure, the Party dictatorship continues substantially unchallenged and undiluted. The Party remains centralized, whatever befalls other institutions. If anything, the stress on indoctrination has increased in recent years. Key positions of power continue to be in the hands of men reared under Stalin. Indeed, the regime periodically demonstrates its continued ability to apply force and intimidation, and to revert to Stalinist abuse and falsification.

There is some disagreement among observers of the Soviet scene regarding the depth of changes and, above all, the probable rate of changes ahead, some holding that social change is likely to take place more speedily beyond a certain "take-off" point, others believing that a deceleration in the dynamism of change is more likely during the coming decade.[2]

Whatever the continuity of its more somber aspects, one may accurately speak of a "liberalization" of certain aspects of Soviet life. An important instance of this process is the greater degree of communication that now takes place between the regime and the public, and among individual Soviet citizens. Greater communication has been crucial in giving rise to genuine "public opinion"—i.e., views and attitudes of private persons which find a form of articulate expression. Since 1953 the state has stimulated or tolerated the public (albeit at times esoteric) expression of divergent views on a variety of issues, even permitting a partial emergence of non-official "opinion leaders"—primarily among the cultural intelligentsia—though without any "guarantees" or any prospect of institutionalization.

In sharp contrast to Stalin's time, there is some increase in communication across bureaucratic lines, even if the present practice is still vastly more inhibited than corresponding American behavior. Within Soviet society, one can now more readily identify groups which collectively make up an elite; and within elite bodies, divergent ideas may now be expressed and opinion groupings formed, by and large, with relatively little risk.

It should be emphasized that it was state initiative, not public expression of demands or hostility to the authorities, that generated this development. Moreover, there are obvious political limits to the area of licit diversity. Whether these limits can in fact be made to hold, and whether official intent will remain observed is another question; but clearly the leadership has encouraged greater communication with a view to its own objectives, not with the intention of countenancing oppositionist sentiments. At its most "liberal," the leadership has done no more than periodically attempt some pre-emptive relaxation in the arts and literature.

A reliable knowledge of Soviet sociography, stratification and mobility, and criteria for ascription to one or another group, are sadly lacking. For the purposes of this Report, one broad distinction must be made between the potentially influential members of the elite (who are not themselves among the top decision-makers of the U.S.S.R.) and the rank and file of the population.

DIVERSITY OF ATTITUDES WITHIN THE SOVIET ELITE

There is circumstantial evidence indicating that the complex of questions relating to disarmament and arms control is very much a part of the broad issues dividing public opinion. To the political elite specifically, large-scale arms-control measures are likely to appear as a component part or an extension of the general "liberal" trend.

While the existence of sharp divisions among Soviet elite groups (on disarmament, just as on other issues) can be identified, there is no sure way of determining which of two suggested interpretations has the greater validity. Whereas one approach extends the political dichotomy—"modernist" versus "traditional" outlooks—into integrated attitudinal patterns among broad segments of Soviet society, the other links differences in elite opinion to divergent functional and perhaps geographic interests. (The two approaches are, of course, not quite mutually exclusive.) Without necessarily discrediting the former approach (which has been followed in much of the political analysis underlying Chapters 2 and 3 above), many analysts incline toward the latter conceptual framework.[3]

It may be presumed that strong dissatisfaction with the prospect of extensive disarmament measures emanates from certain parts of the military, as will be discussed in Chapter 7, and from the Party's ideological elite. It is probable—and true in certain identifiable instances—that the attitude of these two groups finds sympathy among some other officials, managers, and scientists associated with the military establishment.

A hypothesis which warrants further investigation suggests that the same kinds of arms-control and disarmament measures find particular favor among officials and managers of certain (non-armament) industrial and agricultural enterprises, some members of the Soviet diplomatic service, and some economic planners. The one elite group in which the evidence indicates an attitude strongly in favor of disarmament is the "creative" intelligentsia—writers, scientists, and artists. This applies especially to its upper and middle layers centered in Moscow.

The attitude of the bulk of the Party's organizational apparatus, which forms the backbone of the entire Soviet political system, is inherently conservative. This key bureaucratic group, and especially its middle layer, must be expected to be instinctively suspicious of and opposed to any change, innovation, or experimentation which appears unpredictable in outcome or which might lessen the group's authority or control. Finally, residual layers in certain elite groups have no active or articulated attitudes on this subject. An example is the lower level of economic officials within the Party machine.

It is hard to be more precise. In part, this necessary vagueness is due to our lack of information. In part, it stems from the recentness, frailty, and caution which characterize the articulation of private or group opinions where these may differ from the "official" line. Such articulation is, after all, encouraged neither by the habits of political practice nor by an awareness of the possible risks of deviation and dissent. Moreover, as is so often the case in Soviet experience, much depends on the general context in which issues such as disarmament come up for consideration. The opinions of the same group may differ drastically depending on the status of Sino-Soviet relations, of the general détente with the West, of the intensity of memorable crises that might have touched off thermonuclear war, or of domestic conditions generally. It might be fairest to say that attitudes are likely to be formed in large measure in response to (1) broad attitudes toward the outside world, such as suspicion of all "deals" with the imperialist camp, fear of West Germany or the United States, or conversely, a desire for closer contact or identification with the West;[4] and (2) a more functional or even personal view, ultimately reduced to the question: "What will it mean for me?"

It has been argued that even among the most "conscious" members of the Soviet intelligentsia it is usually the quest for personal security, comfort, recognition, latitude, or privacy that is at play, and not a demand for broad political change or even for "rights" for all (or for specific groups of society). Publicly at least, many scientists and technicians (to mention but one important category) do not give much evidence of interest in political affairs or independent political thinking. Yet experience suggests that such appearances may be deceiving; that this is not true among some of the younger scientists; that in fact some of the top scientists, who are very much a part of the Soviet "establishment," do have a strong sense of social conscience and public responsibility and may on occasion have used their powers of persuasion with Central Committee and Presidium members on behalf of specific agreements (for instance, the proposed test ban with a maximum of three annual on-spot inspections). The contacts of recent years also suggest that Soviet specialists (none too surprisingly) are capable of learning, changing their minds, and establishing personal rapport and channels of communication which may conduce to the successful exploration of arms-control agreements.

On balance, most observers seem to agree that it would be an error to think of "the Party" as a separate, single, and superior entity in this network of still inchoate but emerging interest groups. One assumption of the earlier part of this Report has been the existence of individuals near the apex of the Party edifice (for instance, on the Central Committee staff) who sympathize with different policy positions or with particular interest groups. Increasingly Party officials tend to identify themselves with the particular universe to which they are assigned. This tendency has no doubt been reinforced by the splitting of the Party into "industrial" and "agricultural" hierarchies in November, 1962. (For instance, an agricultural Party secretary, who will have top responsibility for farming in his area and will be judged by its performance, will be compelled to act as a spokesman for a sectional interest group.) The same tendency is reinforced by Khrushchev's emphasis on technical competence in Party functionaries, which also involves the recruitment to the Party apparatus of persons whose prior careers have been largely outside this structure.[5]

One possible line of development, therefore, is the increasing dissolution of the solidarity and common characteristics of the Party apparatchik and the corresponding growth in the use of various forms of barter, pressure, and persuasion by spokesmen for different policy and functional groups.

INFLUENCE OF ELITE ATTITUDES ON
SOVIET POLICY

In what circumstances and to what extent do attitudes of various elite groups influence the formation and execution of Soviet policy? One should distinguish between a given set of communications by specific individuals, through identifiable channels, and a more diffuse, hardly demonstrable, awareness of group interests among the top strata of Soviet policy-makers. Another distinction should be made between specific (or technical attitudes bearing on concrete arms-control or disarmament proposals, which are bound to be the province of a few, and general attitudes favoring or opposing disarmament and related ("partial") measures. Such general attitudes need not be based on precise and genuine knowledge; more often than not, they spring from the over-all mood of elite groups and as such are, in one way or another, brought to the attention of policy-makers.

Soviet policy-making remains essentially centralized. Thus divergent views, whether communicated specifically to a segment of the central apparatus, or vaguely made known to other officials at the top, are not likely to be of major influence in determining decisions; groups with divergent views are presumably in no position to dictate or compel policy decisions. On the other hand, such is the nature of politics, even under Soviet conditions, that the leadership ignores the opinions of others at its own peril. The limited autonomy which various elite groups, notably the military, have currently achieved does affect the speed or ease with which relevant policies may be adopted or changed. Though not a veto power, an informal right to be consulted by the regime prior to final decisions thus emerges as a tacit objective—partly already realized—of the crystallizing elite groups.

If a diminution of direct Party predominance (or Party failure on a number of fronts) occurs in the next decade, greater Party receptivity to the attitudes of other elites may be anticipated, including alternative attitudes toward disarmament proposals. Likewise, an extended struggle for leadership, during which two or more contending groups are temporarily in balance, could greatly increase the weight of elite opinion.

If, on the other hand, Party predominance should increase, the influence of divergent attitudes would presumably decline. However, a more firmly entrenched leadership would perhaps feel freer to venture into large-scale arms reduction or disarmament in defiance of some negative reactions among the political elite.

"PUBLIC OPINION" AND SOVIET POLICY

While it is often hard for the observer of the Soviet scene to identify individuals or groups with specific policy positions, it is possible to discover issues which stimulate differing arguments. The "peace issue" and the "consumer-goods issue" probably command the greatest national consensus among the issues for which an attentive public and self-styled spokesmen have emerged since the death of Stalin.[6] Opinion among foreign observers is virtually unanimous regarding the intensity of popular "anti-war" sentiments in the Soviet Union. While not necessarily a logical sequitur, the general "peace" mood may be taken to establish a predisposition in favor of disarmament and arms-control arrangements. The non-differentiated consumer population also forms a huge "lobby." On consumer issues personal demands again go hand in hand with promises and arguments made by the Party leadership in the course of recent years. To a large extent, the groups having a favorable disposition toward disarmament are thus likely to coincide with those favoring more consumer goods, and both tend to overlap considerably with the (perhaps somewhat smaller) group supporting the general "reformism" of the Khrushchev era. While the expression of such views is not sufficiently widespread or audible to provide firm evidence for outside observers, the general mood is sufficiently well known to be credible; and the logic of the syndrome suggests its reality.

In the minds of rank-and-file citizens, disarmament—seen as an extension of "peaceful coexistence"—makes possible the pursuit of other goals; and it provides the savings needed to produce more consumer goods. In the Khrushchev era, the authorities are more attuned to the satisfaction of these consumer demands, more inclined to make changes in structure and policy, and to seek agreements with the "other" camp so as to avoid nuclear war.

It should be borne in mind at the same time that Soviet

foreign policy and national-security policy tend to arouse more popular support than do domestic issues. By its very nature, foreign policy is not subject to verification or to contradiction by personal experience; by and large, the regime has had a near-monopoly on information and interpretation of world events. Moreover, strong Soviet patriotism also tends to reduce the divergence between mass opinion and official policy on the "peace" issue. And the available evidence suggests a widespread fear that influential groups in the West might unleash a new war. In general, it is probable that there is a qualitative difference in non-elite public opinion between attitudes relating to domestic problems and those oriented toward the outside world: while the former tend to be critical and precise, the latter tend to be approving and amorphous.

Soviet leaders will not be induced by mass feelings to accept proposals which, in their own opinion, run counter to their national (or their own) interests. And yet in several ways popular sentiment can make itself felt. For one thing, it can reinforce the position of those leaders who advocate a course it also favors. Thus at all times of divided opinion at the top— and, of course, especially during times of power struggle— popular opinion constitutes, as it were, a "reserve" of one or the other wing. In this instance, sentiment in favor of disarmament and arms control is almost certain to be immeasurably stronger than popular hostility to them.[7]

The present Soviet leadership manifests an undeniably greater interest in public attitudes than Stalin did. This attentiveness is explicable in terms of the dual function that public opinion may perform. It may (or may not) legitimize power and policies in a society. And it may facilitate (or hinder) the attainment of national goals. One source of the government's concern with public opinion is its preoccupation with the need to raise labor productivity. Productivity is directly related to the state of public morale. Morale is, in turn, directly influenced by material incentives and by the degree of public confidence in the wisdom of state policy and its congruence with the individual's own goals, including "peace" and "consumer goods." And, more broadly, public opinion ultimately creates the environment in which the regime seeks loyalty and support.

Public opinion can thus indirectly motivate Soviet leaders to seek (or appear to seek) arms agreements in order to give evidence of striving for "peace," or of releasing resources to satisfy consumer needs. The Soviet authorities have for a

number of years so repeatedly depicted themselves as the advocates of disarmament and their enemies as opponents of arms
cuts and disarmament agreements, that the regime no doubt
expects to earn political credit at home if any disarmament
or even arms-control measures are carried out.

At the same time, the reciprocal aspect of these popular
opinions is the extent to which the Soviet leadership can manipulate this very sentiment. Such manipulation would strive to
attain a substantial internal consensus that the maintenance
of peace depends on building up the economic and military might
of the Soviet Union, so as to discourage Western imperialists
who threaten the peace. Past success in such endeavors of
blaming the outside world for a retarded increase in the
standard of living and, to some extent, for abuses of "vigilance"
and discipline should not be underestimated. Nor should it be
assumed that popular opinion need always be on the side of
the angels. To be sure, anti-war, anti-terror, pro-consumer-
goods sentiments all happen to pull in a direction which some
"modernist" Soviet leaders would seek to promote and which
would be in the interests of the outside world as well. On the
other hand, an intolerant, chauvinistic nationalism, or a self-
centered isolationism are not utterly implausible alternatives
for the popular mood.

The role of public opinion, then, remains uncertain and at
best indirect. It seems clear, however, that what influence it
does have tends to support rather than weaken the advocacy
of disarmament; and future Soviet leaders—whoever they may
be—are likely to be more open than their predecessors to information and opinion from below as well as from abroad.
Hopefully, the channels of communication to and from the
decision-makers will become and remain comparatively free
from the obstructions which have choked them for so long.

Chapter 7

THE SOVIET MILITARY

ESTABLISHMENT AND POLITICS

Traditionally the Communist Party—or, more correctly, its "leading organs"—has had the decisive voice in Soviet policy formulation. When appropriate, the Party leadership has sought to use the professional competence of military men, much as it has called upon the expertise of scientists or the knowledge of engineers, as one input in the process of policy-formulation.

The exercise of political control over the armed forces and their senior commanders, through an intricate network of political officers with its own chain of command, has been a constant feature of Soviet civil-military relations. The competing claims of military efficiency and political reliability have been permanent sources of tension in the Soviet state. In the words of one leading expert, "the inevitable tendency [has been] for the military, at moments of its ascendancy, to seek the efficient non-political army, and to attempt to slip the shackles of political control."[1] But usually the state and the Party have striven to minimize military autonomy and to maximize political pliancy.

The duel was especially acute in Stalin's days. Stalin weakened the military establishment almost fatally by the violent, extensive purge of its commanding staff in 1937-38. The German attack on the Soviet Union in 1941, in turn, gave the Red Army an opportunity to assert itself vis-à-vis the political leadership. The armed forces managed to establish "unitary command" in lieu of the inefficient and abrasive dual Party-military command system which had prevailed until then. Even then the Army was carefully barred from participating in the formulation of Soviet strategy. Its record, however, in winning the war, and its mass base and resonance in the country endowed the Red Army with unprecedented prestige at home and abroad—to such an extent that Stalin, soon after World War II, began to tighten the reins, remove popular commanders, reinstate political surveillance, and seek to reduce it once again to his own serviceable instrument. At the same time, what was later called the cult of Stalin's personality gave him a monopoly of "creativity" in military doctrine and effectively prevented the armed forces in the following decade from adjusting to the imperatives of the atomic era.

The high command was thus in all likelihood one of the institutions which greeted Stalin's demise with relief and expectancy. At the same time, it is well to recall that by 1953 the Soviet military establishment amounted to a major force, internationally recognized, widely feared and respected, commanded by a generation of officers who were increasingly also "good Communists," to whom the problem of disloyalty and subversion no longer loomed with the magnitude or intensity that it had a generation earlier or even during the early months of World War II. The fact remains that until recent years attempts to assert military autonomy from political dictation failed. [2]

While the presumption of continued civilian—i.e., Party—control is strong, tradition is not itself a control mechanism. The ability of the Party to keep the military establishment in its assigned relationship to policy is determined by the effectiveness, stability, and image of governmental and political power. Thus a diminution in the degree of military subordination creates the potential for a corresponding increase in military influence on policy formulation. At other times, however, any attempt by the military to by-pass or speak over the heads of the political leadership—such as Marshal Zhukov's Leningrad speech of July 14, 1957[3]—is bound to be perceived as an intolerable challenge.

It has become customary to distinguish between military influences on national policy, at home and abroad, on military affairs, and on domestic (and elite) politics. So far as the first of these, state and Party policy, is concerned, the direct role of the military has traditionally been minimal. Virtually never in the past has there been any disposition on the part of the Soviet military—either as individual leaders or as an institution—to challenge the dominant role of the Party in national policy formulation. The uses to which military power is put have been determined by the political leadership, and the role of the military has been to furnish advice and to assist in integrating military strategy into national policy, rather than to participate in policy-making. There is no compelling evidence in recent developments to suggest a <u>frontal</u> challenge to this tradition of political primacy.

<u>Indirect</u> influence, however, has been significantly on the increase, albeit subject to violent fluctuations, in the post-Stalin era. This increase is caused, among other things, by the removal of Stalin's iron grip on the institutions under him, by the indispensability of specialists under conditions of increasing complexity in weapons systems and evaluations, and by the all-encompassing nature of present-day military strategy. Out of strictly functional considerations, senior commanders must participate in the political dialogue, either as advisers (who can "stack the deck" by the advice they tender and the demands they make); or as members of political bodies such as the CPSU Central Committee, in which they speak for virtually the entire military establishment. It is true that their effectiveness is significantly reduced when they are not homogeneous in their own political orientation, as seems repeatedly to have been the case. Moreover, there are, by and large, strict and narrow limits beyond which Soviet military leaders will not stray: they are loyal to the system; they will accept a decision once it is made; and they will be sufficiently aware of their own privileged position in Soviet society to be interested in a measure of stability and continuity. Even if they have a few "friends" in the Party Presidium, they cannot always count on them to swing decisions in favor of their preferred schemes.

No doubt, the main lever of their influence is the very control of the visible implements of power—organized armed forces. The Soviet military appear to be increasingly conscious of their own potential to use military force for political ends <u>within</u> the Soviet state. While not inconceivable, actual steps by the military are likely to be extremely risky and very rare. Yet the awareness of the political leadership that an army commander can, for instance, precipitate a "catalytic" confrontation with the West on an East German autobahn, must in itself give Soviet commanders a certain bargaining position.

There are other ways in which the armed forces exert an indirect influence on Soviet policy. An estimate of military intelligence regarding the armed forces of other powers and the "correlation of forces" may stimulate or inhibit Soviet willingness to strike or retaliate. Military options regarding weapons systems and different profiles of strategic forces, or regarding military doctrine and relative readiness for action, are but some of the ways in which "professional" or "technical" advice circumscribes or guides political decisions.

The rash of articles and statements by present or former Soviet army commanders cannot be interpreted as anything but an attempt to boost some and downgrade other political or military leaders by rewriting recent military history. Thus the credit given for victory in the battle of Stalingrad (now Volgograd) has been a good indicator of the political fortunes of an individual leader. Less directly, it has become clear since January, 1960, that the military leadership has the ability to drag its feet in resisting change and thus impose limits on the flexibility of the political chiefs. This residual bureaucratic strength—in addition to direct participation in discussions and consultations—may well have been underestimated as a means of leverage. In some part, this strength is due to the fact that the dividing line between the "proper" concerns of the military and the political universe is increasingly hard to draw in an age when the armed forces have a "legitimate" voice with regard to problems such as the Warsaw Treaty Organization, civil defense, arms control and disarmament, and that vast area of contention—resource allocation.

Close students of Soviet military writings believe that the recent volume edited by Marshal Vasilii Sokolovsky, Military Strategy,[4] may be precisely such an effort to exert indirect pressure on the political leadership. According to this view, the Sokolovsky volume is a document in which the military side (or probably a major faction within it) appears to have scored a point in the strategy debate by getting its view on the record in the first comprehensive exposition of a new Soviet military doctrine.

Had Military Strategy been confined to dealing with strategic concepts only in a technical sense, it would be less suspect of having laid down a challenge. However, the book also sought to identify Soviet military doctrine with the most fundamental conceptions of state interest, and to emphasize its significance as a basis for state policy. This suggests a greater disposition than the military leadership has shown in the past to influence top-level policy-making in a direction responsive to its own concept of national interests, thereby treading upon a terrain once reserved to the political leadership. That the Party leadership indeed regarded the book as such an encroachment would seem to be suggested by some of the comments on the

book which have appeared in the Soviet press.[5] Various other
signs point in the same direction. Marshal Rodion Malinovsky, in an article full of extravagant praise of Khrushchev on
his seventieth birthday, in effect claimed a veto power by
underscoring the fact that, unlike the Stalin era, the Party
Presidium made sure to consult the military commanders before
making relevant decisions.[6]

The disparate purposes of the civilian and military leaders
continue to generate differences in perceptions and policy
preferences between the two groups. The political leadership,
seeking to use military power for political ends, naturally
tends to stress short-term capabilities to the point of perhaps
preferring a "bang" and a "bluff" to the maintenance under
arms of large contingents or the upkeep of vast arsenals of
conventional (albeit obsolescent) weapons. By contrast, professional military interest dictates a primary concern with the
problems of actually fighting—and winning—a war if and when
one should occur. The military interest will thus naturally
tend in the direction of greater preparedness, of playing it
safe, therefore opting for more conservative solutions—e.g.,
regarding force size—and appraising enemy forces "realistically, without under-estimation."

One may speculate whether in the future the political use of
military power is not bound to decline in effectiveness. Given
the recent experience with the "boomerang" of the missile-
gap myth in the United States, with the Cuban crisis and the
Berlin threats, it is possible that in the nuclear age the credibility of untested military threats will fade. But even if this
is to be the case, a source of tension will remain in the continuing control of Soviet decision-making by the political element, and the growing de facto assertion of independence by
the top army leaders. Marshal Malinovsky's public views on
U.S. aggressiveness, on the evils of popular pacifism in the
Soviet Union, on the roles of Stalin and Khrushchev during the
last war, on the probability of war, and on the insufficiency of
deterrence, are all examples of this newly-won autonomy, which
goes well beyond the strict and traditional limits of military
concerns.

One area in which the Soviet marshals traditionally have enjoyed considerable autonomy is, of course, that of military
affairs, such as strategy formulation, the planning and implementation of military training and preparations, and the allocation of the military sector of the budget. More recently, this

area has included problems of military doctrine and related decisions regarding weapons systems, which in the present era have political overtones and implications. Within the limits of broad political requirements, the military have had the major say in these fields.

One should, however, take care not to regard the "Party" and the "military" as two altogether discrete and antipodal bodies in constant opposition to one another. One of the most important trends in recent years has been precisely the alliance between the "modernists" (i.e., moderates) on the political side with the "modernists" (i.e., radicals) on the military. And this seems to have come about not primarily because of a power struggle but rather as the result of an argument between two fundamentally divergent doctrines and strategies.

Thus the unwitting involvement of the military leaders in national policy problems and the traditional concern of these leaders for strategic and military matters are virtually inseparable from, and unintelligible without, an understanding of the third area of military influence—Soviet elite politics.

The outlines of this dynamic relationship are well known, and details have been supplied in several superior studies.[7] In the words of one seasoned analyst,

> The involvement of the military in politics was not achieved as the consequence of a deliberate desire on the part of the marshals to become politicians. Simply on the professional and seemingly non-political grounds of determining the security requirements and military posture of the Soviet Union, the marshals were led to endorse certain policies, and hence to support the factions favoring these policies.[8]

In the face of disunity and maneuvering among the political leadership after Stalin's death, the military leadership found itself drawn into the political arena. It is important to recall that in 1953-57, so far as we know, the marshals stood firmly by Khrushchev in each succeeding crisis. They supported the arrest of Beria in 1953 (with Marshal Zhukov taking Beria's place on the Central Committee); in 1954 and early 1955, they attacked Malenkov's policies in Red Star editorials even before he "resigned." In the Polish and Hungarian crises of 1956, the military rallied to the country's political leadership. They apparently backed parts or all of the emerging Khrushchev line in foreign affairs (e.g., a rapprochement with Tito). And

in the showdown between Khrushchev and the majority of the
Presidium, in June, 1957, the role of the military was unmistakable and, according to some reports, even decisive in assuring Khrushchev's victory by throwing the issue into the full
Central Committee. Yet by virtue of this very victory Zhukov
and the military as a whole were bound to suffer: Khrushchev
no longer faced a divided Presidium, no longer depended on
military support against his political rivals, and could therefore rid himself of the implicit challenge which he saw in
Zhukov's actions and pronouncements. Thus the marshals
lost the opportunity to utilize factional strife within the Party
elite to promote the policies they (or rather, some of them)
preferred. [9]

The alignment of the marshals in Soviet elite politics was
thus made not on personal grounds but in terms of policies
and issues. Though divided among themselves, their collective
weight tended to be reflected in their increasingly free hand in
several fields; these were, notably: (1) military doctrine, especially with regard to nuclear weapons and nuclear war;
(2) insistence on a fair share (or more) of the budget and of
the nation's resources for the military and for related sectors
of the economy; and (3) the "de-Stalinization" of the armed
forces, as measured in the reduction of political controls
over professional officers, the rehabilitation of innocent victims of Stalin's purges, and the promotion and appointment of
senior commanders congenial to this trend.

Ironically, after 1957 the quest for military autonomy and
professionalism was at least partially eroded. Debates and differences have apparently continued on separate but at times
intersecting planes. First, there is the continuing polemic between political and military leaderships, recently illustrated by
the Sokolovsky volume and perhaps barely concealed in Marshal Malinovsky's pronouncements. Second, on various occasions sharp differences over military policy—including especially the size and shape of the military establishment—
have arisen in the CPSU Central Committee. Disagreements
came to the fore in the Malenkov period and again in 1959-60,
when most of the military leadership, we are told, disagreed
with Khrushchev's policies of retrenchment, force reductions,
and a moratorium on nuclear testing. And third, the divisions
within the military profession have tended to leave it split
between conservative and radical approaches to military
affairs.

The military conservatism, in this context, is one following the proclivity to maintain substantial ground forces and conventional weapons (and correspondingly to de-emphasize new weaponry). The military radical, by contrast, is prepared to bank on missiles and nuclear fire-power and, perhaps, to reduce the number of men under arms. In the words of one analyst,

> The conservatives consist mainly of ranking officers in the Ground Forces, who tend to cling to theater-operations concepts, doubt the decisiveness of strategic nuclear weapons, and stress the role of the combined-arms theater forces in future war. The progressives, who are ranking officers in the technical services, stress (more than the conservatives do) the decisiveness of the initial period of war, and thereby imply the obsolescence of large standing conventional forces.[10]

Thus, while on one level the Party moved to reassert its primacy over the armed forces after 1957 (no other military man was advanced to membership in the Party Presidium, as Marshal Zhukov had been), on another level, advocates of more consumer goods and advocates of reliance on nuclear weapons could join in opposition to both civilian and military "diehards."

The intermittent Soviet reduction of the size, budget, and expected role of conventional forces has as its complementary policy the search for a détente with the West and for a shift in resource allocation in the direction of welfare, services, and light industries. Significantly, the apparent Soviet reassessment of U.S. intentions in 1959, coincided with a decision not to give Communist China nuclear weapons or "know-how," the first comprehensive GCD proposal before the United Nations, and the decision to reduce Soviet armed forces by one third. In his report of January 14, 1960, to the Supreme Soviet entitled, "Disarmament: The Road to Durable Peace and Friendship Among Nations," Khrushchev confirmed the new "line": "The air force and navy are, at the present level of weapon development, no longer of the importance they used to be. . . . A considerable proportion of our armed forces has been converted to rocket and nuclear armament. . . . In our time a country's defense potential is not determined by the number of men under arms."[11]

The zigzags during the following years cannot be detailed

here. Suffice it to say that the Soviet Union has seen successive reversals of policy between the "radical" and the "conservative" views and their political equivalents. The budget
cuts announced in December, 1963, suggested a possible or
partial return to the January, 1960, approach. While some
elements among the military elite have fully supported Khrushchev's arguments, it appears that his political decisions have
often prompted military corollaries unacceptable to the profes-
sionals. Indeed, even while Khrushchev succeeded for a time
in deceiving American as well as Chinese Communist observers
regarding Soviet missile and nuclear strength, his futile bluffing over Berlin as well as his abortive Cuban gambit apparently provoked an adverse reaction among the Soviet military, some of whom were inclined to blame the Party for the
Cuban failure. It was surely no accident that Marshal V. I.
Chuikov (in an unusual interview with Red Star, published on
November 17, 1962) cited a telegram which Stalin is alleged
to have sent Lenin during the Soviet-Polish War of 1920.
The telegram's key passage read: "It must be noted, in connection with the attitude of the Central Committee...that our
diplomacy sometimes very effectively spoils the results
achieved by our military victories." [12] When, in his speech
to the Central Committee on December 13, 1963, Khrushchev
raised "the possibility of some further reduction in numbers
of our armed forces," not a single military leader hastened
to express support for the idea. Finally, the same Marshal
Chuikov, Commander of the Soviet Ground Forces, in a major
article sought to demonstrate that the NATO powers were now
"insistently improving their ground forces to accord with
present-day needs," only to conclude that "under contemporary
conditions the ground forces continue to be not only a mandatory
but also a highly important integral part of the armed forces." [13]

Thus the debate went on. There are reports of considerable
earlier opposition to a nuclear test-ban treaty among Soviet
military commanders. There is circumstantial evidence to
suggest that such divergencies still existed when the test-ban
treaty was signed in 1963. The groups within the military establishment which would see the greatest dangers or disad-
vantages in this particular agreement are those with the new-
est equipment—the Air Defense Command and the Strategic
Rocket Command: they would see their opportunities restricted
in proportion to the length and scope of the ban. In most other
instances, it is the ground forces that are most likely to pro-

vide spokesmen for the "conservative" military argument and hence against the policy promoted by Khrushchev.[14]

Despite the continuing policy disagreements on the part of a substantial portion of the military elite, Khrushchev has assumed correctly that the military establishment remains loyal and obedient to the dictates of the Party leadership.

The weight of the military—provided they are not themselves severely divided—is likely to increase at times of factional strife or of a succession crisis, with the marshals conceivably cast in the role of "king-makers." No doubt their support would again be courted by one or another faction. The military apparatus exhibits a unique continuity, a sense of separate "belonging," and an awareness of its own potential. This very potential for influence upon internal Soviet politics would, of course, tend to increase the power of the military in matters involving national policy and strategy.

DOCTRINE AND CAPABILITIES

The reopening of debate on military doctrine and strategy in the Soviet Union was a momentous development. In 1953, two events, Stalin's death and Soviet success in producing nuclear weapons, were the essential elements—the former made the debate possible; the latter made it necessary.

Other studies have analyzed and documented this debate in convincing detail.[15] In brief, the first phase—from 1953 to 1955—saw the gradual reopening of discussion at the instance of the military, prompted largely by the necessity of adapting official concepts to new developments in military technology. The next phase—with the opening of the missile age—stemmed largely from a political effort to adopt a military posture of primary reliance on nuclear deterrence, in part for the sake of political and economic benefits. Finally, after compromises seemed to be reached between the "modernist" and "traditionalist" wings among the proponents of conflicting military theories (as well as among the corresponding political orientations), the Cuban gamble of 1962 dramatized a succession of Soviet setbacks and, in 1963-64, prompted a re-examination of the Soviet doctrine of strategic superiority. The disagreements have clearly not been fully resolved.

The military debate does not address itself directly to disarmament policy, just as unclassified Soviet military writing does not theorize in a serious way on the relationship between different military strategies and various forms of arms control. In its implications, however, the Soviet military debate is highly relevant to the problems of arms control and disarmament.

The development of nuclear weapons and their effect on the military balance have had a fundamental impact on Soviet outlook and policy. An awareness of the destructive nature of thermonuclear war has served as a central motive for the Soviet commitment to "peaceful coexistence" and for Soviet interest in disarmament measures which might reduce the likelihood of such a war. From the declaration (1956) that wars are no longer deemed inevitable to the affirmation (1963) that "the atomic bomb does not adhere to the class principle," it has been a hard but genuine process of adjustment. Not all Soviet responses, it is true, have made for moderation. Some Soviet leaders have looked to military technology as the most promising means to upset the world balance; others have argued in favor of improving the relative power position of the U.S.S.R. in order to prevent the United States from exploiting its military power for political advantage.

There has been, in recent years, a distinct increase in the sophistication and competence of Soviet military writing and in its responsiveness to problems growing out of the current military-technological revolution. Statements on military doctrine now expose real issues bearing on Soviet policy; and, while there is a consensus on a broad range of subjects, unresolved differences of view between what have been called "modernist" and "traditionalist" outlooks have also been brought into focus.

There remains a gap between Soviet and Western contemporary military thought. Soviet writing is generally more permeated with political and ideological arguments. It also conspicuously fails to pay attention to the entire range of relationships between military postures and arms control. Neither does it address itself to the various concepts of "controlled response" advanced in the West in an effort to mitigate the damage to civilian society in the event of a nuclear war. Thus, while Soviet and Western military thinkers have begun to "speak the same language," they are still apt to talk past each other. Yet in the last few years there are indications that Soviet observers and theorists are not only capable of sophistication but are following more closely than ever—and understanding—the best of Western writing on military doctrine, strategy, and arms control.

THE NATURE OF WAR

Among the issues in military doctrine considered and revised in recent years—and in some cases still subject to widely divergent interpretation by different Soviet commentators and officials—only a few can be singled out here. Elsewhere, Khrushchev's reinterpretation of the <u>political</u> doctrine of war has been examined. Since the abandonment of the assertion of the inevitability of war, in 1956, there has also been a distinct decline in the Soviet use of the orthodox concept of just and unjust wars. Yet it was only years later that Khrushchev in effect reversed his 1954 position and came to argue against the Chinese that no victors would emerge from a thermonuclear war. But it remained true that, while general war had to be avoided (the civilian emphasis), one had to be ready to fight and win such a war if it came (the military emphasis).

Since 1954, writes an expert on Soviet military affairs, "the Soviet leadership has lived with an unresolved doctrinal crisis over the question of war as an instrument of policy."[16] Since about 1959, the political leadership seems to believe that the military posture of both the United States and the Soviet Union makes deliberate policy resort to war highly unlikely. (Khrushchev's argument that "men of reason," not "madmen," are in control in Washington in effect underwrites this view.) In substance though not explicitly, this amounts to acceptance of the notion of mutual deterrence, despite the frequent and at times no doubt sincere Soviet concern about Western intentions.[17] Some of the Soviet military leaders, on the other hand, tend to regard the probability of war as somewhat higher—in part unwittingly, as a consequence of their professional concern with the problems of waging war; in part, consciously, in an attempt to justify the kinds of preparedness and expenditures they consider necessary. Marshal Malinovsky, among others, has on several occasions publicly spoken of the aggressive military plans of the United States.

If, as seems to be the case, the prevalent view in Moscow is that the United States will not strike first against the Soviet Union, the possibility of general war shifts primarily to war by accident, misunderstanding, or miscalculation, or else to the escalation of local or limited wars. Ever since November, 1957,

Khrushchev has given considerable publicity to the dangers of
accidental nuclear war and played up all the standard unsubtle
stereotypes of possible derangement or mental failures of individual pilots, geese on radar screens, and the like. On the
other hand—most though not all seem to agree—there have been
indications, especially since the experience of Cuba and the
opening of the "hot line," that the Soviet leadership regards
accidental or unintended war as less worrisome a prospect
than the danger of war from political miscalculation or the involvement of the great powers through the actions of other
states. Khrushchev's private estimates have repeatedly been
rather optimistic so far as the continued prospects of mutual
deterrence are concerned. (The somewhat higher estimate of
the possibility of war in Soviet military analyses, such as the
Sokolovsky volume, which is in no sense an extreme "traditionalist" statement, may well involve a form of special plead-
ing for an increase in defense expenditures; the same may
be true of its novel frankness about the magnitude of American
military capabilities.) Insofar as technical accidents are concerned, there is some speculation that both the U.S. and the
U.S.S.R. have in recent years taken unilateral measures going
far to reassure both sides of the extreme unlikelihood of nuclear accidents apt to initiate war.

More serious, it is believed, is Soviet concern about in-
stabilities created by the proliferation of weapons (and, no
doubt, the prospect of "madmen" coming to power in "enemy"
countries such as the United States). Especially West Germany
and, more recently, Communist China, have been singled out
as likely loci of efforts to initiate or provoke "catalytic"
conflicts which would involve the nuclear powers.

The official Soviet line, frequently expressed, has been that
"limited wars" involving the nuclear powers tend to escalate
into general nuclear war. Herein is concealed an apparent
contradiction, since Moscow also asserts its commitment to
support "national-liberation wars" against the colonial powers.
Such "liberation" might well involve the Soviet Union in a conflict with the Western nuclear powers. In actuality, Soviet
leaders have carefully avoided committing their forces to such
"national-liberation" struggles: Stalin let the Korean War be
fought "by proxy"; Khrushchev has shrunk back from "brinkmanship" and possible involvement in military operations in
Laos, Berlin, Congo, Algeria, Angola, Vietnam, and Taiwan.
Cuba, moreover, provides evidence that even after the nuclear

powers have become locked in a local confrontation, they are capable of acting with sufficient restraint to avert an escalation into nuclear war.

On balance, there remains an ambiguity in the Soviet view of limited wars. It reflects both a genuine fear of escalation (varying in relation to specific situations) and a desire to deter Western responses to local Soviet-inspired or Soviet-supported initiatives by presenting the West with a seeming choice between inaction and nuclear Armaggedon. For some years, there was also a distinctly instrumental facet to the overstatements of Soviet conviction that limited wars lead to thermonuclear war. In this sense the denial of "limited wars" belongs in the same family as the Soviet ridicule and rejection of U.S. efforts to produce a "clean bomb," to establish rules of warfare, or to agree on controlled targeting, as nefarious endeavors intended to make nuclear war more palatable. As one American analyst has put it:

> One of the chief concerns of Soviet propaganda has been to prevent the United States from increasing its freedom of action by a doctrine of limited nuclear war. Soviet propaganda, domestic and foreign, has therefore endlessly repeated that there is no such thing as a limited nuclear war, that any employment of nuclear weapons must inevitably lead to all-out war. [18]

The debate on limited war and escalation continues, but since 1962 the formula used by the civilian press and by the political leadership has become markedly more tentative. Limited wars, it is now held, may expand into general war involving the nuclear powers. [19]

The Soviet debate over the nature of future wars illustrates remarkably well the dichotomy between military radicals and political moderates on the one hand, and military traditionalists and political die-hards on the other. While the former two argue that a future global war will be brief, that intermediate and/or long-range ballistic missiles will be "decisive" (though the meaning of this term is left judiciously vague), and that there is therefore less need of conventional weapons and large ground forces, the latter grouping maintains (as Marshal Zhukov wrote Hanson Baldwin in August, 1956) that "air power and nuclear weapons by themselves cannot decide the outcome of an armed struggle. Along with atomic and hydrogen weapons, in spite of their tremendous destructive power, large armies and a tremendous quantity of ordinary arms will be drawn into military operations." The prevalent opinion (Khrushchev evidently has had to yield since his January, 1960, speech) continues to insist on the possibility of protracted wars, on the annihilation of enemy forces, and on the necessity of having ground forces move in behind the great strikes. Thus the Soviet armed forces must retain diversified capabilities and prepare for prolonged war, even if nuclear strikes can have "decisive" results.

On the other hand, the image of war fought to a victorious conclusion seems to refer to the European theater. The overall military strategy, as discussed in Soviet publications, is applicable to a war restricted to the continent, but not to one involving an overseas power. Moreover, the doctrinal postulate of occupation as a prerequisite of victory is of course inconsistent with the existing Soviet force structure.

Thus, the available evidence regarding Soviet doctrine, force structure, and capabilities leads to the conclusion that the U.S.S.R. has at present no winning strategy—and knows it.[20]

SOVIET OBJECTIVES AND MILITARY POSTURE

The Soviet military posture and outlook have been overwhelmingly defensive. The overriding objective in Soviet military considerations has been the quest for security (or for "invulnerability," if thereby we mean the fullest protection of the Soviet home base). Yet the question remains—what, from the Soviet viewpoint, constitutes or offers the best defense? Above all, does security require military superiority (or at least parity with the potential enemy)?

Russian strategic concepts have traditionally been dominated by the need to preserve the security of the large Eurasian land mass which is covered by the present Soviet Union. As seen from Moscow, the most dangerous frontier has been in the West, bordering on Western Europe across an open plain with no natural defenses. Twice in this century an invasion of Russia was launched from the West European bridgehead, and when World War II came to an end, one of the Soviet government's first tasks was to build itself a belt of like-minded states between the Soviet Union and that part of Europe which was occupied by the armed forces of the West.[21]

However, it was not only (and not primarily) the presence of British, French, and American forces in Western Europe which seemed to Stalin to threaten the Soviet Union during the early postwar period. The major threat stemmed from the possession by the United States of the monopoly of atomic weapons; and Stalin, perhaps attributing to the West something of his own motives, believed that the U.S. would be tempted to use every means at its disposal to destroy Soviet power. He therefore sought a deterrent,[22] and, realizing that he had no power to reach and damage the United States, Stalin decided to build a standing threat to Western Europe by means of a large, conventional army, poised—in Eastern Europe, if possible—to advance through Germany and France to the Atlantic. At the same time the Soviet Union launched an atomic weapons program, a missile program, and the construction of an ocean-going navy, a modern air defense system, and a long-range bomber force. The Soviet Union did not then seriously expect agreement on disarmament proposals. So long as the United States had a monopoly of atomic weapons, the Soviet Union simply advocated their immediate abolition.[23]

Almost at once after Stalin's death, Soviet military men began to debate the meaning of atomic and nuclear weapons in modern warfare, as they had been unable to do in his lifetime. The conclusion they reached in 1955 evidently recognized that the Soviet Union lay at the mercy of the U.S. Strategic Air Command (SAC) whose planes could reach any target on Soviet territory with nuclear weapons and return to American bases. And the degree of damage which such planes could inflict, no longer could be compensated for by a Soviet thrust into Western Europe. So long as Soviet planes could not strike at the continental United States, radical measures were required to reduce the effective threat posed by SAC. This, it seems, was the background of both the Soviet disarmament proposals of May 10, 1955, and the conclusion of the Warsaw Pact, the same week.

Along with many military measures, such as the creation of a new Air Defense Command ranking with the other branches of the armed forces, the Soviet government now adopted disarmament proposals offering the steady reduction of all types of armed forces as well as a system of inspection and the exchange of observers at airfields of the other side. The Soviet Union easily gained the two years' time it needed to mend its strategic posture.

In October, 1957, the Soviet Union sent up the first sputnik.

By mid-1959 the Soviet leadership had come to the conclusion that the number of nuclear weapons held by each side was so great that neither state would deliberately launch a "preventive" war. Khrushchev was therefore receptive to the concept that the U.S.S.R. could rely on a "cheap" but effective deterrent, that is, a force of long-range missiles, backed by a small but efficient force of long-range bombers. At the very time when he was seeking to promote a détente, he could reduce Soviet conventional forces by one third, cut the military budget, and transfer the funds thus saved to civilian sectors of the economy.

As was shown earlier, Khrushchev met a certain degree of opposition to this policy within the Soviet Ministry of Defense. Perhaps the dismissal of senior defense officials in 1960 was connected with this resistance. As it happened, Khrushchev's policy ran into considerable difficulties—from Communist China and from the U.S., as well as inside the U.S.S.R.

In 1961 (and perhaps earlier) the Soviet defense policy was therefore revamped. With the cuts restored to the military budget, the U.S.S.R. unilaterally began a massive series of nuclear weapons tests (one of which yielded a 58-megaton explosion), attempted to intimidate the West over Berlin, and sought to score some significant foreign-policy coups. All these attempts were in vain. As 1962 opened, the hard fact which Khrushchev had to face in the field of defense was that the Soviet Union, in spite of its spectacular "firsts" in missiles and sputniks, was lagging behind the United States in long-range striking power. The gap was widening and would widen still further as the new U.S. strategic missile force—landbased and submarine—came into being.

While firm evidence is lacking, there is increasing agreement that this "gap" was probably the origin of the Soviet attempt to make Cuba into a strategic missile base. If so, this decision, in the spring or summer of 1962, was conceived as a short cut toward partial closing of the Soviet missile gap (or, to be more accurate, the long-range missile gap). From Cuba, the missiles would have placed critical areas of the United States under the more accurate range of medium and intermediate missiles instead of the more erratic and less numerous ICBMs. The United States would have been obliged to build an entirely new Early Warning System facing the Caribbean. Moreover, in the event of war, America would have had to divert half of its strike force to the elimination of the bases in Cuba. The Soviet leadership had manifestly made a total misjudgment of the United States and its President, and of the readiness of the American forces to take direct action once the construction of missile bases had been detected. After a week of crisis, in October, 1962, Khrushchev was back with the same "gap" as before.[24]

Seen in this light, the Cuban gamble was a "last" effort to achieve strategic parity or superiority, since no longer-range reliance on production ratios seemed to spell any improvement in the relative strategic position of the U.S.S.R.

Soviet military doctrine has consistently and candidly required the attainment and maintenance of military superiority. However, the question soon arose whether—given its limited economic resources—the U.S.S.R. could hope to alter the military balance in its favor by technological, political, or other means. In essence, the question has been whether circumstances might combine to persuade the Soviet leadership of the futility of seeking strategic superiority in a technological arms race. The Cuban crisis was uniquely well suited to prompt such reconsideration.

Another approach to the same problem stems from the Soviet endeavor to define a war-winning strategy. The failure to devise a promising formula for winning a nuclear encounter against a powerful transoceanic opponent has apparently become accepted as a fact of life—at least until, or unless, the United States relinquishes its relatively favorable military position or the Soviet Union can capitalize on a unilateral technological breakthrough to upset the military balance.

Once the Soviet policy-makers became aware that it was becoming increasingly difficult for the U.S.S.R. to match U.S. strategic weapons and delivery vehicles, they presumably had— and still have—the choice of resorting to one or more of the following in an attempt to reduce or close the gap. They could attempt to improve the invulnerability of the U.S.S.R. by developing an anti-ballistic missile, by hardening missile sites, and by stepping up civil defense. They could resort to a preemptive strike against the United States (there is no evidence that they seriously considered it); or, in perhaps a more rational gamble (though this move proved to be disastrously wrong in 1962), they could seek to reduce the gap by a "Cuban" type of adventure. Or, on the contrary, they could adopt "softer" policies and seek a more relaxed international climate, as indeed they have tended to do since the end of 1962;

a détente, they may hope, will lower Western "vigilance" and perhaps lower military budgets as well. Finally, arms-control measures are bound to be considered as alternative strategic means of equalizing long-range striking power (in addition to its more elementary "survival" purposes). This suggests that the Soviet policy-makers would expect asymmetrical consequences (in their favor) to result from any specific arms-control measures proposed for this (obviously unpublicized) purpose. For those in the Soviet leadership who feel that a relatively strong Soviet power position must be attained, the most appealing argument might be that arms-reduction and control measures would offer a cheaper and more certain way to cancel out U.S. superiority and to alter the over-all balance of forces in a direction favorable to Soviet interests, than would a continued arms race against an economically stronger adversary.

It is among alternatives such as these that the Soviet policy-makers were evidently choosing in the aftermath of the Cuban fiasco.[25]

One may assume that a variety of pressures in Moscow militated against a continuing attempt to strive for military superiority. Economically, alternative demands on scarce resources made themselves heard; militarily, "closing the gap" seemed both impossible and unnecessary for deterrence; politically, the détente was found especially appealing since there was no evidence of U.S. aggressive designs on the Soviet Bloc. The implicit political strategy of playing for time was fully congruent with the determinist-gradualist ingredients of the Khrushchev "line."

As for the factual basis for the Soviet reassessment, the best available Western sources fully support the argument. As of the end of 1963, the U.S.S.R. was assumed to have in the neighborhood of 100 operational ICBMs.[26] An approximate estimate of comparative strategic strength of the Western alliances and the Communist Bloc as of 1964 reveals several striking indicators of disparity.

	Western Alliances (approximate numbers)	Communist "Bloc"
Ballistic missiles:		
ICBMs (over 2,500 mile range)	U.S.: over 800 [by 1966: over 1,700]	U.S.S.R.: 200
Naval ballistic missiles	U.S.: 250 [by 1966: over 600]	U.S.S.R.: 100
IRBMs and MRBMs (600 to 2,100 mile range)	—	U.S.S.R.: 800*
Bombers:		
Long-range (over 5,000 mile range)	700 [U.S.: 550 "on strategic alert"]	200 [U.S.S.R.: 150]
Medium-range (over 2,000 mile range) —land-based —carrier-based	780 600	1,400 —

*The 750 Soviet MRBMs (of two types—one, with a range of 700 miles, the other, 1,100 miles) are reportedly deployed near the Soviet borders in sufficient numbers to deal with "strategic and semi-tactical targets— such as fighter airfields—in Western Europe, including Britain, and in the Far East." The new IRBMs (with a 2,100 mile range) have a two-stage liquid-fuel engine.

The Cuban fiasco, the test-ban treaty, and the armament reduction in the military sector of the budget in late 1963 form part of a new sequence of policy moves which are evidently based on Moscow's recognition that the U.S.S.R. has to live in a position of strategic inferiority to the United States insofar as numbers of missiles and delivery vehicles are concerned.

Soviet policies no doubt anticipate continued efforts to narrow the gap by a variety of means, such as the retention of Soviet superiority in conventional forces posing a threat to Western Europe and perhaps its extension to Asia; intensive research and development (R&D) aiming at an anti-missile system and an up-to-date submarine fleet; hardening of Soviet long-range missile sites; efforts to secure the closing down of U.S. bases on foreign soil; the creation of nuclear-free zones; and Soviet arms-control initiatives, such as the proposal for the stationing of observers in countries belonging to NATO and the Warsaw Pact, provided these arrangements do not diminish Soviet retaliatory power without at least a comparable reduction in that of the United States.

Khrushchev has evidently made up his mind to live with strategic inferiority at what he regards as the optimum level: a compromise between a minimum deterrent in terms of a credible retaliatory threat to the West and a maximum deterrent in terms of Soviet technological and economic capabilities.

Officially, Soviet military doctrine still tends to stress the need for superiority, although it fails to indicate how and when it is to be achieved. Some Soviet spokesmen, including Marshal Malinovsky, have argued for qualitative superiority rather than a numbers race.[27]

In substance, one may assume that numerical strategic inferiority is tolerable for the Soviet leadership provided that: (1) there is no evidence of aggressive designs against the U.S.S.R. or its allies on the part of the United States or other potentially hostile powers; (2) the Soviet Union is able to maintain a credible deterrent; (3) it commits resources and priorities to research and development, hoping that technological innovation may ultimately upset the unfavorable relationship; and (4) the Soviet leaders are confident that, while for a number of years they need not catch up militarily with the United States, they need not altogether abandon their traditional view of military strength as a measure of political power; and, with their deep-rooted faith in the future, they can, on the contrary, trust in the operation of historical laws to put the Soviet Union and its cause ahead.

It is hardly surprising that there are still ambiguities in this half-hearted accommodation. Clearly not all of its leaders (especially among the military) have as yet accepted the notion that in the nuclear age war is no longer an acceptable "continuation of politics by other means," as Khrushchev-oriented commentators (such as General Talensky) have argued and Party documents in the polemics with Peking have maintained. Soviet military literature (including the Sokolovsky volume) continues to see victory in nuclear war as possible though costly. To the moderates, by contrast, the Talensky argument is politically inviting: the conviction that victory in the nuclear age is meaningless provides the doctrinal underpinning for a rationalization of perpetuating a "second-best" strategic force.

As yet the issue may not have been faced frontally, and for good reasons. Doing so may mean a showdown with powerful military opinion in the U.S.S.R. on the one hand, and with ideological functionaries on the other, who would find it difficult to reconcile recognition of permanent (or indefinite) U.S. strategic superiority with belief in the inevitable replacement of capitalism by Communism throughout the world. Though genuine, the de facto acceptance of inferiority is thus awkward and not irreversible.

Everything else being equal, the outcome of this debate may decisively influence Soviet attitudes toward arms control and disarmament. The prospects for limited and perhaps experimental measures of arms control are likely to improve if the Soviet Union comes to believe that, in purely military terms, such measures may narrow the gap or make Soviet strategic inferiority more bearable.

Chapter 8

MOTIVES AND "MIX"

We began (in Chapter 2) with an attempt to enumerate various considerations which may affect—positively or negatively—Soviet interest in arms control and disarmament. The symbiosis of diverse Soviet motives and expectations—often recommending similar policies for divergent ends—is difficult to analyze and study. The following therefore is but an effort to order the evidence and offer some guidelines for further investigation.

PRIORITIES

The Soviet leadership, not unlike others, is frequently faced with competing objectives and priorities. The following reflects our largely impressionistic ranking of Soviet priorities:

1. Invulnerability of the U.S.S.R.
2. Maintenance of Party controls in the U.S.S.R. and preservation of the leadership in power.
3. "Building of Communism," i.e., in this context, promotion of economic and other forms of development in the U.S.S.R.
4. Maintenance of control and loyalty in the Bloc.
5. Promotion of Communism (or at least its pro-Soviet variants) and "national-liberation movements" abroad.

Some of the objectives here enumerated—e.g., security, in the conventional sense, and the preservation of the CPSU leadership in power—have been attained in large part. Others—e.g., the "building of Communism"—are far from fulfillment. In the Khrushchev era—at least, until 1960-62—the prospects of successfully promoting Communism appeared good in the underdeveloped countries, but remote in the so-called capitalist world. Since the first two goals in our ranking are inherently conservative or defensive in nature, economic development at home emerged as the highest objective, requiring a considerable expenditure of effort and resources.

Our ranking of priorities, or any such ranking, may be

grossly misleading, for the Soviet leadership itself surely has no such pat list to order its decision-making. Nor should it be concluded that the overriding quest for invulnerability necessarily dictates top priority for narrowly-defined strategic considerations. On the contrary, security is a many-faceted objective requiring, in its defensive meaning, political as well as military measures, and prompting, in its most sweeping reading, the equation of total security with total victory of Communism.[1]

Since, moreover, the relative importance and especially the relative feasibility of the various tasks are subject to wide fluctuation and since at any one historical juncture the "mix" of considerations may be far from congruent with the above order, the list of priorities cannot be a key to the detection of Moscow's purposes.

"THE MIX"

To weigh the interplay and total thrust of various considerations, we must know how they combine into actual patterns of motives and policies. Yet the "mix" may well remain unclear even on close examination of specific cases. A few examples will illustrate the frequent impossibility of determining, even in retrospect, which of several coincident sets of events or motives have been responsible for a given development.

The change in Soviet strategic thinking and the espousal of "peaceful coexistence" as the only alternative to nuclear war among the super-powers can be properly related both to the "liberating" consequences of Stalin's death and to the Soviet acquisition of thermonuclear weapons in 1953.

The changes in the Soviet military profile in the past decade might be attributed either to military or to political options. An alignment of military and political leaders (and outlooks) could be identified on either side of the argument over nuclear deterrence—the "rocket" approach to strategy vs. the need for large conventional forces. The same argument could be traced back to 1954: believing that a minimal deterrent on either side ruled out global war, Malenkov evidently urged preparation for limited wars by conventional forces—earning thereby the hostility both of those committed to a "nuclear" approach and of those who denied the possibility of adequate mutual deterrence.

Nor is it possible to determine whether Khrushchev "chose peaceful coexistence" because it was cheaper than a more militant policy, because he wanted to wait for strategic parity (or superiority) in the future, because he realized the destructiveness of thermonuclear war, or because he was predisposed to adopt this rather than any alternative policy in a generalized reaction to Stalinism.

The simultaneity of the crisis in the London disarmament talks in June, 1957, with the crisis in Moscow (the coalition of the Presidium's majority against Khrushchev, followed by the ouster of the so-called "anti-Party" group, including Molotov and Malenkov), and with the successful development of the first Soviet sputnik and ICBM suggests a difficulty in identifying cause and effect.

Nor has the proper place of the Cuban crisis of 1962 been firmly established. The political quest for a détente, the Soviet view of nuclear war, the banking on economic growth and economic warfare, and the wide range of Sino-Soviet disagreements antedate the Cuban events of October, 1962. And yet, the missile crisis was probably decisive in leading to Soviet recognition of the strategic inferiority of the U.S.S.R.

Finally, the test-ban treaty of 1963 demonstrates the difficulty of determining the proper "mix" of contributory motivations. One may look on the treaty as a consequence of the Cuban crisis, with the recognition of strategic inadequacy dictating an attempt to secure a ceiling on the opponent's capabilities and to remove one locus of obvious asymmetry from the confrontation. Or else, one may look upon the test-ban treaty as a fortuitous meeting of Soviet and American terms after several years of failure to be "in phase." This meeting of minds in mid-1963, in turn, may be deemed largely accidental, or else credited to the Sino-Soviet rift, or else explained in terms of comparative weapons technology. The test-ban treaty may be considered a natural consequence of the prevalent Soviet insight, since the mid-fifties, into the calamitous nature of nuclear war. Or else one may surmise that Soviet military and scientific advisers considered additional testing to be of modest value at this stage and therefore came to support the efforts of the political arm to make a virtue of abstemiousness.

An expert reporter on Soviet affairs is well justified, then, to conclude that "even in crisis, at the worst moments of doctrinaire conflict, reading the Russians is an imperfect art."[2] A few rules of thumb may deserve reiteration, nonetheless, in trying to determine the sources of Soviet attitudes toward arms control and disarmament.

At an earlier point, we established the general priority of domestic over foreign goals. At another, we spoke of the derivation of specific politics from broad, general policy orientations. Arms-control and disarmament measures are likely to be "dependent variables," subject to alternating treatment as the political situation changes. (The frequent lack of Soviet interest in arms control "for its own sake" may be derived from this deference to a larger political vantage point. If so, even proposals favorable to the U.S.S.R. may prove unacceptable unless the "whole situation" is favorable.)

The whole Leninist outlook and tradition are essentially political. The stress on political action and political organization was at the root of Lenin's arguments against his populist, syndicalist, "economist," and anarchist rivals. Political considerations have been decisive throughout the entire Soviet period, and the political leadership has held a virtual monopoly of policy-making. Moreover, in the Stalin era virtually all facets of Soviet life were "politicized" to a point where political sensitivity became second nature.

This is not to neglect the role of other criteria. The most obvious exception concerns those cases in which by decision of the political elite, economic or other needs are given top attention. Thus, a political option in 1921 postponed political changes and social engineering in the country until the economy was put back on its feet. The same kind of decision more recently underlay the program to develop the fertilizer industry, the revision of wage scales, the increase of cash payments to collective farmers, the purchase of wheat abroad, and other economic measures of the Khrushchev era.

Both economists and non-economists are agreed on the subordination of economic objectives to political objectives on the Soviet scene. No doubt scarcities are a real and at times serious factor for the Soviet leadership to contend with, and their totality is bound to constitute a form of nagging pressure on the decision-makers. These constraints are not such as to compel Soviet political decisions in the arms-control field. They may make more welcome or palatable or economical or reasonable certain decisions which are taken by the po-

litical leadership against the background of a broad political
assessment of gains and costs.

Still, the matter must not be dismissed too lightly. Not only
does economic achievement have a special and crucial place
in Bolshevik thinking; in the strategy of what we have called
painless revolution, it is an essential substitute for violence
and for grass-roots revolution which would hopefully propel
Communism to international victory. Indeed, this relative
"upgrading" of an economic road to Communism has earned
the particular scorn of the Chinese Communists, to whom
Khrushchev's "goulash Communism" smacks of sheer bourgeois opportunism.

It is often impossible to make a clear separation between
military and political inputs into decision-making.[3] Arms control itself is, after all, a phase of security policy, which by its
nature concerns both realms. In fact, as the discussion about
Soviet secrecy should make clear, security considerations—
whether political, military, or both—are now believed to have
distinct priority over ideological and "traditional" factors.[4]

There has been an unpublicized increase in the influence
of top military commanders. The military still cannot overrule
the political decision-makers, while the political leadership
may dictate to the military (e.g., it may determine force
size by committing itself to the support of certain "national-
liberation" wars). Yet military capabilities—and their limitations—are closely intertwined with political goals and tactics.
Thus military procurement policy has been directed toward
"poker-game" situations like Berlin or Cuba, in which each
side tries to use the threat of war for political gain. While
they have a handicap in a strictly strategic encounter, the
Soviet leaders have in maneuvering near the brink an advantage in their short-term immunity from accountability,
in their ability to manipulate resources and evidence, and in
their freer and fuller use of secrecy and surprise. Indeed,
these advantages may have restrained Moscow from seeking
arms-control agreements at an earlier date.

In return, military considerations can also seriously affect
political decisions. In the thermonuclear age the separation of
the two realms is well-nigh impossible. As John Erickson
puts it,

The difficulty was amply illustrated in the Cuba crisis.
If the decision to support Cuba was political, the military-

nuclear exploitation of this act was a military move aimed
at the strategic balance. The delicacy of this relationship
between strategy and diplomacy, or ... the degree to which
policy might be engulfed by strategy, also illuminates the
strain implicit in the 'advisory' role of the military.[5]

At the very least, the political leadership's own reading of the
need for military security and its estimate of military capabilities circumscribe the radius of possible political action.
But ultimately, even recognizing the inherent military aspects
of arms control, there remains the priority of political considerations. However strong the objection of individual military
commanders to this or that political measure, once a political
decision has been made, all senior men, including the dis-
senters, are expected to agree and go along—or else lose their
posts.

A vital problem area remains. Certain Soviet policy-makers
have evidently come to favor arms control primarily as an
"equalizer" of the strategic imbalance or as a "gap reducer."
Others—perhaps including Khrushchev—favor the same measures for rather different reasons, stemming from a general
political orientation best summed up by the term, détente.
As a later discussion will show, the inferences drawn here-
from are significantly different for the two groups.

Ideology is an essential element of the political mind, but
it is also a source of possible tension between "practicism"
(as it is sometimes referred to by Communist theorists) and
"dogmatism" (as the moderates at times speak of it). Elsewhere it has been argued that two opposite trends must be
borne in mind. The ideological element in Soviet thought, perception, and conduct has uniformly been more important than
many Western observers have been prepared to recognize.
We find, however, that ideological preconceptions have begun to
diminish. It is premature to speak of the "erosion of ideology"
as an accomplished fact rather than as a tendency, however
strong.[6] It is true that official pronouncements are less and
less helpful as a guide to Soviet views, say, of the United States
or as a reflection of the conduct of Soviet officials "backstage."
The attenuation of ideological determinants would indeed be
hard to demonstrate if we judged by statements rather than by
behavior. And yet, most observers would not—or at least not
yet—see the Soviet-American duel as reduced from the excesses

of the Cold War to a natural competition between two "conventional" great powers, in the nature of traditional diplomacy.

Moreover, certain assumptions and categories of perception remain fundamentally unaltered, even while some parts or levels of ideology change a good deal. This is why, it appears, hostility against the non-Communist world may survive along with major social changes and major ideological revisionism. On the other hand, the example of Yugoslavia suggests that a sincere commitment to one particular variant of Communism can prove to be compatible with an outlook which expresses or requires no active hostility toward the outside world. It is probable, as a general proposition, that Communism as a "state" takes precedence over Communism as a "church."

As with any systematic world view, there is an inherent tendency for those professing faith in Communism to seek some consistency of criteria by which options and decisions may be made. This by no means precludes the existence of logically-incompatible or unreconciled divergencies in the outlook or conduct of a given individual, group, or party. But it does support the view that such labels as "revisionism" (as now applied by the Chinese or by the "neo-Stalinists") refer to meaningfully and logically interrelated views and attitudes. If this is so, it may be futile to argue that a given step or position is motivated by this political or that economic or some other reason. Rather, there is often—though surely not always—a cluster of connected positions identifiable on a wide range of different issues. The preceding chapters pointed to this hypothesis.

Thus, there is a logic connecting Communist responses to a great variety of seemingly unrelated issues; if completely consistent, "modernists" and "traditionalists" (or "soft" and "hard" Communists) could be expected to line up on opposite sides on each of these issues. For example, there is an interlocking plausibility to a moderate or "modernist" Communist approach to all of the following:

De-Stalinization; rehabilitations; availability of more consumer goods and housing; budgetary reallocations involving a reduction in military spending; partial demobilization; missile-cum-nuclear warhead strategy and a finite deterrent; exploration of a limited détente with the West; in certain countries, peaceful accession of Communists to power; increase in commercial, cultural, and other contacts abroad; recognition, however reluctant, of the irreversibility of centrifugal tenden-

cies in the Socialist camp; an attempt to see the world without
bias or preconceptions, even if this means reconsideration of
some old stereotypes about the capitalist world; recognition of
the destructiveness of thermonuclear war; avoidance of violence
at home and abroad; resistance to making sacrifices for uncertain or remote goals or causes and to inordinate risk-
taking; exploration of disarmament agreements; greater leeway
for intellectual and scientific experimentation; an emphasis
on incentives rather than coercion.

A serious caveat must promptly be injected, however. It is
not suggested that such linkages are either uniform or firm.
It is misleading to assume that the advocacy of relaxations
or reforms at home necessarily involves a conciliatory attitude abroad, much less a readiness to conclude reasonable
disarmament agreements. "Modernism" at home, in other
words, need not preclude an aggressive foreign policy, though
the odds would be against their widespread conjunction under
the present conditions of Soviet politics. The Sino-Soviet
dispute may well contribute to a "straightening out" of inconsistencies in individual Soviet positions. And yet—as in the
United States—it would be grossly misleading to attribute all
shifts within the elite to changes along the axis of "hard" and
"soft" policies. The "anti-Party" group in 1957, for instance,
proved to be a curious agglomeration of "left," "right," and indifferent Communists who agreed on one single issue only—
getting rid of Khrushchev.

The artificial separation of logical strands does obvious
violence to the reality of human decision-making, under pressure and in a bureaucratic environment, with accidental and
irrelevant considerations entering into play more often than
not. Indeed, one of the most powerful forces determining how
the balance tips in any one case is simply inertia. Another,
one suspects, is happenstance of alignments within the leadership on other, more or less irrelevant issues at any given
point in time, with consequent fortuitous combinations. But
these are elements not susceptible to systematic investigation or prediction.

Having issued all the appropriate caveats on the difficulty
of deducing Soviet motives from the record, it remains to point
out a pattern of rationality in Soviet responses—a rationality
demonstrable even where the relative weight of different causa-
tive "inputs" cannot be ascertained. Rationality as here used

implies neither reasonableness nor infallibility; rather, it requires a responsiveness of policy-makers to relevant changes on the domestic or foreign scene.[8]

An examination of the evidence shows that there is indeed a fairly consistent correlation between shifts in Soviet policy with regard to arms control and prior "objective" events. Whether these events provide the evidence on the strength of which the leadership is willing to reconsider, or whether they reinvigorate factional strife and give the momentary victory to this or that position, cannot be determined; either hypothesis might fit the facts.

What are some of the recent bench marks? If we take Khrushchev's January 14, 1960, speech to symbolize a turn toward unilateral partial reduction in military force and budget, and a shift from ground to missile forces, we would identify the preceding external events as the "spirit of Camp David." The Soviet Premier's visit to the United States, his encounters with President Eisenhower, and his GCD proposal at the United Nations were evidently both responses to a quest for, and a move toward, a limited détente with the West.

Similarly, as seen from Moscow, the U-2 incident on May 1, 1960, demonstrated that Khrushchev could not rely on Eisenhower's good will or word; it thus destroyed one of the pillars of the Soviet policy which, among other things, sought to see the U.S. as "peaceful" and "friendly" toward the U.S.S.R. By exposing the inadequate protection of the Soviet Union, the U-2 flight and the publicity surrounding it must also have provided the occasion for some arguments in favor of stronger defenses or larger military appropriations.

Yet we cannot pretend to identify the circumstances without fail. For instance, what prompted the shift on the intellectual front, symbolized by Khrushchev's remarks at the Manège on December 1, 1962—as well as its termination in April-May, 1963—remain subjects of speculation, and little more. Such ignorance should not negate the hypothesis here advanced regarding the fundamental rationality of responses. Leaving aside the military aspects of the equation, similar causation can be found preceding each of the shifts and crises from Malenkov's replacement, in February, 1955, to the November, 1957, Plenum.[9]

Such a finding is of some general significance. For, in our complex world of nuclear weapons and automation an assumption is being made—implicitly or explicitly—that responses "by the other side" to moves and threats will be rational. Our evidence would support the view that, in spite of all the personal impulsiveness, aberrations, and intuition, and all the differences in style of leadership, a fundamental rationality pervades the Soviet policy process. In this regard, it does not seem to differ significantly from that of other powers.

Part III

THE OUTLOOK

Chapter 9

THE SOVIET RECORD:
FROM GCD TO ARMS CONTROL

THE DUBIOUS LEGACY

The history of Soviet disarmament policies and proposals spans nearly half a century. It is a peculiar record of contradictory approaches and pronouncements, with a perplexing yet characteristic ambiguity. While, in the early years, some Soviet pronouncements affirmed the utter impossibility of disarmament under existing conditions, others passionately pleaded for total disarmament. That record cannot and need not be reviewed here.[1]

First at Genoa (1922), then in Moscow, and soon afterward in Geneva, Soviet diplomats began submitting proposals—for a "general limitation of armaments," then for a proportional arms cut by Russia and her neighbors, then for immediate and total disarmament. In seemingly indefatiguable endeavors Maxim Litvinov offered now a four-year plan for complete disarmament, now a graduated reduction of armaments or a one-third cut, adding new compromise proposals and amendments as his motions and draft conventions were, one after the other, turned down, whittled down, or ignored by the Preparatory Commission and the Disarmament Conference in Geneva (1927-33).

In recent years Moscow has claimed that V. I. Lenin, from his sickbed, instructed Soviet diplomats and negotiators in 1922; the Leninist aura of legitimacy is cherished by the Kremlin, whatever the twists of the "general line." Actually, just as with peaceful coexistence and the non-inevitability of war, Moscow's current attempts at establishing the Leninist orthodoxy of its disarmament policy are highly debatable. Lenin and his associates had, after all, been candid enough in their days to deny the possibility of any firm and binding compacts among inherently hostile states in an inevitably fluid world. As has since been suggested, the Leninist out-

117

look affirmed, in essence, that in a system of capitalist
powers, negotiated disarmament was impossible; in a Communist system, negotiated disarmament was unnecessary.[2]
Soviet international lawyers, Comintern politicians, and Communist ideologists, journalists and diplomats were frank to
admit, in the 1920's, that they—and presumably the Soviet
government—had no illusions: they did not expect any disarmament agreements to be negotiated, concluded, or carried
out. Yet disarmament and the broad Communist-sponsored
"fight for peace" made appealing causes to champion—and
important ones.

The "peace" movement was again to be a major theme of
Soviet political propaganda after World War II. Under Stalin,
the Soviet Union's many mouthpieces gave considerably more
publicity to the partisan mass appeals sponsored by this or
that "progressive" body—the Stockholm Appeal, the "Ban
the Bomb" campaign, the synthetic protests against the alleged use of bacteriological warfare by the United States in
Korea—than to the futile and interminable sessions on disarmament around the U.N.

Once again, the Soviet Union was unwilling to limit its
freedom of action by tying itself to an international arms
agreement, unwilling to limit its sovereignty by admitting
foreigners to inspect its armed forces, resources, and industry; unwilling to limit its self-esteem and its freedom of
action by agreeing in advance to abide by the decisions of a
non-Communist majority. Moscow made sure to voice and
circulate its own proposals which, in this period, were aimed
at depriving the United States of its newly-acquired monopoly
(and later, of its superiority) in atomic weapons and means
of their delivery. Soviet policy made agreements impossible.
Ideologically-rooted preconceptions and realistic assessments of Russia's military and economic weakness fused
more than once to shape Soviet foreign and disarmament
policy.

The post-Stalin leadership proved to be dynamic and flex-
ible enough to reach accords which heretofore had been
frustrated, restore contacts which had been severed, and
seek friends and influence outside the Communist camp.
Concurrently, in the disarmament negotiations, a new spirit
of what to many Western diplomats appeared to be welcome
reasonableness began as a trickle in 1954, dramatically
manifested itself in 1955, and two years later led to the

submission of a Soviet "package" no longer limited to pre-dictably unacceptable proposals. On the contrary, the 1957 package incorporated precisely what the West had been urging—a step-by-step approach to the successive adoption and implementation of what the Soviet Union called "partial measures."[3]

Preceding chapters have outlined the extent and the limits of change that Soviet outlook and policies have undergone. New political priorities, new military requirements, new doctrine, and new opportunities seemed to herald at least the possibility of new departures in many areas—"security" included. Yet the ballast of established purposes and pro-grams, mutual suspicion, and unchanged underlying causes of conflict between "East" and "West" remained, so that dis-armament negotiations and discussions continued without hard results for several more years.

Unevenly and often unpredictably, Soviet policies and po-sitions have, since 1955, inched—despite zigzags and relapses —toward greater flexibility and efforts to reach at least limited agreements. Earlier we developed the hypothesis that, in some key circles in Moscow, the basic outlook on disarmament underwent a change precisely at this time. Indeed on several occasions Soviet proposals seem to have put Western negotiators on the defensive, leaving them in embarrassing uncertainty about their government's willing-ness to "buy" this or that scheme. While the West withdrew some of its pre-1954 proposals in the period under consider-ation (and did so primarily for military reasons), on other issues, such as general and complete disarmament, the West-ern powers were in effect stampeded into vying with the Russians in a popularity contest over programs which, one suspects, most thoughtful American and British observers deemed utterly unrealistic to start with.

To the general public, meanwhile, Soviet disarmament policy seemed to be as contradictory as ever. World atten-tion, riveted on crises such as Hungary, Berlin, the U-2, and Cuba has, in recent years, tended to displace awareness of the quietly-developing momentum of change in what used to be the Communist Bloc. Indeed, as was argued earlier, both the quest for a certain relaxation of tensions and the awareness of Soviet inability to formulate a "winning" strat-egy, in the foreseeable future, were present well before the Cuban crisis of October, 1962. Yet, in retrospect, it was

evidentally the double impact of Cuba and the Sino-Soviet
dispute that precipitated (with zigzags, to be sure) the new
course formalized by the signing of the partial test-ban
treaty. Way stations on the road to it were Khrushchev's
offer of three on-site inspections for an underground test
ban (December, 1962), and (after what appears to have been
a related policy dispute within the Soviet leadership) the
cessation of Soviet jamming of BBC and Voice of America
broadcasts; the signing of the so-called "hot-line" agreement (June 20, 1963); the near-coincidence of President
Kennedy's American University speech indicating a readiness to explore an improvement in Soviet-American relations, and the Chinese Communist note of June 14, 1963,
exacerbating relations with the CPSU to a point from which
a return to reconciliation seemed well-nigh impossible.
Still, it is well to recall that "the Sino-Soviet schism is not
the cause of the Soviet turn towards a détente with the West,
and the détente has itself been only the final occasion for a
break that had long been in the making."[4]

From Moscow's point of view, the new policy has appeared
to pursue several goals—a general relaxation of tensions; a
demonstrable success to point to in intra-Communist debates; an insurance against Western pressures in the aftermath of Cuba; in turn, with the reduction of immediate
outside threats, a rekindling of divisions within the Atlantic
alliance; hopefully, the establishment of precedents or a
pattern of responses that would permit further political and
economic accords and changed relationships beneficial to
the U.S.S.R.

The "raw material" on the changing Soviet terms is
amply available and has been published and commented
upon at considerable length.[5] If we could now filter out the
tactical or temporary zigzags, what core of attitudes and
goals would remain?

THE SOVIET ATTITUDE: CONTINUITY AND CHANGE

The Soviet attitude toward disarmament, over the years,
reveals both constants and variables. One unchanging purpose has been the propaganda exploitation of a popular and
appealing idea at home and abroad. From Litvinov's assertion that "we shall not let a single opportunity slip for the

most intensive propaganda for peace and disarmament," to Khrushchev's statement that GCD is "a potent weapon with which to rally the people," political warfare has been a distinct, and hardly surprising, element of the Soviet purpose. The change in recent years, if any, has been the stress on the feasibility of disarmament agreements, as contrasted to reiteration (in "Chinese" fashion) of the necessity of struggling and winning before disarmament can become a reality.

In the period from 1922 to 1935, it seems clear, the Soviet authorities put forward the most radical and imaginative disarmament proposals, realizing full well that they had no chance of acceptance, but knowing also that the rejection of these proposals would in itself redound to the benefit of the Communists. The Soviet attitude, in other words, reflected no expectation that the West would agree to disarm. Had it done so, Moscow might well have found itself in a highly embarrassing situation.

It was easy and tempting to make "disarmament," like "peace," the central theme of a political warfare campaign, which was likely to be the more effective, the simpler and cruder the terms. Thus there emerged an inverse relationship between the expected propaganda gains (requiring generality and inflexibility of slogans) and the willingness to negotiate seriously about specific wording, technical details, and problems of implementation. The broad and sweeping sloganeering obstructed the view of political negotiation as an exercise in the art of the possible. Only later was Moscow to shift from a policy of total proposals to a "policy of little means," breaking up the master plans into "partial measures" and thereby at least making possible a move from rhetoric to the roundtable.

Soviet resistance to some of the more "sophisticated" Western concepts—such as "arms control" itself, or "war control"—stems partly from the fact that subtlety and compromise make poor propaganda. To grant that there can be a "clean bomb" or a total war without victors or that one can agree with the archenemy about a sequence of unilateral restraints is to acknowledge a measure of legitimacy and respectability for the foe. In fact, even "to advocate a system of stabilized deterrence is to lose the moral force and emotional appeal of a radical disarmament position."[6] But here, just as with the notion of coexistence itself, some changes have been made—as the "hot-line" agreement made clear.

At no time has the Soviet Union, in discussing or considering disarmament, permitted itself to forget that its security needs remained uppermost. Virtually all Soviet disarmament proposals between 1945 and 1955 would have had the result of reducing American strategic superiority. When the U.S. had a preponderance in air power, the U.S.S.R. proposed inspection stations at air bases and the reduction of strategic weapons systems. More recently, under conditions of U.S. missile superiority, the U.S.S.R. has pressed for the destruction of delivery vehicles in the first stage of the Soviet GCD proposal. It has insisted on the abandonment of military bases on foreign territory and a variety of other steps which would give it an asymmetrical advantage. The U.S.S.R. is of course hardly unique among the nations in formulating its proposals so as to envisage, as a consequence of acceptance, an improvement in its relative power position.

Another constant of Soviet policy over the years has been the attempt by the U.S.S.R., as the inferior party, to immobilize its possible enemies. This pattern showed up as early as December, 1922, and was manifested in such gambits as the Litvinov Protocol, which brought the Kellogg-Briand Pact's provisions into force among the Soviet Union and its neighbors.

Soviet security, Moscow seemed to be reasoning, can be advanced by different means—by non-aggression treaties and by alliances, by industrialization and by building up the Red Army, by appeasing possible enemies, and also by disarmament measures. The post-1945 Soviet demand that the U.S. surrender its atomic weapons is perhaps the best case in point.

The strategic calculus, however, cannot be considered the sole or overriding factor. Moscow has had to reconcile disarmament programs with political and ideological considerations as well. For, as has been shown, there was, and there was bound to be, a Bolshevik predisposition against disarmament. There was, after all, a strong tradition against "trafficking with the enemy"; there was the belief that no deals with the "other" camp could be made to "stick"; there was the whole movement's basic commitment to change—sweeping and secular—and therefore no belief in an international equilibrium. Only gradually did the notion emerge that during periods of "ebb," between rounds of revolutionary upheavals, the Soviet state could legitimately be interested in the "temporary stabilization" of international power relations and in fact be eager for an extended "breathing spell," during which it could recover and rebuild. The acceptance of the notion of temporary stabilization was to provide a precedent to be cited later, thus compounding an ambiguity which the Communist movement has sought to slur over: the simultaneous assertions that conflict was inevitable (and hence disarmament, too, was impossible or nonsensical other than as a delaying device) and that peaceful coexistence was a legitimate strategy to pursue.

Here the post-Stalin era brought some clarification. As of 1959, Khrushchev was prepared to argue that it was possible to advance to the higher stage of Communist society while pursuing, all the while, a policy of peaceful coexistence. The actual application of this insight in Soviet policy or negotiations, of course, has lagged substantially behind the evolution of Soviet doctrine to the point of accepting coexistence as an imperative of our age.[7]

The qualitative change stimulating Soviet interest in concluding agreements with the United States—if not on disarmament, then on certain partial measures—must be considered a response to internal and external changes after Stalin's death. The acquisition of nuclear devices by the United States in such numbers as to permit it at all times to inflict intolerable damage and devastation on the U.S.S.R. helped make concepts such as mutual deterrence—heretofore scorned as implying a fallacious and dangerous interdependence of opposites—and, more broadly, the necessity of dealing "with the enemy" more plausible. Unwittingly, the realization that the security of the Soviet state and people is henceforth locked into agreements with—and hence, after a fashion, placed at the mercy of—the leading "capitalist" state serves to undermine more than one orthodox Marxist assumption, especially at a time of additional pressures and doubts generated by the Sino-Soviet rift.

The desirability of certain agreements with the United States must have impressed the Party leadership, since it has realized that the Soviet military and economic establishments could not readily keep up with, let alone overtake, their American equivalents—except perhaps at a price Moscow has been unwilling to pay. Having once reached this realization, the Soviet leadership, far from jettisoning its objective of "invulnerability," could opt for a finite deterrent, entirely satisfactory for defensive purposes but not capable of matching American output. Such an option presupposed a tissue of Soviet beliefs about intentions and capabilities, which would appear to be propitious for a serious Soviet pursuit of disarmament measures.

This is especially true in view of the contributory pressures from the Soviet economy. Competition for scarce resources invites a many-sided tug-of-war between the various elite groupings. With an increasing sensitivity of the leadership to pressures on behalf of a higher standard of living, it could not but welcome an opportunity to reduce, however slightly, the percentage of the budget devoted to the armed forces and the arms industry.

FROM GCD TO "FIRST STEPS"

Khrushchev's widely publicized appeal to the United Nations in 1959 for general disarmament recalled Soviet proposals made thirty years earlier. With some hesitancy, one is obliged to conclude that even GCD cannot be dismissed as a mere propaganda effort. Of course, such a sweeping and simple program makes far better "copy" than partial, complex, and differentiated control systems.[8] But there is more to it than this, even if one grants that the Soviet authorities themselves cannot believe total disarmament to be possible at present.

The positive role of GCD may be, most modestly, ascribed to the unconscious Communist need for an ultimate objective to which short-term moves can be related. GCD is, after all, nothing but a collection of arms-control and peace-keeping measures phased over time. At the same time, general and complete disarmament may be regarded by the Soviet leadership as an elaboration, or a more radical formulation, of the doctrine of peaceful coexistence. Yet, it is appropriate to ask, can one conceive of Moscow's willingly diluting its own power in a disarmed world? Most unlikely; but this argument seems logically compelling to some Communists: There are but two possible outcomes to the present confrontation between "capitalist" and "Communist" states: the "Pyrrhic" victory of Communism after a disastrously destructive war, or else the gradual advance of Communism, imperceptibly inching toward world-wide success without nuclear war. If the faith persists in time as Communism's ally and companion, the certainty of eventual victory can only reinforce the wish to refrain from war. Here is the basis of present Soviet groping for a new theory of painless revolution.

Some Communists—though clearly not all—are prepared to maintain that, unlike capitalism, their cause is not dependent on the use of force for the achievement of its own objectives, because organic historical forces underlie and steer its advance. GCD, from this vantage point, amounts to a device for clearing the tracks of obstructions, so as to permit unimpeded passage to the Communist "locomotive of history."

More concretely, one may sum up Communist arguments in favor of a disarmed world in this fashion:

1. GCD would eliminate the possibility of war and thus the possibility of damaging the prospects of Communist success.

2. GCD would deny the imperialists the force to restrain revolutionary forces throughout the world.

3. GCD would weaken the ties that bind the West together.

4. GCD would probably promote the socialist at the expense of the capitalist economy, and would at the very least permit very considerable savings in capital, manpower, and resources.

5. GCD would give the Soviet Union a major success to take credit for.

To be sure, there are costs and risks the Communists would have to face as a consequence—assuming they could reach the goal. In sacrificing its military power, the Soviet Union would lose a key element of its ability to exert political pressure. Within the Communist camp the Soviet position would be further impaired. Whatever international peace-keeping and/or inspection organ is brought into being would command certain rights which heretofore Moscow has refused to give any foreign power or agency.

Implicit in the Soviet argument for GCD is the assumption that the elimination of the military component in the race between the two camps would shift correspondingly greater weight to techniques and forces other than overt war: revolution, guerrilla warfare, subversion, "public opinion," economic competition, and so forth. In these forms of struggle, they believe, the Communists have an inherent advantage over the enemy camp.

One aspect of any prospective general disarmament which has not received much attention—perhaps because of the unlikelihood of realization—goes to the heart of the differences between the Soviet and the Western views on disarmament. However arrived at, GCD would cause considerable destabilization and invite widespread chaos. Western observers are apt to respond to this prospect with real concern, whereas Communist leaders tend to welcome the fertile environment for revolutionary action which GCD would thus create.

It is reasonable to assume that, desirable or not, GCD is not now viewed in Moscow as a practical goal. Indeed, given the Soviet-Chinese falling out, it would be foolish for the U.S.S.R. to press for or proceed to general disarmament. One hopeful measure of greater realism has, therefore, been the recent Soviet willingness to move from general pronouncements in favor of GCD to negotiations of limited and specific agreements. [9]

Despite their willingness to accede to limited agreements, however, Soviet officials have long and strenuously resisted the entire Anglo-American approach to "arms control." Not stabilization at a high rate of armaments but destruction of arms, has been the standard and pat Soviet verdict.

Yet there are those in Moscow, too, who hold that an armed world is a safer world than a disarmed one. In the last few years they have had little opportunity to express their views; sometimes they do so by indirection; sometimes they may not be conscious of "speaking prose." Soviet suspicion of American and British intentions in developing a complicated and considerable body of thought and research on arms control is hardly surprising. Yet, after berating this concept on many occasions, Moscow has come around to a more moderate position (or at least some Soviet spokesmen have). Thus Igor Glagolev, one of the leading Soviet social scientists writing on disarmament, explains in a footnote: "In capitalistic countries persons active for peace use the term 'arms control' for measures limiting the use of nuclear weapons, whereas in reactionary circles it is understood to mean the disguised arms race." [10]

Actually, while resisting the label, the Soviet Union has repeatedly engaged in "arms control," as American experts define it. For instance, the Soviet proposals for preventing surprise attack (1955), taken at face value, amounted to arms control. More recently, the "hot line" has provided a classic example. The Soviet authorities have, after all, unilaterally imposed reasonable limits on their own financial commitment to the production of existing weapons and the development of new ones. Occasionally Soviet writers even seem to agree with the U.S. view that hardening of missile sites on <u>both</u> sides or the <u>non</u>-withdrawal of U.S. forces from Europe serves to stabilize the balance of deterrence. [11]

The concept of "mutual deterrence" itself is still far from unanimously accepted in Moscow. Ever since Marshal Zhukov rejected it in 1955, many of the Soviet marshals have refused to adopt it. Marshal Malinovsky has apparently never conceded that deterrence assures adequate security. On the other hand, the Sokolovsky volume on military doctrine does speak of a "nuclear stalemate"; and Khrushchev—especially since Cuba—has made clear his belief that mutual deterrence has in fact been achieved. [12]

VARIETIES OF ARMS CONTROL

Because of the absence of Soviet typologies of comparable adequacy, we must resort to an "American" catalogue of partial measures to be reviewed. Since the Soviet position on specific measures is overt and manifest, no attempt is made here to trace the shifts in Soviet policy toward them. Nor are we qualified to discuss these attitudes in terms of weapons technology and its implications.

1. Preventive Measures

Moves intended to control arms or delivery vehicles not yet existing or not yet deployed have the attraction of avoiding the impairment of facilities or weapons systems already relied upon for security.

One of the central concerns of the whole international security complex is how to <u>limit weapons research and development.</u> "The haunting fear of vulnerability in the face of potential new weapon developments by the other side is the source of much of the dynamism which powers the arms race." [13] By its very nature, verifiable limitations on scientific and technological research are extremely difficult to devise and to enforce. There is at present no likelihood whatever of Soviet agreement to effective limitation of research and very little likelihood of formal agreement, under mutually-acceptable conditions, on restraints in developing qualitatively-superior weapons or delivery systems. A meaningful advance in this area would presuppose a basic change in Soviet outlook regarding inspection. Moreover, as was suggested elsewhere, research and development are among the major areas of Soviet reliance for future "breakthroughs" to change the balance of power.

Given the limitations on resources available for military needs, it is far more realistic to expect each side unilaterally to desist from the further development of certain weapons or systems so long as the other side adheres to a similar commitment. This might be true of anti-ballistic missiles (ABM); there is apparently no evidence that the Soviet Union is committed to their development. No formal agreement to desist is in prospect; nor is there any prospect of Soviet agreement to limit size and deployment of submarine fleets.

The agreements not to test nuclear weapons (in three environments) and not to orbit weapons of mass destruction, among other things, set a partial limit on military R&D. One may assume that the Soviet Union would accept similar measures which would have the effect of slowing the tempo of the qualitative arms race without involving inspection and without preventing certain further scientific or technological research. The testing of new and "superior" ballistic missiles or warheads may belong in this category.[14]

More serious and probably more promising of success are endeavors to prevent the spread of weapons and delivery vehicles. In some cases, such as chemical and bacteriological warfare, agreements would evidently have to be declaratory; without inspection provisions, they might be negotiable. The subject which has received major attention, however, is a possible treaty pledging the non-proliferation of nuclear weapons. Basically, Soviet and American interests seem to coincide here; and agreement would not spell significant unilateral advantages for either potential signatory. There is evidence of Soviet concern about the acquisition of independent nuclear capabilities by either China or West Germany; other states have appeared to share some of this concern that a newcomer to the "nuclear club" could precipitate a "catalytic" thermonuclear conflict. While, on both scores, this fear may be much exaggerated, military doctrine in both camps would agree at present that "an increase in the number of nuclear powers would increase the danger of thermonuclear war many times over" (Soviet memorandum of January 28, 1964).

The major impediment to agreement here is the Soviet position on the NATO Multilateral Force (MLF). Whatever the balance of considerations for and against it in the West, there is no reason to question the fact that Soviet statements on the MLF reflect actual concern about its anticipated effects and prospects—including the eventual acquisition of independent nuclear capability by West Germany. At the same time the Soviet Union may be prepared to pay a substantial price for effective prevention of proliferation.

The Western powers have apparently taken cognizance of "legitimate" Soviet concern on this score; thus, in replying to the Soviet note of July 11, 1964, the United States offered to give formal assurance, under international law, that it would not turn over control of nuclear weapons to any of its allies not possessing an independent nuclear capability. [15] The Soviet Union is thus left with the embarrassing choice between sacrificing a political trump—the "anti-warmonger" line in its propaganda against the Bonn regime—and sacrificing what increased security it would derive from an accord banning the transmission of these weapons or information on their manufacture to other states. There still would remain the insurmountable obstacles to a non-proliferation agreement: France and China. The de facto situation, it is true, is that the Soviet Union, the United States, and Great Britain are already acting with restraint in not assisting further proliferation.

Preventive measures also encompass efforts to reduce the risk of war. In addition to the Khrushchev message to all heads of state, on December 31, 1963, proposing a treaty renouncing the use of force in settling territorial or boundary disputes—a rather curious document—[16] the Soviet Union has given some attention to the prevention of hostilities set off by accident, communications failure, miscalculation, or "third-party genesis." As of 1964, none of the possible measures in this field are on the Soviet Union's current agenda for the Geneva negotiations.

In fact, though not in law, the nightmare of nuclear war-by-error appears to have become a good deal less likely in recent years, and Moscow seems to be aware of this fact. Despite its eloquent alarums—about the proverbial flock of geese on radar screens, about bomber pilots blacking out,

and other scenarios involving human or technical failure—the
Soviet leadership seems satisfied that it (as well as its potential adversaries) possesses an improving ability to dis-
criminate between an isolated incident and a large-scale attack. The improvements in communications (such as the "hot
line"), unilateral moves such as the hardening of missile
sites,[17] and the perfection of reconnaissance satellites and
warning systems, are but some of the measures already
adopted to reduce the risk of war initiation by accident. A
non-proliferation agreement would presumably add some
further reassurance. Khrushchev's designation as Commander-
in-Chief of the Soviet Armed Forces (in peace time) suggests
a possible analogy to administrative restraint on the use of
nuclear weapons in the United States, where only the President may authorize their use.

The dangers of war-by-miscalculation have evidently declined, too. Moscow has been visibly impressed by the sense
of restraint which has characterized the behavior of the nuclear powers in several international confrontations; indeed,
this is what certifies their leaders as "men of reason."
There is little else to be done to prevent miscalculation,
other than to improve communications between adversaries,
including the development of personal relationships of confidence with adversary representatives, both in and out of
diplomatic channels; and to strive for precision in critical
situations so as to permit the other side to predict adversary
behavior with the greatest possible probability. It is only fair
to say that Soviet equivocation over "national-liberation" wars
only adds to the uncertainty which Moscow professes to de-
plore.

2. War Control

Measures to mitigate the consequences or reduce the destructiveness of war have been of no interest to the Soviet
Union. In part, Soviet refusal to discuss matters such as
limited targeting, "clean bombs," or controlled response
builds on a political tradition of righteous indignation at such
efforts as devices intended to make war more palatable.

In addition, since the U.S.S.R. is concentrating on the perfection of a "poor man's deterrent" with high-yield warheads
designed to produce a maximum number of casualties, there
seems to be an assumption on the Soviet side that—whatever

actual Soviet behavior would be in the case of a nuclear strike—it has an advantage, lacking force size and quality for a "counterforce" strategy, in promising not to spare any cities. Since 1958 or 1959, some people in the Soviet leadership may have realized that the Soviet Union could achieve about as much, politically or militarily, with a force one third the size of the American, as they could by raising this force, through great exertion and diversion of resources, to half of that of the United States. There is apparently no particular reason to expect an early change in this general approach.

At the same time, the "hot-line" agreement may be considered not only a means to help prevent war but also a war-control device. Further means for adversary communication, for bargaining or termination of conflict, without involving limitation on weapons or on the use of weapons, may provide areas for fruitful exploration.

3. Strategic Force Reductions

With the exceptions noted below, there seems to be virtually no chance, in the foreseeable future, of an agreement on the reduction of Soviet strategic forces, even if the U.S. were to agree to cut a larger proportion of its own forces simultaneously. The reduction of the inferior Soviet missile and bomber forces would be taken in some quarters to be a significant diminution of Soviet international power. Moreover, the forces in being are not costly to maintain, and no political incentive seems to offer any countervailing attraction to justify Soviet cuts in strategic forces. Since, furthermore, effective reduction agreements would in the Western view require inspection to verify retained forces, weapons, or delivery vehicles, the U.S.S.R. may be expected to refrain from any moves in this field other than as (1) a possible result of informal reciprocation, and (2) a (possibly inspected) destruction of some delivery vehicles without verification of retained levels.[18]

A related area susceptible of further exploration is suggested by the cutback in the production of fissionable materials, in early 1964, and by the possible transfer of some quantities of fissionable materials to peaceful uses. However, such moves might be more properly considered as primarily confidence-building rather than affecting the strategic balance.

4. Limited Stabilizing Measures

There appears to be some Soviet interest in a variety of widely different measures designed to increase what the United States would call the stability of deterrence. Closely related to these is the whole range of war-prevention measures, discussed above, in which both sides have parallel interests.

Many "preventive" measures—precisely because they are "limited" and hence easily feasible—may also be considered primarily political in nature; that is, they contribute to a climate in which both sides may give evidence of greater willingness to explore limited settlements and accords; indirectly, the establishment of such a limited cooperative relationship between adversaries may in itself be said to lessen the hazards of war.

A somewhat special case is the proposed limitation of military budgets. While there appears to be some interest in this, on both sides, it is hardly necessary to point out that the actual Soviet "defense" budget is in part concealed under other categories in the official budget, as published. Without elaborate (and, for all practical purposes, unrealistic) inspection procedures, it would be farcical or naive to accept Soviet budgetary data at face value.[19] Moreover, the very definition of defense expenditures raises major difficulties, as the outlay for space research and exploration exemplifies.

These, and other, objections do not, of course, apply to reductions in military budgets undertaken by either side as a matter of self-interest without necessary expectation of reciprocation. Such unilateral reductions are engaged in with greater confidence, of course, if there is some assurance of at least a gross equilibrium or symmetry of trends.[20]

Another measure first proposed by the U.S.S.R. in May, 1955, revived in July, 1963, and incorporated in the Soviet memorandum of January 28, 1964, pertains to the establishment of observation posts on both sides of the Iron Curtain in Europe. This proposal, although usually put forward in the larger context of measures to prevent surprise attack, to bring about disengagement or nuclear-free zones, might be separable. The probability of agreement is substantially greater if reciprocity in the location of such inspection points is maintained and if, to start with, Western observation posts in the Warsaw Pact area are located on East European territory outside the U.S.S.R.

5. Confidence-Building and Symbolic Measures

Not being technically descriptive of a given body of measures, this category overlaps with other subjects of negotiation. Measures in which the U.S.S.R. has been interested include, in addition to preventive steps, a non-aggression pact between NATO and the Warsaw Treaty Organization (WTO); an agreed ban of what it describes as "war propaganda"; and the exchange of military personnel for study or observation, or as a form of hostages.

The value of such gestures should not be exaggerated; while they help create an environment propitious for negotiations, a fundamental readiness to seek and reach accords must precede them if they are to lead to more substantial arms agreements. And yet a sequence of modest agreements, such as the Antarctic Treaty, may be pointed to as demonstrating—presumably to skeptics in Moscow, too—the possibility of a new trend. In terms of maintaining a momentum of agreements in the year following the signing of the test-ban treaty in August, 1963, one may point to the banning of weapons of mass destruction in orbit; the extension of the safeguard system to large atomic reactors, voted by the International Atomic Energy Agency, for the first time with the affirmative votes of the Soviet Union; the negotiation of a declaration of legal principles for outer space; agreement allocating radio frequencies for space operations; success in negotiating a consular convention between the U.S.S.R. and the United States; reduction in the defense budget; conclusion of a new two-year cultural exchange agreement; cut in production of fissionable materials; possible implementation of the civil aviation agreement initialed in 1961, and perhaps other, less publicized moves. Declarations unilaterally denying oneself the first use of nuclear weapons might fall into the same category, though whether this would constitute a symmetrical abnegation for both sides is another matter. [21]

For example, if the West agreed to a pledge of "no-first use" of nuclear weapons, the Soviet Union would be able to

exert pressure against Berlin with some confidence that
the West would not retaliate. The Soviet proposal for a non-
aggression pact carries the same overtones; Moscow evidently hopes that a non-aggression pact would enable it to
use other means to gain advantages in Berlin.

These are all instances of a willingness to exercise some
restraint in exploiting military power. The Western powers
so restrained themselves over Hungary in 1956; both sides,
in their own ways, did in Cuba in 1962 and, less dramatically,
over North Vietnam in 1964. Since then the concept of self-
imposed restraint—not totally dissimilar from the imposition
of self-restraint in economic competition—has become better
understood and appreciated.

Some arms-control experts would argue that there is for
all intents and purposes an unwritten and unspoken "no-first-
use" understanding in existence. The strategic assumptions
underlying the development of military establishments in
recent years, in effect at a considerable cost denying the
nuclear powers their own nuclear weapons, make no sense
unless one assumes that the adversary, too, understands the
reasoning involved.

It remains to say a word about possible reasons for Soviet
interest, year after year, in formal, declaratory, and presumably symbolic moves such as a non-aggression pact and
the banning of "war propaganda." There is perhaps no secret
meaning at all behind Soviet interest in the NATO-WTO treaty.
It would, specifically, provide a most circuitous form of de
facto recognition of the East German regime by the U.S. and
its allies. But even without this prospect, Moscow would
generally favor such a treaty. As an upstart suffering from
isolation and inferiority, the Soviet regime—even when its
power position was well established—retained a peculiar
yearning for protestations of "parity" and whenever possible
has sought occasions for the affirmation, by friend and foe,
of equality and legitimacy for itself or, as in this instance,
for its Bloc of allies.

The proposed ban on "war propaganda" may be seen as
an extension of the Soviet "peace" campaign. Peace propaganda, to be effective, must always remain short of its goal;
once peace is assured, there is ipso facto no more need for a
peace "campaign." Hence, perhaps, the last-minute Soviet
refusal to sign the agreement banning war propaganda when,
most reluctantly, the United States consented to it in May,

1962. The volte face evidently took the Soviet delegates in
Geneva by surprise, too. It appears to have been the work of
the appropriate higher levels of the Soviet hierarchy to whom
the agreement had been submitted for final approval. The
"working" diplomats may have been overruled in this fashion
—it used to be said in Moscow that the diplomatic clerks need
not know the revolutionary algebra of their masters—because
the aim of floating the proposal was not its acceptance but
propaganda. On the other hand, more substantive disagreements within the Soviet elite may have been responsible for
the change.

At the same time, the propaganda ban may be regarded in
Moscow as something of a test of Western responses. There
are various precedents, after all, for Soviet interest in such
token moves. The esoteric gestures that preceded the Nazi-
Soviet negotiations in the spring of 1939 included, as one of
the earliest steps, the cessation of mutual attacks in the
press and on the air; twice in recent years Soviet attempts
to promote a limited détente with the U.S. were accompanied by the suspension of Soviet jamming of Western
broadcasts beamed at the U.S.S.R. In the Sino-Soviet dispute
the several efforts at reconciliation since 1960 began with
the suspension of public attacks between the two principal
parties. Especially with regard to the non-Communist world,
willingness to conclude such agreements may well be taken
as evidence that Moscow believes there are "not madmen but
men of reason" in control of the enemy camp.

The view that the campaign, not the conclusion of the
agreement, is the central Soviet interest here is supported by
the fact that, in spite of its 1962 embarrassment, the U.S.S.R.
has persisted in bringing up the subject of a war propaganda
ban at Geneva. There is no reason to believe that either the
acceptance or the rejection of this proposal would affect
progress in arms-control negotiations.

Nonetheless it is worth underscoring the growing Soviet
emphasis on confidence-building. In Soviet diplomatic notes
and in Khrushchev's pronouncements, frequently no distinction is made between "relaxing international tensions" and
confidence-building. In the official Soviet view, moves which
conduce to either are justified in themselves, but especially
because they pave the way to further agreements. Khrushchev
has said that the first year after the signing of the test-ban
treaty taught that, "given a certain fund of confidence, one

can move toward lessening of international tensions and achievement of understanding in various fields, and not only through official agreements but by a policy of 'mutual example.'" [22]

6. Conventional Force Limitation

Soviet conventional forces—as distinguished from forces geared to transcontinental combat—are primarily designated as European Theater forces, with four possible missions: to act as an indirect deterrent against the United States; to help assure the maintenance of order and control in Eastern Europe; to be prepared to destroy a considerable number of specific targets in Central and Western Europe; and to reinforce Soviet political demands or threats against the NATO area, particularly against Berlin.

In recent years the strategic and deterrent uses of the European Theater forces must have become a less formidable threat to the West and less important to the Soviet deterrent posture. The political need for and the propriety of Soviet forces in Eastern Europe seem likewise to have declined. It is most unlikely that the Soviet Union would plan to initiate forward moves against Western Europe. These European Theater forces, moreover, are hardly needed to assure the U.S.S.R. of victory in war since the Soviet Union does not now expect such a war (a fact borne out by the present Soviet strategic posture).

The U.S.S.R. could of course make a reduction in its European Theater forces part of a larger "package" negotiated with the United States. But the odds are distinctly against this—if only because of the perennial German question. Moreover, in the past the Soviet Union has cut its forces unilaterally—largely for internal reasons (such as manpower shortage or the shift in military doctrine and capabilities to missiles). At the same time—as the earlier discussion of military and civil approaches to force size suggested—it would not be surprising to find Soviet commanders biased against force reduction.

Among various kinds of force limitations, the most likely would be an agreed ceiling on the number of men under arms. With regard to a limitation of deployment (partly discussed under regional arrangements), the U.S.S.R. has been insistent indeed in its efforts to have the U.S. abandon its overseas bases which, it alleges, "encircle" the U.S.S.R. While the strategic utility of some American overseas establishments is presumably vanishing, the situation is sufficiently asymmetrical to make an agreement under which both sides withdraw from foreign territory objectively a setback for the United States.

Given the over-all Soviet attitude toward war control, it is implausible that the U.S.S.R. would agree to any advance limitation on the use of weapons or on targets to be attacked in case of war. Such agreements might be concluded only if in Moscow's view they were (1) unilaterally favorable to the Soviet Union, or (2) meaningless: Khrushchev has remarked, on occasion, that once a power found itself at war and losing badly, it would not feel bound by formalities keeping it from resorting to nuclear weapons.

7. Internationalization

The Soviet attitude toward the creation of a veto-free international police force (with or without its own second-strike capability to deter potential aggressors or to punish "guilty" parties) and the whole concept of an international peace-keeping machinery has been singularly negative. As part of its inordinate "sovereignty" syndrome, the Soviet leadership has always been suspicious of supra-national organizations which it does not control.[23] It has regarded the prospective international peace-keeping authority as a fig leaf for "predatory imperialist interests." It is likely to fear that such an agency might take charge of directing political change, especially in underdeveloped areas, through legal and political processes which would undercut precisely the kind of "revolutionary" development which Soviet observers have taken for granted as the wave of the future. Furthermore, the technical approach of a United Nations affiliate would be out of keeping with the overriding politicality of the Soviet approach.

At root, the Soviet approach reflects a vision of security in a disarmed world vastly different from that (or, more correctly, those) held in the United States. While the dominant Western expectation calls for an agreed code of international conduct, an international police force, and perhaps some authority to act (or to recommend action to the U.N.) where necessary to preserve the peace, and a larger role for the International Court of Justice, the Soviet view quite candidly rejects any supra-national authority, any compulsory jurisdiction or arbitration by an interstate organ, and postulates the existence of sovereign states, presumably for as long as "peaceful coexistence" lasts—i.e., until Communist victory is complete.[24] If this is true of a future disarmed world, Soviet suspicion of international authority and force is bound to be even greater in an armed world.

Some specialists, it is true, have pointed out that there may be room for exploration on this question, nonetheless. Thus, military forces of individual Communist states might be permitted to participate in international pacification, not as part of a U.N. peace-keeping operation but as autonomous national units assisting local "liberation movements" (potentially, a hazardous prospect, too, if one cares to rewrite the scenario of the Congo, Suez, or Cyprus operations). Perhaps more realistic is the thought that Soviet and East European contingents could contribute to the manning of multi-national ground control posts in Central Europe, if these are developed by agreement among the powers. Verification procedures offer another possible device for the involvement of Communist states, at least marginally, in such international activities.

It is not excluded that the Soviet Union would agree to international peace-keeping forces in specific cases where it has no political choice or would expect anti-Western effects (as it did in the first stages of the U.N. Congo action in 1960, and to some extent in the Cyprus action in 1964). But it insists that such forces consist of separate national contingents and be organized on an ad hoc basis. Its failure to give financial support to U.N. peace-keeping forces is well-known.

In principle, Moscow has repeatedly recognized the need for an international disarmament or inspection authority— for the future. Soviet interest in and speculation about the nature of such an agency, which was generated in the months following the Soviet GCD proposal in September, 1959, was wiped out with a vengeance as a consequence of the "experience" with the Congo operation in 1960. And while it recommended, for the first time in July, 1964, that the U.N. Security Council provide itself with the peace force envisaged under the Charter, there is no indication whatsoever that the U.S.S.R. would be willing to support such a force without a Soviet veto over its entire operation.

It is only when we come to administrative bodies or pro-

cedures requiring no surrender of sovereignty and possessing no forces of its own, that we find examples, in increasing
numbers, of Soviet interest and support. Multilateral international control commissions (for instance, in Germany and
Laos) have been acceptable to the U.S.S.R. The United Nations
was able to carry out peace-observation or mediation functions in Indonesia, Israel, and elsewhere, thanks to the absence of Soviet obstruction. The Soviet Union has itself
brought issues before the General Assembly and the Security
Council as a means of placing inhibitions on other powers.
And it has welcomed the neutral ground the U.N. provides to
use the organization or its Secretary-General (as in the Cuban crisis of 1962) for informal contacts, peace-keeping, and
negotiating purposes. That, however, is a far cry from inter-
nationalization as a way of securing the peace.

8. Regional Measures

There is no reason to doubt the seriousness of Soviet interest in formalizing, under international law, nuclear-free
zones in areas where no nuclear weapons now exist. Such an
attitude is congruent with Soviet interest in reducing the possibility of war, especially war instigated by third parties (whatever the official Soviet doctrine about supporting "national-
liberation wars"). The creators of nuclear-free zones can cite
the Antarctic Treaty as a precedent; there, of course, the
situation was exceptionally clear-cut, and the arguments and
temptations to alter the de facto denuclearized status were
minimal. The Soviet advocacy of nuclear-free zones may include the expectation that they would serve to "educate" the
United States to accept such arrangements, presumably in the
hope of later extending them to areas around the perimeter of
the U.S.S.R. or its allies.

Moreover, the creation of a nuclear-free zone amounts to
a non-proliferation measure, and a good case can be made
that the latter was a not insignificant consideration when
Moscow urged nuclear-free zones that would have encompassed both China and Germany. [25]

Often the choice of timing and location have indicated
that the Soviet authorities have been guided by political,
rather than security, considerations in proposing the establishment of this or that nuclear-free zone. In the Mediter-
ranean, for instance, it would involve the unilateral renunci-

ation of Western positions. Political considerations have also, no doubt, been responsible for Soviet withdrawal of such proposals by silence (e.g., on the Far East) or explicitly (e.g., on Latin America, with regard to which evidently Cuban remonstrations led to a change in the official Soviet position at the U.N. in November, 1963). Similarly, Soviet proposals regarding a nuclear-free zone for the Middle East and another for the Indian sub-continent have been modulated, over the years, with changing Soviet awareness of potential political complications.

While such zones need not yield asymmetrical advantages for either of the two major powers, the Soviet Union might expect to benefit from the relatively greater restriction which the establishment of nuclear-free areas would put on the actual or potential deployment of Western military power. Nonetheless, there are no insuperable obstacles to agreement with regard to certain areas, such as sub-Saharan Africa.

On the other hand, the Soviet Union has shown comparatively less interest in arms embargoes. Perhaps this is because of its awareness of the dire consequences such embargoes might have for certain "national-liberation" movements. While this does not preclude the possibility of future agreements—formal or informal—not to send or permit any arms into particular areas, Chinese Communist activity in the non-Western areas has in effect put Moscow on notice that Peking will disregard any such understandings on arms restraint and, by implication, would challenge Moscow to provide tangible aid to the struggling "liberation" movements.

The problem of arriving at agreements on nuclear-free zones along the perimeter of the Soviet Union and its allies raises even greater difficulties. Here Soviet interest has been most intense. Especially with regard to the two Germanies, the creation of a buffer so as to avoid the confrontation of hostile forces can be applied either to nuclear disengagement or to conventional demilitarization.

In one form or another, military "disengagement" from Germany or Central Europe would be possible if either side abandoned its position on the future of Germany.Without such a change, a withdrawal of forces—even bilateral and phased— would almost certainly be viewed by one side or the other as significantly weakening its political position in Europe.

The centrality of the German question in this context can

hardly be exaggerated. In Khrushchev's mind, it seems, the whole question of arms control is ultimately linked with the question of Germany. Strategy plays a significant part in arms-control diplomacy over Germany. Soviet forces in Berlin being superior to American forces there, the U.S. must make compensatory efforts in other parts of the globe each time a crisis arises. Thus Germany is the single most sensitive area where both major powers seek, directly or indirectly, to influence the existing situation—by altering it or by preventing change. The military commitment of both sides is here most highly concentrated. Many observers therefore see a direct relationship between the political confrontation there and the willingness of either side to enter into arms-control agreements.

That Gordian knot this Report is, happily, not called upon to cut. It is relevant, nonetheless, to indicate a near-consensus that there is in the U.S.S.R. a genuine fear of West German developments. Not that German conventional forces are likely to be considered a serious menace; above all, the possible provocation of conflict, quite possibly leading to or aiming at the involvement of the nuclear powers, and the prospect of Bonn's sooner or later acquiring an independent nuclear capability may indeed be genuinely disturbing to the Soviet leadership and population alike.

If finally one considers that this is a matter of considerable import to Germany's eastern neighbors as well, one can only underscore the obvious fact that this conundrum invites an urgent re-examination of the entire complex of problems relating to Germany, stabilization in Europe, NATO and WTO, and the various schemes—from "freezing" to "thinning out" to "disengagement"—with which the present volume hardly concerns itself. The future of arms control and disarmament as well as the future of Germany call for such a reconsideration in terms of changing priorities both of the Atlantic alliance and of American-Soviet relations. [26]

Chapter 10

SECRECY AND INSPECTION

One of the most stubborn and most persistent issues that have frustrated disarmament agreements has been the Soviet attitude toward secrecy, inspection, and control. What many foreign observers consider to be an unwarranted or exaggerated Soviet penchant for secrecy has inhibited agreement on the sort of verification which other powers consider imperative for the conclusion of meaningful agreements.

THE ROOTS OF SECRECY: NON-RATIONAL CONSIDERATIONS

Both rational and non-rational causes have been cited to account for Soviet rigidity on this subject. The assumptions made regarding the nature of Soviet attitudes are of some moment, for if the roots are primarily irrational, the attitudes will be extremely difficult to moderate, eradicate, or dispel. If, on the other hand, they are largely rational and perhaps manipulative, there may be "objective" means for circumventing or modifying the attitudes and the formidable obstacles they raise in the way of disarmament agreements. Moreover, the estimate of causes would presumably permit deductions as to the probable effect of specific arms-control proposals and the likelihood of their acceptance by the U.S.S.R.

Among the "non-rational" factors frequently adduced, Russian historical traditions and cultural patterns are often viewed as major sources of the penchant for secrecy.[1] Various commentators have referred to sundry stereotypes— Byzantine "secretiveness and deviousness," Tatar authoritarianism, Muscovy's isolation from the Renaissance, "traditional Russian xenophobia," "Oriental despotism," the images of the Marquis de Custine's Journals, collective Russian paranoia engendered by a sense of cultural backwardness or continual exposure to the threat of invasion—in explanation of what they consider to be a tradition of Russian secrecy or, at the very least, suspicion of the world abroad. While few

142

would deny some such "Russian, not Soviet phenomenon" with its roots "in the deep, dark past" (to quote Edward Crankshaw, though one might equally well cite numerous other writers), specialists on Russian affairs are overwhelmingly disinclined to consider this a major part of the explanation of Soviet policy on inspection and control.

Some observers see, however, a persuasive argument by inversion: If it is true that the Russian "peasant" character or the proverbial Russian soul have been distinguished not by guile but by openness, lack of discipline, and expansiveness in word, drink, and passion, one might regard the institutionalization of secrecy as a compensating device. In reply it should be argued that modern Soviet society has been unwittingly eroding this aspect of Russian character and, hopefully, any compensatory mechanism as well. Modernization and industrialization have, especially in Bolshevik garb, generated and required a purpose-oriented outlook, disciplined behavior, and a self-inhibiting social commitment which amount to a surrogate for the "Protestant ethic."

Numerous commentators have spoken of a keen Soviet sensitivity to all revelations of inferiority, coupled with a highly-developed sense of self-righteousness. While the labeling of large groups as subject to "paranoia" or "inferiority complexes" is a dubious (and scientifically unsound) procedure, there is for the layman an element of plausibility in the belief that some deep causes of insecurity may explain part of the story of Soviet secretiveness.

One need not (as some scholars would) extend one's explanation of the Soviet use of deception and concealment as a "defense against being taken in," to psychoanalytic theories of Russian fears of "succumbing" or being "penetrated." One may grant that there may indeed be deep "irrational" roots to the propensity to give "inordinate" emphasis to sovereignty, with all its symbolic paraphernalia—an impulse both compensating for past inadequacies, iniquities, and inferiorities, and corresponding to the self-image of the Communist movement's mission and future glory.

Another influence is the frequent projection by the Soviet leadership of its own suspicions, aggressive drives, and deviousness (however motivated) onto Western policy—such as, for instance, U.S. insistence on inspection. The attribution of the worst possible motives to the "capitalist" world is familiar to readers of Soviet materials. Even where such arguments are manifestly propagandistic, one is inclined to suspect that at times Soviet functionaries come to think in the patterns they are attempting to manipulate.

It has also been argued that specific elements in Bolshevism and its Marxist-Leninist heritage tend to engender a hyper-attachment to secrecy. The conspiratorial background of Lenin's movement, its use of Aesopian language in self-protection, its suspicion of (and assumption of undying hostility on the part of) the outside world, the elitist sense of exclusiveness, and the habitual inclination "to cultivate falsehood as a deliberate weapon"[2] can legitimately be considered characteristic of the Soviet temperament.

The state of mind nurtured by the dichotomic, combative streak in Marxism-Leninism leads readily to genuine disbelief in the sincerity of Western fears of Soviet aggression and in Western good will with regard to disarmament. This state of mind tends to preclude any facility for "open-minded" and above all for non-affective thinking. To the extent that the affective style is indeed typical, it tends to make for serious distortions of perception and reinforces the Soviet propensity for secretiveness.

The pre-Revolutionary and especially the Stalinist experiences have led to the institutionalization of secrecy in Soviet society. The sense of permanent conflict and the expectation of punishment for dealing with the (class) enemy—no matter whether real, potential, or imaginary—as well as the latitude of meaning given to "State Security" and the arbitrary application of comprehensive and capricious State Secrets Acts—all suggest a strongly subjective approach.

Furthermore, the effects of institutionalized secrecy are heightened by the bureaucratic tendency of lower-level functionaries to exaggerate policy directives and overreact to superior orders. Yet this is hardly a uniquely Soviet phenomenon.

Finally, beneath the overlays of traditional, ethnic, and cultural factors, beneath the assumptions of "national character" (whatever that may be), beneath the fiducial components of pseudo-scientific ideology, and unproven hunches about ancestral memories and collective neuroses, lies a psychological explanation of Soviet attitudes, which at times seems irresistibly tempting to the layman as much as to the diplomat and the journalist. Psychological factors can be useful in explaining Soviet behavior primarily in cases where it makes a significant difference precisely how the individual Soviet leaders perceive, and are predisposed to respond to, given situations. No doubt, in specific instances the personalities at the helm provide the unique element essential for an explanation (as did Stalin, e.g., in his refusal to believe the evidence of the impending German attack in 1941). As a rule, however, such an approach has seemed to be unnecessary and uneconomical by focusing on the unessential. Where psychological factors do play a role, their impact will presumably be reversed only when the persistence of the pattern of secrecy ceases to "make sense" and becomes dysfunctional.

Together, all the considerations noted above, and no doubt others, constitute the non-rational components of the Soviet approach. While in different degrees the hypotheses may be valid (and some experts would argue that they are not), these considerations are not essential to the problem before us. Even if all the non-rational elements could be made to disappear, the question would operationally remain substantially the same.

THE ROOTS OF SECRECY: RATIONAL CONSIDERATIONS

In our judgment, the prime determinants of the Soviet stress on secrecy and obstinacy with regard to inspection are to be found in the objective situation confronting the Soviet leadership—the political, economic, and military realities of the day. Though subjective elements no doubt reinforce these trends, functional considerations are sufficient in themselves to account adequately for Soviet policies in this domain. First and foremost, "secrecy" is explicable as a function of political control. The instrumental "uses" of secrecy by the Soviet authorities reveal an awareness of the asymmetrical advantage which they possess therein over the non-Communist world.

As a device to maintain the regime's grip on the social order, the secrecy complex complements the Stalinist drive to atomize all social groups, to maintain the barriers to communication within the country between rank and file and elite, and between different elites. ("It is difficult even for a member of the Central Committee to know what is going on in the Soviet Union," remarked one participant in a position to have known.) The Party and the state have jealously maintained a monopoly of communications media in the land.

By the same token, the Soviet leadership is concerned about foreign endeavors which—wilfully or not—might undermine the political control structure. Reduced to simplest terms, the very existence of alternative loyalties, appeals, and ideologies has always been an object of Soviet concern. [3] This follows logically from the whole conception of the single "guiding" party, itself guided by the single truth. It is illustrated by the record of official behavior toward the presence of alien, non-Soviet, bodies on Soviet territory. Thus Stalin in 1942-44 would not allow Allied planes or troops to be stationed in the Soviet Union, even when such a move would have been advantageous to the U.S.S.R. In a moment of dire need (as it seemed in the summer of 1941), Stalin had in effect urged the transfer of British arms and troops to the Soviet front, but he promptly canceled the invitation when the military situation was eased. In a year of greater strength and self-confidence, the U.S.S.R. dragged out negotiations for a U.S. strategic bomber base at Poltava and for a U.S. meteorological station in eastern Siberia, preparatory to an attack on Japan. In both instances, these moves were demonstrably beneficial to the U.S.S.R. in the course of fighting the war, but they were potentially subversive of that monopoly of loyalty and controls which Stalin had come to insist upon. To give another example, all the standard totalitarian fears of divided loyalty were no doubt evoked (as they have been on other occasions by pan-Islamic or Ukrainian nationalist or other divisive propaganda) by those massive and enthusiastic demonstrations which Soviet Jews staged for Israeli Foreign Minister Golda Meir in 1948. The subsequent bitter official Soviet hostility to Israel was in some degree the result of these demonstrations.

Secrecy also serves as a device to reinforce elite cohesion by strengthening "in-group" feelings based on varying degrees of access to hard data. By maintaining internal barriers to the flow of information, it helps secure the status of the top leaders who are presumably in possession of unique knowledge; and it reduces the possible influence of the rank and file on policy formation.

Secrecy can also be viewed as a weapon in Soviet political warfare, both domestic and international. Thus Soviet news media almost never report the occurrence of accidents, disasters, or disorders within the U.S.S.R., presumably out of a calculated policy of minimizing adverse information and not shaking confidence in the fundamentally optimistic assumptions about progress here and hereafter.

Soviet secrecy policies are thus in no sense limited to foreign visitors or to military affairs. In the political, economic, and military fields, secrecy serves both to cloak weaknesses and to keep a potential enemy (not to mention any ally) guessing about elements of strength. The concealment of weak spots may well be the far more significant of the two uses. An "open-door" policy was understandably intolerable to Stalin, for such a policy would have entailed the dread political exposure of Soviet forced labor camps, low living standards, mass deportations, and miscarriages of justice. The great discrepancy between official Soviet statistics and subsequent "corrections"—either by successor regimes in the U.S.S.R. or else by Western analysts or agencies—supports the view that the covering up of weakness is a major Soviet concern, for such a concealment makes more difficult the correct assessment of over-all Soviet strength.

Concealment has also operated in the interest of economy. Since the "other side" is not certain of the completeness of its intelligence data, secrecy may serve as the equivalent, e.g., of hardening a certain number of additional missile sites. The myth of the missile gap, after all, grew out of Soviet secrecy. Secrecy, moreover, obscures the direction and rate of military research and development, thus presumably increasing the chances for a technological "end run."

From a military standpoint Moscow must regard secrecy as an important asset. As an integral part of the Soviet defense posture, secrecy (Soviet military doctrine appears to maintain) confers on the U.S.S.R. an advantage over "open societies" with regard to intelligence about target location, force size and armament, warning systems, and technological innovation. Particularly under conditions of American military superiority the U.S.S.R. stands to gain advantages from a policy of calculated secrecy, which serves as a partial equalizer for strategic inferiority. [4]

Secrecy prevents an accurate estimate of Soviet capabilities. In this sense, the Western view of the Soviet Union as "an enigma wrapped in a riddle" has been an asset to the

U.S.S.R. Time and again the United States has credited the Soviet armed forces with greater strength or combat readiness than has turned out to have been warranted. Such was the case in the mid-fifties with American assumptions about the possible adoption of a "pre-emptive" surprise-attack strategy by the U.S.S.R and concomitant estimates of the military establishment supporting such a strategy.

Finally, it is highly probable that Soviet leaders—military, security, and political alike—believe Western insistence on "inspection" to be part of a systematic and none-too-subtle effort to legalize espionage and subversion inside the U.S.S.R.[5] For two generations they have talked about the world-wide capitalist conspiracy, which was bound to attempt an overthrow of the Soviet system. Here, they were bound to feel, was precisely what the enemy had been waiting for.

Khrushchev has more than once alluded to the intelligence tasks of "so-called" technical inspectors whom the U.S. would send. Time and again he has accused Western powers and Western citizens of violating Soviet sovereignty and abusing Soviet hospitality. "In short," he has concluded with regard to U.S. inspection demands, "set them at the table and they will put their feet on it" (or, in a variant exclamation, "let them into your house, and they'll break into your bedroom"). It need hardly be added that occasional foreign statements about the espionage uses of inspection as well as discovered acts of spying have not served to dispel such suspicions; and that the Soviet Union for its part has a far better opportunity than is reciprocated to obtain the intelligence it may require about the United States, without territorial inspection.

The establishment of an independent inspectorate would thus invite risks and troubles for the Soviet single-party regime. The cost of inspection, under the circumstances (unless based on non-territorial verification or on unmanned and automated devices), would be considerably higher for the Soviet Union than for a pluralistic society. This is a matter of especial touchiness at present: At a time when the elite is trying to ease some controls without jeopardizing its own power, it is understandable that a particular sensitivity would attach to U.S. pressure or arguments concerning inspection. To Moscow, inspection easily shades into espionage or control. At least in some significant measure, this

Soviet response is not a "programmed" or fictitious one but a reflection of sincere concern.

The changes which have occurred in the Soviet Union over the past decade have not left secrecy attitudes untouched. As we would expect, the leaders' attitude toward secrecy is an integral part of a broader pattern of perceptions and policies. It is thus in harmony with Soviet "reality" as perceived by them. It is more resultant than determinative. By the same token, it is less likely to be altered in and of itself than in conjunction with a change in the basic pattern of Soviet perceptions and values.

The changes since Stalin have been of uneven magnitude. Within the elite, the pressure for broader participation in, and consultation prior to, policy formation has included demands for wider access to information. Internal communications and initiatives within the elite have increased strikingly since 1953. Soviet citizens have had greater access to foreign information in Soviet libraries; they have had increased contact with foreigners through exchange programs and greater Soviet participation in international organizations and conferences. Other moves have reflected a growing Soviet consciousness of "public relations" as well as a willingness to take modest risks for the sake of abolishing the accoutrements of "Stalinist" secrecy and controls, such as the elimination of preliminary censorship for the foreign press corps in Moscow; the establishment of direct telephone and radio links abroad; the cessation of jamming of broadcasts from the Voice of America and the BBC; the contemporaneous release of information on Soviet manned space flights (previously announced only after their successful completion); the appearance of telephone directories and city guides, as well as far more plentiful statistical and archival data. Where previously certain areas of the Soviet Union were carefully shielded from foreign visitors, the U.S.S.R. now encourages tourism, e.g., in Uzbekistan, in an attempt to present its accomplishments in Central Asia as a model for others in Asia to emulate.

Finally, technological change may render many military secrets both impossible and less important to keep, while improvements in material and political conditions are apt to reduce Soviet reluctance to accept reasonable inspection proposals out of fear of exposing "shameful" spots to foreign observers.[6]

The hesitant relaxation that has occurred in Soviet life since 1953 is a hopeful sign. Needless to say, the policy of secrecy has hardly been breached in the military and security realms. The limits of change are sadly and soberingly apparent; some areas of the U.S.S.R. remain taboo to foreigners; exchanges have involved only a minute number of Soviet citizens; many of the improvements have been little more than retreats from Stalinist excesses. There is no basis for asserting that important relaxations in secrecy—as they affect international agreements—are bound to follow in due time. If the basic Soviet calculation was rational, it presumably continues to be so, and continues to deny the justification for any significant departure from present security practices. And yet, by the same token, the evidence suggests that a calculation of costs and benefits can lead Moscow to a lowering of secrecy barriers where such lowering is felt to be in the Soviet interest.

VERIFICATION AND INSPECTION

The Soviet refusal to accept the inspection schemes advanced by the U.S. and the U.K. as essential parts of arms-control and disarmament proposals must be seen as basically a political decision, less weighted down than are comparable American decisions by attention to technical detail. By the same token, Soviet opposition to inspection is not caused by a desire to cheat or to make cheating easy (though the Soviet armed forces must be expected to cheat if the "need" should arise).

Despite their customary denunciation of Western verification proposals as ostensible efforts at espionage or subversion, Soviet pronouncements have generally recognized "in principle" the legitimacy of demanding proof of non-violation of agreements. Soviet negotiators, however, have shown virtually no interest in reciprocal opportunities to inspect analogous Western facilities. Soviet officials and scientists have shown no awareness of the complexity of the problem and have given no evidence of research or curiosities comparable in sophistication, detachment, or originality to the best efforts in the West. Instead, the tedious bargaining about on-site inspections of a nuclear test ban, and arguments about the relative priority of disarmament or inspection have yielded not agreement but bitter exchanges of tu quoque as well as sterile maneuvers among predictably unacceptable positions.

Nonetheless, the Soviet authorities have, since 1959, shown themselves capable of breaking the ice—or the secrecy—when in their estimation the balance of costs and gains in security or propaganda has been compelling. Western newspapermen, for instance, were permitted to be present at ceremonies in East Germany capping a conventional force reduction. Similarly, foreign observers were invited to witness the disbandment of a Soviet tank division in Byelorussia soon after the January, 1960, speech of Khrushchev. In the wake of the Cuban crisis the U.S.S.R. permitted overflights by U.S. planes and aerial inspection of the removal of missiles on Soviet ships. On several occasions Khrushchev has apparently been prepared to agree to one, two, or three on-site inspections a year (whatever the obstacles which might have arisen in the implementation of such an ancillary agreement to a nuclear test ban).

Implicit in this and other compromises is Soviet acceptance of the principle of sampling and probability in the approach to verification. Some of the Soviet responses to the "open skies" proposal have at least recognized the desirability of such non-territorial inspection. The Soviet Union has urged agreements stabilizing or cutting military budgets with some (probably inadequate) auditing of central records. Characteristically, virtually all of these examples refer either to activities outside the territory of the U.S.S.R. (East Germany and Cuba, air space and outer space, as well as the Antarctic Treaty) or to agreements which, in the view of non-Communist experts, are inherently easy to evade (budgetary inspection).

Even the timid steps just indicated support the view that, while it creates substantial impediments to any extensive disarmament program, the Soviet outlook is not necessarily incompatible with large-scale verification.[7] Maintaining secrecy and coping with the problems raised by verification procedures are less important objectives to the Soviet leaders than the avoidance of nuclear war. If they came to believe that the choice lay between arms reduction and a marked increase in the danger of war, it is likely that the Soviet policymakers would consent to a meaningful form of verification. Such a choice, to be sure, does not appear likely to confront them in the immediate future. But this is not likely to be the only circumstance, either, under which the Soviet leadership would accept fair verification. It is to be noted that the Soviet system is probably not so fragile that it could not stand a degree of intrusion. Technology may lend a helping hand by providing less intrusive means of verification as time goes on.

Since different ways of penetrating the veils of secrecy and verifying compliance involve different costs to the Soviet leadership, one may hypothesize about the relative accepta-bility of various forms of verification. It is significant (and encouraging) that both sides appear to regard verification—or inspection, as a particular form of it—no longer as a guar-antee against violation or against aggression but rather primarily as a deterrent; in this light, partial inspection looms as a device tending to "keep the other side honest."

Any forms of verification, to be acceptable to the U.S.S.R., must fall within the limits set by the constants of Soviet strategy—i.e., it must not jeopardize the quest for invulner-ability and the maintenance of internal dominance by the CPSU. The fact that only very few forms of verification seem to be "strategic" (and hence difficult to sanction) and most are "tactical" in nature (to use Soviet political jargon) at least suggests a certain political and ideological feasi-bility.

Many arms-control agreements designed to prevent war or to slow or limit the arms race require no territorial access for verification: this is true, for instance, of the non-deployment of space vehicles and of anti-ballistic mis-sile systems, and the non-proliferation of nuclear weapons. Presumably these would be among the measures to which the U.S.S.R. could most readily agree.

Unilateral verification suffices to assure adequate com-pliance with some other agreements, either through espio-nage or else through mechanical devices. In the view of some observers, unilateral means of verification already yield considerable data to the West. If so, the U.S.S.R. has now fewer secrets to keep—and to give away—than it did even four or five years ago. Once both sides can inspect ade-quately without the permission of the other, the military value of secrecy and, therefore, the utility of opposing territorial inspection may be expected to decline. Such a development might readily provide, at an early stage, for joint access to information thus gathered. We are in no position to assess the technological likelihood of such optimistic expectations, but military specialists have asserted this to be the trend.[8] It is interesting that Khrushchev has reversed himself with regard to reconnaissance satellites which he had vigorously condemned ever since 1960. Claiming, in mid-1964, that the Soviet Union, too, was using space satellites for photographing U.S. military bases, he indicated that he knew the United States was using them to photograph Soviet installations such as missile sites.[9]

In other instances, it is necessary to limit agreements to exchanges of unilateral affirmations of non-use. In view of the "impossible" detection problem, this is evidently true of bacteriological warfare.

Presumably those arms-control measures which are subject to unilateral verification by existing personnel or by existing facilities are potentially acceptable to the U.S.S.R. Another potentially acceptable category consists of the agreed destruction of specific quantities of given weapons or materials, witnessed by foreign observers. By definition, such selective destruction involves no problem of unwanted inspection.

If Soviet apprehensions as to foreign inspection are largely political or else based on fear of discovery of military objects and targets other than those explicitly subject to inspection, one may assume a greater degree of acceptability to the U.S.S.R. of unmanned automated stations as a means of verification. The "black box" is presumably the best example of this type. Its fate supports the above thesis but also underlines the fact that in practice considerable difficulties are likely to remain even if "in principle" a given device or agreement appears acceptable.

In the Soviet view, non-territorial means of verification are generally preferable to territorial inspection, and inspection by automated systems is preferable to inspection by foreigners. This approach carries the implication that Soviet authorities would prefer disclosure of any evasions to foreign governments (capable of "reading" the instruments) to exposure of any evasions (or demonstration of compliance) to the general public at home and abroad by permitting foreign inspectors on the grounds.

While various forms of non-territorial and non-physical inspection thus possess a certain attractiveness, Soviet authorities are likely not to support "psychological" inspection.

In fact, they are sharply opposed to any scheme under which foreign (national or international) agencies would be entitled to subpoena, interrogate, or solicit communications from individual Soviet citizens without a prior Soviet veto. Such efforts at "subversion" of Soviet sovereignty and stimulation of spontaneity are bound to clash directly with rational as well as irrational elements in the leadership's image of Soviet controls. Any scheme for "institutionalized disloyalty," such as has been suggested by certain quarters in the United States, is predictably unacceptable to the U.S.S.R.[10]

All these generalizations are subject to considerable fluctuation in response to the broader political and strategic context. If one examines a standard enumeration of specific verification measures, however, such as that given below, one finds that most of these measures do not require a substantial change in Soviet attitudes or values. One might hazard the opinion that of categories 1 to 9, measures 1 through 4 can be acceptable at present, and 5 through 7 are potentially acceptable to the U.S.S.R., given a generally favorable context and perhaps successful experience with simpler accords. On the other hand, categories 8 and especially 9 refer to measures which are qualitatively so different from the earlier ones that it would be unrealistic to anticipate Soviet acceptance of them in the foreseeable future.

Here one significant difference in outlook becomes apparent: in the Western view, precisely such a "carte blanche" for foreign inspectors as that indicated under 9 is a requisite for the ultimate goal of significant strategic force reduction. Such free roaming could be allowed only after a profound change in Soviet attitudes, since the Soviet authorities would never know in advance what the inspectors were about to do and where they were about to go. Yet no less significant than the suggested cut-off point between feasible and unfeasible measures is the extent to which arms-control measures with limited access for verification do provide substantial further opportunities for agreement and implementation.

ARMS CONTROL AND VERIFICATION MEASURES[11]

Degree of Access	Arms-Control Measure
1. External verification—Adversary: requires no cooperation or acquiescence by country being inspected.	Warheads: ban or restriction on underwater and atmospheric testing; large missiles: testing, transfer; aircraft: production, deployment, transfer; submarines, conventional and nuclear: size of fleets; booster: testing, presence in orbit; deployment of troops outside national boundaries.
2. External verification—Cooperative: requires cooperation or acquiescence (for example, special reports, or agreement not to jam).	Military expenditures: gross budget information; arms-free zones outside U.S. or U.S.S.R. territory.
3. Existing internal verification—Cooperative: access by presently acceptable diplomatic personnel and tourists, with present restrictions.	Reduction of force levels (e.g., mass demobilization).
4. Invitation to witness destruction or divestment of declared items.	Agreed destruction or divestment of specific quantities of any weapons or materials.
5. Significantly increased internal verification—Cooperative: by diplomatic personnel and travelers.	Ban on AICBM system: deployment.
6. Access to declared facilities.	Ban or restriction on fissionable materials: production; warheads: testing in outer space; production, detection of purpose; AICBM: R&D, testing and production; anti-submarine devices and weapons: deployment.
7. Access to or stationing of observers at specified borders, airfields, depots.	Significant preparation for aggression.
8. "Quota inspection" of suspected undeclared facilities; zonal inspection.	Large missiles: future deployments; nuclear warheads: underground testing and production.
9. "Carte blanche": unrestricted access.	Large missiles: stockpiles; nuclear warheads: transfer; smaller missiles: all control; fissionable materials: transfer.

To these forms of verification should be added agreements providing for the stationing of observers outside the territory of the U.S.S.R. and the United States. Exchanges of observers in Central Europe, or between NATO and the Warsaw Treaty Organization (minus the two major powers) would not involve Soviet sensitivities to the same extent as would manned posts within the U.S.S.R. Moreover, such relatively modest war-prevention measures (primarily, against surprise attack) would give the Soviet Union (as well as the West) some experience in operating in the presence of an equivalent of foreign inspection. Since inspection might, in an initial stage of disarmament, involve the observation of "declared" forces only, no "carte blanche" would need to be issued. One can readily visualize a series of steps by which such accords, if successful, could be extended at later dates—from ground to air inspection and installation of radar equipment in the "enemy" zone; from Central Europe to wider areas, eventually including equivalent zones of the U.S.S.R. and the U.S. While success would not be easy or immediate, it cannot be ruled out.[12]

While the Soviet Union has in recent years declared itself ready to permit observation of destruction of equal or equivalent quantities of weapons or materiel, it has generally refused to admit the necessity of inspecting retained forces, especially as far as undeclared or hidden arms are concerned (except as sampling is implicit in some of the above items). Our group has no competence to determine the extent to which the prevalent Western doctrine, which considers such inspection essential to substantial arms reductions, is sound and immutable. On this score, at any rate, the likelihood of Soviet "surrender" appears to be little better than nil.

While granting some limited improvement in the prospects it must be recognized that the Soviet leadership is certain to remain suspicious and wary of all forms of verification that give foreigners access to its territory or, worse, access to its citizens. Soviet leaders are likely to remain even more reluctant to surrender their control or veto over inspection procedures to foreign governments or international agencies. Even when they accept inspection provisions as part of arms-control and disarmament "packages," they will predictably strive to minimize the scope, the time, and the frequency of intrusion, and to reserve for themselves the greatest possible opportunity to "repair" any resulting "damage."

It remains to raise the question of probable consequences of inspection. While U.S. behavior can facilitate the acceptability of certain agreements, it is also important to recall that certain American actions, prone to be perceived as attempts to "penetrate" or "undermine" the Soviet system, are apt to be counter-effective and actually result in a hardening of control and an increase in Soviet secretiveness. Moreover, fear of intrusion by a large number of foreigners is very likely to be a persuasive argument for use by those in the Soviet Union who argue against disarmament. Proper U.S. actions would be ones making Soviet officials feel increasingly comfortable living with "alien elements" in their midst.

It is essential to differentiate between the prima facie purposes of verification, and secondary advantages or opportunities. Not only would attempts to "reach the Soviet people" behind the backs of their leaders be frustrated and doomed to failure when made part of verification procedures, but they would in all likelihood jeopardize the entire program while also defeating their own ends.[13] Indirect goals, however attractive and desirable, such as the "opening up of Soviet society," the building of precedents for future extension of agreements, and the establishment of higher loyalties—all these must be eschewed if the immediate purpose of verification of arms-control measures is not to be defeated.

Actually, even without secondary purposes, the impact of inspection agreements would in all likelihood be considerable. While the assertion that institutionalized inspection is bound to have "a dissolving effect on the Soviet system" is quite excessive, the experience would be significant, in and of itself, in bringing home to Soviet citizens the realization that agreements with the "capitalist" world have been and are being concluded and observed, and that, moreover, the security of the Soviet Union—as of the United States—is in some degree dependent on foreign powers. But it is precisely because Soviet authorities are likely to be aware of the possible consequences of foreign contacts that it is realistic to approach arms-control agreements only from a narrowly functional point of view. In other words, in order to anticipate favorable Soviet responses, Western proposals may wish to approach the problem of inspection by asking what types of verification Moscow would find acceptable and then devising appropriate agreements. Such considerations may also bear on the sequence of possible measures, for, it has been suggested, the smaller the degree of disclosure required for confidence, the earlier a given measure can come in a sequence of steps.

Chapter 11

THE CHANGING CALCULUS

Soviet-American relations have proved capable of far greater modulation than many observers would have thought possible even a year or two ago. Both the Soviet Union and the United States have been attempting, in their different ways and at different rates, to adjust to the rapidly changing needs and opportunities of the nuclear world. In their mutual relations, there was and there is some learning and rethinking to be done.

The Soviet system—its institutional and social forces—has turned out to be both more brittle and more variable than had been supposed. The leaders and the people have proved to be no supermen; they are subject to error and ignorance, passion and greed, idealism and ambition. This much, we should have known.

No longer is Russia sealed off from the world, as it was in Stalin's last years. It is not an "open society," and will not be at any early date. But Soviet society has regained some modest life and spontaneity of its own; and it has shown itself to be keenly sensitive to what it can hear and see abroad. Within narrow limits, the outside world may be in a position to influence some Soviet attitudes, beliefs, and choices.

U.S.A./U.S.S.R.—INFLUENCES AND INTERACTIONS

The dynamic view of Soviet-American relations is reinforced by what has been called the "reactive" element in Soviet policy. In an earlier chapter it was argued that, by and large, Soviet policy has been rational—in the sense that it has responded with changing conduct and expectations to changing conditions abroad. It has evolved in response to a variety of stimuli, one of which has been American behavior.

While this reactive element is real, it is difficult to isolate, for it is naturally interwoven with other components, such as the Soviet assessment of the balance of military power, the estimate of political conditions and opportunities throughout the world, and the perception of domestic and Communist Bloc needs and politics.

The evidence regarding the reactive nature of many Soviet actions, it might be added, runs counter to some widespread stereotypes. It would seem to disprove, once again, the notion of a Moscow "master plan" for Communist advance and "take-over"—presumably, a rigid calendar whose fulfillment is centrally determined and decreed and whose political compass, once set, is doggedly obeyed. The evidence also disproves the notion that initiatives and stimuli invariably originate (or must originate) with the Soviet side. Far more correct, it seems, is the image of varied interaction, with stimuli and responses—either conscious or unwitting—on both sides.

A review of Soviet disarmament policies suggests that actual changes in American conduct, doctrine, military procurement and deployment have influenced Soviet decisions.[1]

Soviet reactions and their bearing on political uses of military capabilities are related to the "containment" conception which is implicit in the Soviet strategy of peaceful coexistence.[2] The strengthening of the Soviet home base—politically, economically, and militarily—goes hand in hand with the expectation of "revolutionary situations" abroad and the disintegration of the "imperialist" world. Soviet military power, it appears, is assigned a more indirect role than has at times been assumed abroad; it is to serve, among other things, not only as a deterrent to moves against the Soviet Union and its allies, but also as a deterrent to "counterrevolution," that is, to Western "interference" with revolutionary processes in Asia, Africa, and Latin America.

What kind of American policy is most likely to encourage relevant changes in Soviet attitudes and conduct that we would welcome? The question, deserving of separate investigation, proves to be a surprisingly complex one, with exceptions for every possible rule. There are two broadly contrasting views as to why and how desirable progress in Soviet disarmament policy might come about. In one case, Soviet cooperation or moderation is likely to be a by-product of domestic Soviet liberalization and relaxation, for which an essential Western permissiveness and open-mindedness are a necessary but not a sufficient condition. In the other, a changed Soviet attitude would result from having Soviet political momentum checked and ambitions frustrated by a "hard" Western line which holds out the continuing choice between an intensified and all-too-costly arms race and an assurance of security by arms control and arms reduction.

The evidence is inherently ambivalent. Like others, Moscow has a tendency to exploit moments of strength; at the same time, such moments provide good opportunities for it to reach agreements. While relative weakness invites disarmament as a device to reduce the "gap" or prevent it from growing, relative strength, too, may invite disarmament so as to "freeze" the strategic advantage for political benefit.

In the past, the most effective spur to changes in Soviet outlook and the moderation of Soviet foreign policy has been adversity in the environment—internal weakness (e.g., in the early years of the Soviet regime, and a decade later, during collectivization of agriculture and the first Five-Year Plan) or firm resistance of other powers to Soviet probes (e.g., the policy marked by the Truman Doctrine and the Marshall Plan, after World War II, and the U.S. stance during the Cuban crisis of 1962). It is not true, however, that its willingness to yield is proportional to the Soviet Union's relative inferiority or failure. There may exist some optimum point of perceived adversity, which we cannot define and which may not be fixed.

Moderation by the U.S. does not necessarily evoke similar moderation by the U.S.S.R. In the past, at least, many Soviet advances were predicated on the "softness" of the outside world. Paradoxically, not routine coexistence but crises have usually sparked negotiations leading to new agreements. Moreover, so long as Moscow perceives (not without reason) in the ideological implications of coexistence a possible danger to the total dedication of its citizens, the Soviet leadership will be sure to insist on the impossibility of doctrinal compromise with the West. In fact, experience suggests that a period of détente usually brings about an ideological tightening up at home. As in 1946-47, this tightening may follow previous tolerance of contacts with the outside world; at times the two have been virtually simultaneous. Significant in this connection is the fact that, on both occasions which one may take as intended moves toward a relaxation with the United States—following the Camp David meeting of Khrushchev and Eisenhower, and again following the failure of the Cuban gambit—a new campaign aimed at "ideological" conformity was initiated in the Soviet Union. One may look upon this simultaneous effort as an attempt to provide some additional "waterproofing" of the Soviet population in the face of greater exposure to and contact with the West.

In periods of obvious military inferiority, the Soviet Union has traditionally concluded that it could not afford to commit itself to extensive disarmament. It must assume that such agreements would require inspection of retained arms, which would demonstrate to the whole world Soviet military weakness. Moreover, the Soviet leadership is bound to fear that under such conditions the United States would halt the disarmament proceedings and begin to apply heavy pressure on the Soviet Union in order to secure substantial concessions. In general, consenting to disarmament under such conditions would mean, to the Soviet Union, settling for the least favorable terms.

If, on the other hand, the Soviet leadership became convinced that the U.S.S.R. would continue to lag, irrespective of the resources invested, it would be more likely to develop a genuine interest in a disarmament or arms-control proposal which would reduce the tempo of the arms race, reduce its cost, and perhaps reduce the magnitude of the "gap."

The closer to parity the two forces are, the better the "objective" chances for agreement would seem to be—but also, paradoxically, the greater the internal pressures on the inferior party to make the extra effort to push ahead to parity or beyond.

The prospects for Soviet interest in significant agreements would be poorest in case of a clear Soviet strategic superiority over the West. Even the experience of the "missile gap" suggests that the Soviet Union would seek to exploit the new balance so as to wring concessions from its adversaries.

Such generalizations, however, unrealistically assume a static political environment and an unchanging state of expectations. If the Soviet leaders should conclude that, for economic or political reasons, the strategic margin could be maintained only at a huge cost and strain, they might prefer to "freeze" their advantage by means of arms-control agreements so as to derive the commensurate political benefits.

Soviet willingness to change policies may relate, moreover, to political alternatives. To cite but the most obvious example: Having taken cognizance of the U.S. edge in missiles in 1963, the Soviet leadership wished to ascertain whether an attempt to move to a political détente would be reciprocated or rebuffed by the United States. At such critical moments, subordinate or symbolic factors as well as extraneous considerations (such as China) may suddenly loom with heightened importance. So does the American posture (in this case, President Kennedy's American University speech).

At other times, the key determinant seems to be not the absolute strength or weakness of the Soviet Union but rather the optimism or pessimism of its leadership—whether their country or their Bloc would be stronger or weaker at some future point; whether or not waiting would inevitably redound to the advantage of the U.S.S.R. (as Communists have been prone to assume). Yet this is not an overriding factor, either. Soviet interest in disarmament increased both at a time of relative euphoria within the Khrushchev leadership, in 1958-59, and at a time of obvious setbacks, following the Cuban crisis of 1962.

No single element, in other words, can be a master key to Soviet responses. With some oversimplification, one might be tempted to suggest that, in military but not necessarily political terms, Soviet willingness to conclude substantial disarmament agreements, would be most likely under conditions of American military superiority without concomitant American bellicosity.[3]

Some specialists have astutely advanced the argument that strategic asymmetry is a prerequisite—and provides an impetus—for an arms agreement. Similarly, to favor an agreement on arms limitation or control, each side must see in it a distinct benefit to its relative security, prestige, or power. Two states are therefore more inclined to enter into an arms-control agreement if each believes that time is on its side to the extent that their expectations and national policy objectives are in conflict. Just as with U.S. and Soviet economic aid to unaligned countries or with their cultural exchange agreements, the probability of agreement is greater, the more the reciprocal expectations of the two signatories diverge.

The danger point may occur when the leadership becomes aware of its own miscalculations. Would a succession of failures and hard choices lead the Soviet policy-makers to reconsider the assumptions underlying their present strategy? Whether at that time they would be more likely to revert to a more militant policy or, for all intents and purposes, indefinitely postpone the achievement of their own long-range goals, cannot be foreseen. But, to the extent that the outside world prefers their present stance to a more extreme one, it is important that the Soviet Union be convinced (or remain convinced) "that it must perforce and that it can comfortably and honorably live within a balance of power which is decidedly in our favor."[4]

Given increasing confidence, on both sides, in the gross equilibrium in world affairs, neither the United States nor the Soviet Union is likely to give top priority to disarmament questions. Despite the formal importance attached to it—for instance, by its inclusion in the new CPSU Program,[5] and the attention given it in Khrushchev's addresses at the United Nations and elsewhere—a look at the record of Soviet foreign policy shows only few clues to arms-control policy. One reason herefore has been precisely Soviet willingness to subordinate it to other and more immediate tasks. The fact, for instance, that Moscow, promptly, after voicing its proposals for a troika to administer international organizations (with equal Communist, Western, and neutralist contingents) extended this demand to the Geneva disarmament talks revealed a willingness to torpedo the disarmament negotiations for the sake of a momentary, futile, and politically irresponsible gambit.

That incident also underlines a difference between American and Soviet approaches to disarmament. For the United States, disarmament has been primarily a technical problem. For the Soviet Union, it is above all a political problem. Precisely for this reason Soviet officials are concerned to maintain and to demonstrate the consistency of their policy with the "general line." Hence Soviet arms-control and disarmament postures are bound to be influenced by developments in other fields to a greater degree than is true of the West.

By the same token, it is important for the United States not to create the impression of inconsistency, of tactical diversions and divergencies, of advancing proposals and amendments which are bound to be perceived by Soviet negotiators as "gimmicks" or "jokers" not worthy of serious attention. Any suspicion on their part that they are being trapped or deceived is likely to boomerang with a vengeance.

For the same reasons, there are obvious limits to the utility of negotiations. Tactful communication does not necessarily improve chances of success; different styles and attitudes may have but a marginal value in influencing the results—if the Soviet negotiators have instructions to stick to conditions unacceptable to the West. There is probably some "feedback" to Soviet policy-makers from the negotiating table. But, while there is evidence of thorough and accurate reporting by Soviet representatives to their superiors at home, it is conjectural how much the impressions of the practitioners are conveyed to, even less how much they influence the judgments of, their masters.

At the same time, if negotiations are carried on with a genuine desire on both sides to arrive at a reasonable agreement, there is available a wealth of technical advice that stems from years of cumulative experience in such negotiations. It ranges from the nature of the forum, the size of the group, and the physical settings, to the importance of personal trust and the establishment of rapport among key negotiators, and the great opportunities often provided by informal contacts, away from the official sessions.

What little evidence is available suggests likewise that there is every benefit to be derived from using other, academic, governmental, and personal channels to explore points of view and opinions with Soviet citizens. Informal and unofficial discussions of the type conducted by the "Pugwash" Conferences on Science and World Affairs may help to identify specific disarmament measures of mutual interest and to explain, in an atmosphere of greater mutual confidence than is normal among negotiators, the reasons for specific U.S. policies. Such discussions, furthermore, may possibly encourage modifications of Soviet policies. To be effective, U.S. nationals involved must have a close relationship with their Soviet counterparts and must possess scientific competence as well as a good knowledge of American policy.

Particularly at times of crisis it is important to have developed relationships of confidence with adversary representatives through diplomatic and if necessary extra-diplomatic channels. "The great value of personal confidence in such communications, when it is possible, is likely to be more than the public can be made aware. This may be one of the most tangible aspects of the limited adversary relationship."[6]

PACT OR PING-PONG?

One novel problem—since the conclusion of relevant agreements is itself a recent phenomenon—is the best form of arms-control agreements, from the Soviet point of view. The nuclear test ban of 1963 was a formal treaty—not so much for reasons of enforcement as for reasons of symbolism. The signed agreement, ratified and deposited, may be assumed to have satisfied the Soviet affinity for formalism and literalism in international agreements. Since then, it may be possible and preferable—from the Soviet point of view and, as Moscow sees it, perhaps from the American point of view, too—to opt for successive exchanges of (reasonably symmetrical) unilateral steps which, put together, may amount to "limited cooperation."

The basic prerequisite for any such "informal arms understanding"[7] must be the conviction by both parties that a gross equilibrium exists. Without a sense of relative stability of deterrence, neither side would be willing to make even modest unilateral moves; with stability, presumably, a single failure to reciprocate a modest move would not seriously disturb the over-all balance. A second necessary presupposition for continued reciprocity (one, however, not articulated by the Soviet Union) would be a rational "reading" of the signals of one side by the other.

An advantage of step-by-step procedures lies, in part, precisely in the ease and informality with which progress can be made. Moreover, this procedure would appear to be far "safer" for the U.S.S.R. than more public methods in that it would avoid continued dickering with the Chinese.

Informal reciprocal or unilateral arms-control measures have actually been practiced for some time, perhaps without the explicit realization of one or more of the participants that they were engaged in what, by current American terminology, could be described as arms control. In some instances, there has been in effect a commitment to restraint; thus, in 1956 the Soviet leadership probably thought the United States had implied it would not forcibly enter the territory of any country in the Socialist camp. The forbearance of both the United States and the Soviet Union in not introducing their own forces in certain other areas—for instance, Laos—or in limiting military confrontations to proxies has rested on similar mutual hints and inferences.

From the Soviet point of view, an interest in maintaining the level of international tension below certain limits (at least during the present phase of Soviet policy) acts as a restraint against actions which would be unduly conducive to

Western mobilization or cohesion. Soviet political control over its military establishment, Soviet determination not to transfer nuclear arms even to its own allies, and Soviet limitation of its own resources committed to arms development all constitute informal arms-control measures.

Similarly, each side is evidently prepared to hold off with certain measures as long as its opposite number is. While we have no adequate information on the subject, one may surmise that this is true of all-out civil defense and of anti-missile defense systems. Some moves in other areas may also contribute to predisposing the participating powers to further reciprocal moves. The exchange of Soviet Colonel Abel for U-2 pilot Gary Francis Powers would seem to be such a case. The suspension of jamming of Voice of America and BBC broadcasts to the Soviet Union may be taken to represent an esoteric invitation to a further sequence of steps leading to a limited détente. Chairman Khrushchev has indeed acknowledged Soviet awareness of such gestures in calling for a continuation of what he labels a "policy of mutual example."[8] Moscow undoubtedly considered its stated budget cut of 600 million rubles, announced in December, 1963, to belong in the same complex, and it virtually said as much with regard to the announcement of the reduction in fissionable materials production in March, 1964.

The Cuban crisis of 1962 brought perhaps the most sophisticated series of responses, including Soviet acceptance of the legitimacy of U.S. interest in seeing the Soviet missiles removed, and American willingness to view (and presumably count) them from a distance, without demanding close examination. Moscow may even conclude that, in the future, a unilateral thinning out of troops could be carried out by either side—should security considerations permit—without the outcries of "betrayal" that would accompany a formal accommodation with "the enemy camp."

In all likelihood, there are a considerable number of arrangements, positive or negative, which the Soviet Union now views as belonging in this sequence of informal trade-offs and implicit matchings. The utility of such procedures for arms control appears indeed to be real and not inconsiderable. In fact, from the United States position it may well be argued that an essential step toward effective arms-control agreements is the widespread acceptance of the likely continuation of political conflict within the framework of a mutual interest in introducing some safeguards to reduce the hazard of war.

Yet two words of warning should be voiced. On the one hand, states do take action not wishing an identical or reciprocal response by the opposite side. The U.S. missile program beginning in 1961, for instance, presupposed American ability to convince Moscow that the Soviet Union could not readily keep up that race. Yet at times the detection of signals differentiating between moves meant to be and remain unilateral and those meant to elicit a symmetrical response, may not be foolproof. Moreover, the powers may well come to a point at which the nature of the weapons or delivery systems involved would require publicity, simultaneity, and formal verification arrangements—e.g., reduction of strategic forces. At that point, one may assume, both sides would deem formal agreements to be indicated. It is most probable, however, that in the short run—and perhaps beyond it—the Soviet leadership will favor resort to the policy of "mutual example."

SENSE AND NONSENSE

It would take a long catalogue to list—let alone, to subject to thorough criticism—basic flaws and errors regarding Soviet affairs, in the rapidly-growing literature on disarmament and arms control. Such an effort would be both pretentious and unnecessary here. Yet brief cognizance should be taken of a few "untenable" or at least highly debatable views.[9]

One assumption expressed with bothersome frequency is the ostensible "identity" of Soviet and American positions and problems. However significant the parallels, the present Report should leave no doubt that, in our opinion, this point of view is hard to defend when it comes to assumptions, apperceptions, and long-range goals.

No less misleading is the increasingly widespread argument that, having jettisoned Stalin and Stalinism, Khrushchev's Russia is (and its successors will remain) "pragmatic" in outlook. Granted that important changes in ideology have taken place, the attribution of "eclecticism" and "pragmatism" to basic Soviet perceptions and motivations still seems not only premature but also misleading in terms of inferences it encourages to be drawn.

One may readily dismiss the assumption that the arms race and other problems are bound to "resolve themselves, given some good will." There is little evidence suggesting that either "waiting for convergence"[10] or trying to "muddle through to diversity" is likely to be a wise course.

More substantial and worthy of a hearing is the view that disarmament negotiations have become nothing but exercises in "gamesmanship," which (to use Joseph Nogee's definition) amounts to "the technique of utilizing the discussions for propaganda purposes" and proceeding to "reject the proposals of the other side without appearing to sabotage the discussions." While there has been a considerable amount of shadow-boxing, the conclusion of several agreements and treaties in 1963 and 1964 would seem to invalidate this argument as a basic or adequate analysis.

Another argument avers that, while Communism (as it has been known in this country and abroad) has been a "Stalinist phenomenon," now the Soviet regime (or the leadership, or the country) has found a way out of terror and prejudice, or else that, in a thorough break with its own past, the CPSU has adopted a decision "to seek substantial disarmament by every means." This is likely to be a rosy exaggeration of atmospheric and, one hopes, genuine changes without considering the proper historical background, the political context, and their possible upset.

At the "pessimist" end of the spectrum, the most formidable argument to take cognizance of—and to dissent from—comes from men like Robert Strausz-Hupé and Stephen Possony, who in effect maintain the impossibility of credible agreements with Communists, in general, and on disarmament, in particular.[11] The views of that school come close to others who insist on the utter immutability of Communism (or of Russia). This includes those who deny that there has been or will be any significant change over time; those who refuse to see meaningful differences among Communist Parties and states; and those who fail to allow for differences among individual members of the Communist movement.[12] The available evidence, we are convinced, leaves little room to argue (as proponents of these views have done) either the adequacy of deriving Soviet goals and policies from what may be called quotation-mongering from Marxist-Leninist "classics," or the impossibility of diversity within a totalitarian elite (as previously the same analysts were prone to insist on the impossibility of diversity among Communist Parties and states) or, finally, monolithic conspiratorial coordination by Communist regimes that allows no occasion for error, hesitation, confusion, or independence of mind.

Entirely different from the "pessimist" arguments—yet, in our view, no less erroneous—are explanations readily advanced for Soviet "irrationality" or "secretiveness." In this vein one is apt to hear that Russians have always regarded force and violence as proper means for self-advancement; or else, that Soviet aggressions are the product of fear and humiliation inflicted on Lenin's regime after 1917; or, that the Russian "national character" (or the "Russian soul") explains "uniquely Russian" traits—which may be credited to Byzantine, Mongol, or other influences. An attempt was made in an earlier chapter to dispose of these views.

Let us also beware of the assumption that "our problem with the Russians" is merely one of communications, past misunderstandings, or residues of prejudice—that in fact "the problem" lies with us rather than with them.

There is one other school of thought which has found support among serious experts: "tension reduction." It assumes that international conflict is the product of hostility, which must be broken down; and that any cooperative action—in the fields of health, science, cultural exchanges, or trade, for example—is likely to overcome suspicions, create a sense of community, attenuate tensions, and ultimately reduce armaments.[13]

None will question the desirability of reducing tensions; indeed, all arms control may be considered a form of tension reduction. Symbolically, tension-reducing gestures may contribute, if only marginally, to the negotiations of agreements. Khrushchev has welcomed confidence-building as a prelude to new agreements, much in the way some American "tension-reducers" would. Fundamentally, however, underlying Soviet-American differences are not susceptible to resolution in this fashion, and expectations that they are, are bound to be grievously disappointed. Nor is it clear whether (1) arms control should be negotiated in order to reduce or overcome international tensions and conflicts, or (2) tensions should be reduced in order to make arms-control agreements possible. In either case, once means and ends are sorted out to make arms control the goal, tension reduction demands "the convergence of values and purposes in the two societies." Most Soviet-affairs specialists will wish to dissociate themselves from this point of view.[14]

By contrast with the above (in our opinion, fallacious) theories, it seems far sounder, first, to acknowledge the basic differences of our two systems and societies, and then, to follow the advice of one of our participants: in negotiating with the Russians, "start with the assumption that they are normal human beings, and keep to this unless the contrary is proven." Or as John Strachey wrote,

> The Russian authorities in general, and the Russian defense planners in particular, have apparently had much the same preoccupations, made some of the same mistakes, suffered many of the same anxieties, and come to many of the same conclusions, as those of the West.[15]

WHAT LIES AHEAD?

It would be wisest to desist from any outline of possible future trends. Sovietologists have an execrable record of predicting. Moreover, even if the major trends are correctly defined (or divined), their translation into actual policy must not be taken for granted. Finally, zigzags have characterized Soviet policies in the past and presumably will continue to do so in the years ahead. And no moment is more likely to precipitate dramatic shifts and crises than that when the succession to the leadership must be determined—or fought out—as it will be in the not-too-distant future.[16]

In the absence of a major catastrophe or war, present political trends are most likely to continue. An overthrow of the Soviet regime can be ruled out. On the other hand, the perennial tension between conservative and reformist elements may be expected to continue, in a variety of forms and forums. While a partial reascendancy of the "die-hards" can by no means be discounted, the continued predominance of moderate forces appears to have far better prospects. It is underlined by the cumulative momentum of recent steps—advocacy of a détente, test-ban treaty, fertilizer program, modest toleration of loyal non-conformity, reconciliation with Tito, refusal to compromise with Peking, defense of "goulash Communism," adjustment to strategic inferiority. However, neither the orientation itself nor the men behind it enjoy immunity from change.

In future leadership contests the contenders are likely to vie for broad public backing (whether direct or indirect) within the U.S.S.R. They therefore may be expected to compete for support by means of a variety of "liberalizing" postures and promises. The harshness of the conflict with Communist China is likely to engender further polarization of the opposing Chinese and Soviet views. This, in turn, is likely to strengthen moderation of Soviet outlook and conduct. In the interim between now and the next Soviet succession crisis centrifugal forces in the Bloc, as well as the thrust of useful if limited contacts with the West, may, at the very least, help to establish a momentum which would be hard to break.

The question of the rate of future policy changes remains open. While some specialists expect a continuation of recent trends and, beyond a critical point, perhaps a gathering momentum, others foresee an early loss of dynamism and, in substance, a Soviet proclivity to avoid risks and changes. The latter observers would attribute some of the changes of the past decade to the unique needs of de-Stalinization. An increase in rigidity would seem particularly probable under any future leadership which, having come to maturity in the Stalin days, would be likely to lack imagination and flexibility but would instead tend to rely on bureaucratic routine in the conservative Party and state machines.

One may expect continuing adaptations in the field of ideology. Almost certainly these will serve further to "erode" the formal ideology, although attempts to slow down this process or to conceal it are not precluded. At any rate, despite the reality of "erosion," it is at least quite premature—and could be dangerous—to assume that the entire corpus of Communist beliefs and attitudes is irrelevant to Soviet attitudes and behavior.

There is substantial agreement about the probability of further social change in the Soviet Union, but less than a consensus on its direction and scope. Not everyone would predict a "mellowing" of Soviet society, but it still seems more likely than not. One may anticipate less opportunity for social mobility and, in general, a certain "settling," with a concomitant increase in self-identification and crystallization of social groups, especially elites. Most significantly, the slight broadening of the base of policy-making is likely to permit spokesmen for social and functional "interest groups" to express their views more freely and perhaps to apply some efforts at persuasion on behalf of their favorite schemes.

One such emerging group consists of those who manage and plan the Soviet economy. Though these people are not themselves agreed on all issues, many of them apparently desire a greater use of rationalized—"objective" and impersonal—criteria in making management and economic planning decisions. Their efforts in this direction are likely to bring them into conflict with other groups, especially the Party apparatus. Within managerial circles, cleavages may develop between those who might be considered a part of the Soviet "military-industrial" complex and the rest, such as those in light industry; or between bureaucrats and planners intent on central planning and tight control, on the one hand, and those economists, officials, and managers who advocate meaningful decentralization, on the other. In any case rationalizing the economy does not necessarily mean (or help) liberalization of policy—though it might.

Another group certain to acquire a distinct political profile and point of view is the military leadership. In fact, the present role of the military may already be greater than is popularly assumed. While in recent years it has been customary to think of the marshals as spokesmen for a "tougher" line, there is no inherent reason why this has to be so; in fact, in foreign affairs—be it on Berlin or "overseas"—the evidence suggests that the military have been cautious and reluctant to take dangerous initiatives. On the other hand, they yield to no one in their suspicion of the "main enemy" and "likely adversary"; and they are likely to be hostile or at least indifferent to reforms from which the defense establishment would derive no benefit.

As a third elite group, the Soviet intelligentsia has surprised many Western observers by its inclusion of an amazingly hardy core of alienated men and women, particularly of the younger generation. In fact, the growing insistence of members of the creative intelligentsia on the realization of values often honored in name only—progress, justice, freedom—has been one of the most striking (and to the Soviet leadership, most bothersome) phenomena of the past decade. Reluctantly, the Party has been obliged to reconcile itself to the existence of

intellectuals who want a private life and apolitical creativity;
but it cannot yet abandon its view of the arts and letters as
"weapons to be kept in battle readiness." Whether the years
ahead will bring tolerance and emancipation here, also remains
a matter for speculation.

A fourth elite group, the Party apparatus, looms as a
colossus barring the path to change. Despite all the official
efforts to "re-educate" the Party, to "bring it closer to the
masses," and to modernize its outlook and procedures, the
Party apparatus remains generally sluggish and conservative.
Functionaries resist "volunteer" groups and "spontaneity";
they dislike secret voting and mandatory rotation of officials;
many resent the growing role of non-Party specialists consulted
by the leadership and the novel concept of the "Party of the
whole people." Time and again in the Khrushchev era, observers have had the impression that the Party machine can
very effectively "drag its feet" so as to obstruct implementation of a favorite scheme of the seemingly unpredictable leadership. The inherent conservatism of the Party machine cannot
be eradicated overnight; in fact, new cadres may "catch" the
orthodox spirit. Here the prospect is one of slow and uncertain change.

No mention has been made thus far of the vast "rank and
file" of Soviet people. This is so not because they do not matter or because they have no opinions or attitudes, but because
their views have no immediate bearing on policy. Not in their
mass disloyal, they will presumably go along with Soviet policy—especially if it assures them of continued peace abroad
and improved living conditions at home. Yet the Soviet
citizenry presents the leadership with further dilemmas. Not
the least of these is the "problem of reconciling the urgen-
cies of heavy industry and defense with consumer welfare."
In the words of a leading authority,

> While the welfare concessions sponsored by the Khru-
> shchev regime are modest in absolute terms, they do
> move in a direction which the Soviet people can only wel-
> come. Such improvements in the standard of living as have
> taken place since Stalin's death have served to blunt the
> edge of discontent and to bring worker and regime closer

together. At the same time appetites have been whetted rather than satiated, and the Soviet leadership faces its own continuing revolution of rising expectations.[17]

In the Soviet economy one should not expect radical new departures—not because such departures are not objectively called for, but because (1) Soviet officialdom hesitates to tinker with a going, even if at times sluggish, concern, and (2) ideological obstacles to drastic change remain in such areas as decollectivization of agriculture and decentralization of planning and industry. Some experimentation with new forms and techniques, some crash programs to remedy severe ills, and some innovation may be expected—along with a determined effort to increase labor productivity, promote automation, improve quality, rationalize planning, and step up the use of synthetics. But the far-reaching changes which the Soviet economy needs are not likely to come during the next few years.

In military technology and doctrine, most probably no fundamental changes will occur in the next few years. Such a view is advanced with some misgivings, as we are keenly aware of our lack of competence and information in this field.[18]

There remains the question whether developments in weapons technology are more likely to move the U.S.S.R. toward disarmament or away from it. Part of the difficulty in providing even a tentative answer stems from the impossibility of determining how heavily Soviet leaders count on advances in military technology and science to yield a qualitatively significant improvement in the strategic posture of the U.S.S.R. In the short run, whatever the opinions are in military and scientific circles, there is no indication of any Soviet plans or moves which are in obvious conflict with what we take to be the standard view within the Soviet political leadership, namely, that it is now impossible to get a war-winning capability which would make the initiation of war by the Soviet Union a rational policy.

At present neither side is likely to back out of an agreement out of a desire to exploit a technological breakthrough. Nor does the fear of such a "break" provide a significant incentive for either side to agree to strategic force reduction or limitation. Whether or not the Soviet Union would violate an existing agreement if and when it was in a position to score a breakthrough, can hardly be predicted without a knowledge of specific circumstances.

The most plausible assumption to make on the basis of the various projections is that there is room for various arms-control agreements and "partial measures" to be concluded by the U.S.S.R. in the 1960's; but that there is no great likelihood of a far-reaching strategic disarmament agreement acceptable both to the Soviet leadership and to the United States. Still, meaningful disarmament is not impossible. If it were to occur, it would probably bring in its own wake further changes on the Soviet and on the world scene, most of which should be welcome to the United States.

DILEMMAS AND OPTIONS

In the past decade the Soviet Union has come face to face with the thermonuclear world. It has found it awesome and sobering, exhilarating but complicated beyond belief. Confronted with the staggering challenge of adapting itself on the run to the needs and opportunities they perceived, Stalin's heirs have been eager but perhaps unable fully to recognize the scope of their own problems at home and abroad, in theory and in practice. This has been true despite all the successes scored, all the dynamism and enthusiasm generated, and all the wrongs set right.

The first promise of technological superiority over the West and the subsequent threat of obliteration have combined to intensify the historical pendulum swings of Soviet political development between overconfidence and fearful doubt, between faith and manipulation, persuasion and coercion, reality and utopia, domestic needs and foreign ambitions, revisionism and orthodoxy, determinism and voluntarism, super-power and underdevelopment, West and East.

In its search for a "general line," the Soviet leadership has been impaled on the horns of a major dilemma. How high a price is it willing to pay, and how great a risk is it willing to take, in order to promote the change to which it remains committed? The Soviet state has never been stronger: its arsenals of nuclear weapons and its accomplishments in science and space; its economic growth and its drive to make friends and influence people around the globe—all this, it would seem could but confirm the rosiest belief in the inevitable progress of its cause. That much more intense has been the feeling of frustration which has pervaded Soviet policy-making in recent years. In large measure, it has stemmed from the coincidence and magnitude of the problems facing the U.S.S.R.

An elite bred on the notion that the way to advance is to maximize its power, has come to realize that in the nuclear age one cannot and dare not simply convert one's investment in power into political dividends. A movement wedded to the belief in its own inevitable progress and the inevitable doom of the enemy camp has witnessed the most profound split it has ever experienced, while the "other" camp survives with superior strength and without anticipated crisis. A Party taught the infallibility of its leaders and the scientific nature of its creed, has come to know of its dead master's crimes and to sense the inadequacy of its doctrine. The issue of disarmament, which the Soviet elite recognized to be crucial in this decade, has further challenged some core assumptions and confronted Soviet policy-makers with awkward and difficult options.

Is disarmament to be a warrant of survival or a ticket to victory, a life insurance or a battle plan? Is arms control to be part of a broad Soviet quest for détente, or is it intended to be a strategic booster to augment Soviet power? In the unceasing dialectic of Soviet apperception, is it a phase of conflict or of coexistence? Is it likely to stimulate—or is it a part of—a chain reaction of accords with the non-Communist world; or is the number of agreements which can be concluded soon to be exhausted, without much ado? Are partial measures to increase security "habit-forming"; or is their roster, like a laundry list, to be discarded once its purpose has been served?

Does the Soviet disarmament plan offer a true accommodation between the two "world systems," or is it an ingenious form of struggle? Or is it both, and if so, how? Communists ask themselves these questions, much as non-Communists do. The whole notion of common positive interests with the adversary was, when it first appeared, as suspect and unfamiliar to Soviet observers as it must have been in the United States— whether in its "non-zero sum game" formulation or in more practical and primitive terms. The political advantages which could be derived from strategic power now had to be balanced against the dangers inherent in its use. Both reckless bluffing and cautious conservatism in the management of force and violence sprang from the liaison of Communism with nuclear power. Soviet questioners have had increasing difficulty in providing certain and simple answers.

Marxism-Leninism itself allows of several different read-
ings, depending on the interpreter's values and point of view.
In good Communist terms, one could show that disarmament
must never be anything more than propaganda; and one could
also show that it must not be allowed to remain sheer propaganda. One could argue, in orthodox fashion, that the world-
wide victory of Communism must precede disarmament—that
"general disarmament can be realized and the source of war
removed only when imperialism is wiped out by revolution"[19] —
but one could equally maintain that disarmament would ease and
assure that very victory.

Two very different Communist tempers are visible here.
Perhaps they have always co-existed, at opposite poles of the
dialectic, with many Communists somewhere in between. Now,
with the authority of the center impaired and discipline in the
world movement disrupted, the two approaches face each other
with all but irreconcilably divergent impulses and implications.

One is the optimistic faith in the future, which favors innovation, is prepared to refrain from violence wherever possible
because it does not believe it necessary, is able to assess the
limits of the possible, and seeks friends and allies. History,
moving in necessary stages, strikes its proponents as an ally
which will, in any case, run its predestined and victorious
course; but (in Khrushchev's phrase) one cannot "whip the
horse of history" to make it go faster. Here a dose of gradual-
ism and flexibility combine with a pinch of romanticism but
also reason. Here also are some who believe in the future Communist society, in the withering of the state, in the betterment
of man—and in disarmament as one way of speeding the process, reducing the power equation between the two camps to
its simplest terms. They are confident that mankind disarmed
will head—more safely and more simply—where it was destined
to head anyway. Henceforth, Khrushchev has told American
visitors, nothing must interfere with the inevitable process.[20]

The opposite Communist temper is impatient, power-ori-
ented, willing and eager to organize and manipulate, and prepared to intervene as if to twist the arm of an unwilling Clio.
For the good of the cause, it sanctions any means; it frowns
neither on the rewriting of history nor on coercion, purges, and
concentration camps. In a Mao or Castro, its expression
includes the belief that there are no mountains too high to
scale, no obstacles that human will and effort cannot overcome.
In a Stalin, it led to an indefinite postponement of utopia, a

pessimism about man, and an impulse to direct and control everything. This conflict-oriented statist tends to ignore the blissful images of the good society that is presumed to lie ahead. So long as "we live not on an island but in a system of states," defense—and, by definition, the strongest possible defense—is an elementary necessity. This Communist has no time for, and no understanding of, arms control and disarmament; he has learned not to trust friend or foe.

As they encountered the problems crystallized by the specter of thermonuclear war, Soviet leaders began to move in different directions—without any clear lines of demarcation and sometimes, it may be, without themselves knowing where or how far to go. Some found themselves worried about the dangers of "relaxation" and pacifism, about the need for greater militancy against the foreign foe and against the spread of a "consumer-goods mentality" at home. They yearned for the simpler, if more austere and risky yesterdays: they, after all, had survived! Others indignantly rebuffed and rebutted the growing list of Chinese charges of treason, and found themselves welcoming more elbow-room in thought and in work, and more opportunity for contacts abroad; they sympathized with the substance if not with the label of "goulash Communism" and argued against the "metal-eaters" and "militarists."

Many, no doubt, have been confused, vacillating, refusing to take clear-cut stands, seeking cover and concealment. If we knew more, we could perhaps construct a typology of Soviet attitudes not totally unlike that which American analysts (such as Robert Levine, in his The Arms Race) have suggested, with a spectrum in which either the avoidance of war or the promotion of Communism, in its Soviet variant, is given "systemic" and "marginal" priority.

The strategic conception of "peaceful coexistence" assumes that war is neither desirable nor necessary for victory. It is rooted in the premise of successful economic development in the Soviet Bloc, and in the growing ties and affinities between the Soviet Union and the non-Western world. What if it now turned out that neither affluence at home nor influence abroad have come close to expectations? What if, in addition, the Soviet Union must settle for an unfavorable balance of power without, for the present, any "winning" strategy?

The Soviet leaders could not be expected, at first blush, to accept the notion of being second best, lastingly and without foreseeable relief. Whether the continuing belief in future victory will prove to be a clever insight or a consolation prize for the naive believers, only the years ahead will tell. As the faith erodes, a revisionist unmindful of Bolshevik proprieties might yet be tempted to expound as Moscow's ideological centerpiece a novel theory of permanent coexistence. But that day is not yet in sight.

If, for the nonce, nothing could be done to overcome American superiority—or, at least, done within the margin of cost and safety which the leadership was prepared to sanction—something had to be anticipated to alter the power relationship with the United States. Yet precisely the kind of item of military hardware which research and development held out to be most promising—such as the anti-ballistic missile—would, if procured, have a dangerously destabilizing effect on the international scene. And in a thermonuclear setting, strategic destabilization could be fatal to Communists and "capitalists" alike.

To those who understood all this, and more, the simple world of Marx and Lenin no longer provided adequate formulae. They were on their own. But these inferences the leadership, understandably, preferred not to ventilate in public. Meanwhile, it had to make policy decisions, regardless of its brave public posture on general and complete disarmament. To advocate or to perfect a system of mutual deterrence means to acknowledge a degree of interdependence with the "imperialists" which Moscow has heretofore rejected; in turn, its commitment to a change in the political status quo seems to demand a measure of independent and vigorous action which risks upsetting the strategic balance. Faced with this problem, Moscow has sought some formula by which to combine the stabilization of deterrence with opportunities for political destabilization—for having its cake and eating it, too.

In practice, the natural instinct is to play it safe and to hold on to existing power—to that which, after all, has been the key to the rise of the Soviet Union to the status of a superpower. "It seems safe to say that...the Soviet leaders will continue to regard Soviet military power as an indispensable safeguard of their security and a strong support for their political strategy."[21]

This does not preclude successful further negotiations and arms-control agreements in the years ahead. Deals and détentes are by no means alien to Communist experience and morality; in fact, willingness to engage in them is one of the many hallmarks of a "right" swing in the Communist line. The Soviet Union has participated without qualms in technical concerns such as the Universal Postal Union and the international allocation of radio wave lengths; more than that, ever since Lenin, it has made a virtue of "using" whatever constellation of forces has appeared most suitable. Lenin himself was prepared to accept funds "from the Kaiser" or from a Russian industrialist, or to take "ammunition and potatoes from the Anglo-French imperialist robbers." In this respect arms control has not been considered to be very different from a cultural exchange treaty or a foreign trade protocol: each involves a legal agreement between two or more states to provide certain goods or perform certain services.

Previously, there was no need, and hence no effort made, to incorporate any implications of such dealings into the substance of Communist thought. Now such an attempt is being made. In the disarmament field, after all, cooperation with the major adversary is for shared purposes or for parallel purposes— on a level well in excess of what had previously been sanctioned. There is, manifestly, uneasiness about collaborating with the enemy; and Soviet officialdom has evidently been prepared not to ask too insistently what might be the theoretical foundation of such an adversary relationship as distinguished from more superficial, purely instrumental tactics. The Chinese do ask this question, however, and taunt Moscow with it. The CPSU can answer only in terms of the danger of nuclear weapons and the dominance of "reasonable" men in the enemy camp, adding that of course no ideological compromise is to be brooked.

Despite zigzags and changes, the general thrust over the recent years has been the intensification of pressures on the Soviet leadership for a breathing spell in the arms race. Indeed, the present offers a unique concatenation of such pressures. Here, after all, is a world situation of gross equilibrium, which is more of an impediment to a power ultimately committed to total change than to a power more or less willing and able to live with the status quo. There is some reality to the "relaxation of tensions." There is more of a lull in the arms race than the world has seen in twenty-five years. At the same time, Moscow has evidently recognized its numerical inferiority in the strategic balance with the United

States. Economic shortages are once again imposing strains
and stresses far more vulgar and humiliating than Khrushchev's
recent visions of tomorrow's Communism would have led one
to expect. The Sino-Soviet rift and the arrogation of independence by Communist states and Parties throughout the world
have been, as Moscow openly recognizes, sources of weakness
for the U.S.S.R. There may still be time, technically and politically, for agreements on non-proliferation, nuclear-free zones,
ground rules in that novel cooperation among adversary states.

On one level, Moscow no longer asks for an "all or nothing
at all" approach; the political leadership approvingly cites
President Kennedy's call (in his American University speech
of June 10, 1963) for step-by-step progress in "a series of
concrete actions and effective agreements which are in the
interest of all concerned." On another level, however, there is
still a bothersome lack of comprehension—or studied incompre-
hension—of precisely those categories which, to many Western
observers, seem among the most promising. A senior disarmament specialist in Moscow, for instance, still echoes the theme
that "arms control" amounts to an evasion of the central issue,
which in his words is the choice between "militarism or disarmament . . . either yes or no, either 1 or 0. There is no third
alternative."[22]

None can tell how far it can all go. It is likely that any other
leadership in Moscow would also welcome an arrangement that
would lower the cost of deterrence and reduce the risks of
unintended war. Those are likely to be the most tangible
benefits of Soviet-American arms-control agreements. There
is nothing in sight to indicate that the old, hard barriers have
melted. There is no foreseeable inspection of the sort the
West deems essential; no prospect of strategic force reductions
of any significant size.

Yet, while the odds are against a major break, it is well to
remember that "anything is possible" in the years ahead.
Ideas, it has recently been remarked, change more rapidly
than technology, and less predictably at that. The Soviet Union,
moreover, is at a particularly fluid stage of its development.
One can heartily agree, therefore, with the following view of
an expert on Soviet military affairs:

The prospect that the Soviet military search for a war-
winning strategy may prove unrewarding , or that victory
in a nuclear war, even if attainable, may come to look increasingly barren, does not mean of course that the Soviet

leadership will find it necessary or even possible to seek a disarmed world as the only alternative answer to the problem of Soviet security. The intermediate ground between armed peace and a disarmed world is broad and unexplored.[23]

In that exploration, the United States can help.

Limited common action, limited test ban, limited détente: these promise some alteration of conduct, perhaps some change of attitude, but not—at least, not yet—any reduction in the underlying causes of world tension. But more important perhaps than dramatic accords could be the growth of mutual self-restraint—tacit or otherwise—and of a sense of ineluctable interdependence.

One's modest optimism must be tempered by the insistent recollection of other men and other generations, of countries, parties, groups manipulated and deceived, time after time, into believing that Communism had at last changed its essence (or, in the minds of some, had reverted to it). This danger, too—the risk of total error and deception—does exist, and it is important to know it. Yet in the light of the evidence, this danger seems small, compared to the far greater danger of rigidly denying the reality of change within the U.S.S.R. and consequently rejecting any opportunity we now have—perhaps for the last time—of agreeing to survive.

BIBLIOGRAPHY

No effort was made to make the following bibliography exhaustive. It does not, in particular, indicate the extensive records of international conferences and organizations concerned with arms control and disarmament. These and other additional titles are listed in several of the bibliographies and reference works indicated in the following section.

BIBLIOGRAPHIES AND REFERENCE GUIDES

Clemens, Walter C., Jr. A Bibliography of Soviet Disarmament Policy 1917-1963. Stanford, Cal.: Hoover Institution, 1965.

Collart, Yves. Disarmament: A Study Guide and Bibliography on the Efforts of the United Nations. The Hague: Nijhoff, 1958.

Fischer, George. "Soviet Disarmament Policy, A Survey of Recent Sources." Cambridge, Mass.: Center for International Studies, Massachusetts Institute of Technology, 1961 (processed).

Hammond, Thomas T. (ed.). Soviet Foreign Relations and World Communism: A Selected Annotated Bibliography of 7,000 Books in 30 Languages. Princeton, N.J.: Princeton University Press, 1964.

    Includes a selection on "Soviet Policy Toward Disarmament," compiled by Walter C. Clemens, Jr.

Stevenson, Eric, and John Teeple. "Research in Arms Control and Disarmament 1960-1963." New York: The Ford Foundation, 1963 (processed).

U.S. Department of State. "Soviet Military Doctrine: A List of References to Recent Soviet and Free World Publications on Soviet Military Thought." External Research Paper, No. 141, 1963 (processed).

_____, External Research Staff. "Studies in Progress or Recently Completed: Arms Control and Disarmament." Washington, D.C.: Government Printing Office, 1963 (processed).

BOOKS AND ARTICLES

Barnet, Richard J. Who Wants Disarmament? Boston: Beacon
Press, 1960.
_____. "The Soviet Attitude on Disarmament," Problems of
Communism (Washington, D.C.), X, No. 3 (May-June, 1961),
32-37.

Beaton, Leonard, and John Maddox. The Spread of Nuclear
Weapons. New York: Frederick A. Praeger, 1962.

Bechhoefer, Bernhard G. Postwar Negotiations for Arms Con-
trol. Washington, D.C.: Brookings Institution, 1961.
_____. "The Soviet Attitude Toward Disarmament," Current
History (Philadelphia), XVL, No. 266 (October, 1963), 193-99.

Becker, Abraham S. "Soviet Military Outlays Since 1955."
Santa Monica, Cal.: The RAND Corporation, 1964 (processed,
RM-3886-PR).

Bialer, Seweryn. "I Chose Freedom," News From Behind the
Iron Curtain (New York), V, No. 10 (October, 1956), 3-15.

Bogdanov, Oleg V. Vseobshchee i polnoe razoruzhenie. Moscow:
"Mezhdunarodnye otnosheniia," 1964.
_____. Iadernoe razoruzhenie. Moscow: Institut Mezhdunarod-
nykh Otnoshenii, 1961.

Brennan, Donald G. (ed.). Arms Control, Disarmament and
National Security. New York: George Braziller, 1961.
    A revised edition of the symposium originally published
as a special arms-control issue of Daedalus: Journal of the
American Academy of Arts and Sciences (Cambridge, Mass.),
Vol. LXXXIX, No. 4 (Fall, 1960).

Bronfenbrenner, Urie. "Social-Psychological Factors Affecting Soviet Reactions to Arms Control Proposals." Washington, D.C.: Institute for Defense Analyses, 1962 (processed).

Buchan, Alastair. "The Age of Insecurity," Encounter (London),
XXI, No. 6 (June, 1963), 3-10.

Bull, Hedley. The Control of the Arms Race: Disarmament
and Arms Control in the Missile Age. New York: Frederick
A. Praeger, 1961.

Brzezinski, Zbigniew. Ideology and Power in Soviet Politics.
New York: Frederick A. Praeger, 1962.
_____, and Samuel P. Huntington. Political Power U.S.A./
U.S.S.R. New York: The Viking Press, 1964.

Clemens, Walter C., Jr. "Ideology in Soviet Disarmament Policy," The Journal of Conflict Resolution (Ann Arbor), VIII,
No. 1 (March, 1964), 7-22.

_____."Soviet Disarmament Proposals and the Cadre-Territorial Army," Orbis (Philadelphia), VII, No. 4 (Winter, 1964), 788-99.

Coffey, Joseph I. "The Soviet View of a Disarmed World," The Journal of Conflict Resolution, VIII, No. 1 (March, 1964), 1-6.

Crane, Robert D. (ed.). Soviet Nuclear Strategy—A Report of the Study Program on Soviet Strategy. Washington, D.C.: Center for Strategic Studies, Georgetown University, 1963.

Crankshaw, Edward. The New Cold War: Moscow v. Pekin. Baltimore: Penguin, 1963.

Dallin, Alexander. The Soviet Union at the United Nations: An Inquiry into Soviet Motives and Objectives. New York: Frederick A. Praeger, 1962.

_____."Russia and China View the United States," The Annals of the American Academy of Political and Social Sciences (Philadelphia), Vol. 349 (September, 1963), pp. 153-62.

_____, (ed.), with Jonathan Harris and Grey Hodnett. Diversity in International Communism: A Documentary Record, 1961-1963. New York: Columbia University Press, 1963.

Davis, Kathryn W. The Soviets at Geneva. Geneva: Librairie Kundig, 1935.

Dinerstein, Herbert S. War and the Soviet Union. Rev. ed.; New York: Frederick A. Praeger, 1962.

_____."Soviet Goals and Military Force," Orbis, V, No. 4 (Winter, 1962), 425-36.

Dougherty, James E. "The Disarmament Debate: A Review of Current Literature," Orbis, V, Part I, No. 3 (Fall, 1961), 342-59; Part II, No. 4 (Winter, 1962), 489-511.

_____. "Key to Security: Disarmament or Arms Stability," Orbis, IV, No. 3 (Fall, 1960), 261-83.

Dulles, Allen W. "Disarmament in the Atomic Age," Foreign Affairs (New York), XXV, No. 2 (January, 1947), 204-16.

Erickson, John. The Soviet High Command: A Military-Political History, 1918-1941. New York: St. Martin's Press, 1962.

_____. "The 'Military Factor' in Soviet Policy," International Affairs (London), XXXIX, No. 2 (April, 1963), 214-26.

Fainsod, Merle. How Russia is Ruled. Rev. ed.; Cambridge, Mass.: Harvard University Press, 1963.

_____. "Khrushchev's Russia," The Australian Outlook (Melbourne), XVII, No. 3 (December, 1963), 233-59.

Fischer, George. "The Role of Public Opinion in Soviet Politics," Public Opinion Quarterly (Princeton), XXVII, No. 4 (Winter, 1963), 621-22.

_____ . Science and Politics: The New Sociology in the Soviet Union. Ithaca, N.Y.: Center for International Studies, Cornell University, 1964.

Floyd, David. Mao Against Khrushchev. New York: Frederick A. Praeger, 1963.

Gallagher, Matthew P. "Military Manpower: A Case-Study," Problems of Communism, XIII, No. 3 (May-June, 1964), 53-62.

Garthoff, Raymond L. Soviet Military Doctrine. Glencoe, Ill.: The Free Press, 1953.

_____ . Soviet Strategy in the Nuclear Age. Rev. ed.; New York: Frederick A. Praeger, 1962.

Gilpatric, Roswell L. "Our Defense Needs: The Long View," Foreign Affairs, XLII, No. 3 (April, 1964), 366-78.

Glagolev, Igor S. (ed.). Ekonomicheskie problemy razoruzheniia. Moscow: Akademiia Nauk S.S.S.R., 1961.

_____ , and V. Larionov, "Soviet Defence Might and Peaceful Co-existence," International Affairs (Moscow), No. 11 (November), 1963, pp. 27-33.

Gouré, Leon. Civil Defense in the Soviet Union. Berkeley, Cal.: University of California Press, 1962.

_____ ."Notes on the Second Edition of Marshal V. D. Sokolovsky's 'Military Strategy.'" Santa Monica, Cal.: The RAND Corporation, 1964 (processed, RM-3972-PR).

Griffith, William E. Albania and the Sino-Soviet Rift. Cambridge, Mass.: The Massachusetts Institute of Technology Press, 1963.

_____ . "The November 1960 Moscow Meeting," The China Quarterly (London), No. 11 (July-September, 1962), pp. 38-57.

Griffiths, Franklyn J. C. "Origins of Peaceful Coexistence," Survey (London), No. 50 (January, 1964), pp. 195-201.

_____ ."Proposals of Total Disarmament in Soviet Foreign Policy, 1927-1932 and 1959-1960." Unpublished Certificate Essay, Russian Institute, Columbia University, 1962.

Grossman, Gregory. "The Soviet Economy in the Post-Stalin Decade," The Realities of World Communism, ed. William Petersen. Englewood Cliffs, N.J.: Prentice-Hall, 1963.

Grzybowski, Kazimierz. "Peaceful Settlement of International Disputes in the Communist Bloc," Washington, D.C.: U.S. Arms Control and Disarmament Agency, 1963 (processed).

Hahn, Walter. "The Mainsprings of Soviet Secrecy," Orbis, VII, No. 4 (Winter, 1964), 719-47.

Henkin, Louis (ed.). Arms Control: Issues for the Public (The
American Assembly, Columbia University). Englewood Cliffs,
N.J.: Prentice-Hall, 1961.
    See in particular J. Malcolm Mackintosh, "Disarmament
and Soviet Military Policy"; and Harry Willets, "Disarma-
ment and Soviet Foreign Policy."
Horelick, Arnold L. "The Cuban Missile Crisis: An Analysis
of Soviet Calculations and Behavior," World Politics (Prince-
ton), XVI, No. 3 (April, 1964), 363-90.
_____."'Deterrence' and Surprise in Soviet Strategic Thought."
Santa Monica, Cal.: The RAND Corporation, 1962 (processed,
RM-2618).
Hsieh, Alice L. Communist China's Strategy in the Nuclear
Age. Englewood Cliffs, N.J.: Prentice-Hall, 1962.
Hudson, G. F., Richard Lowenthal, and Roderick MacFarquhar
(eds.). The Sino-Soviet Dispute. New York: Frederick A.
Praeger, 1961.
Ivanov, K. "The National and Colonial Question Today," Inter-
national Affairs (Moscow), No. 5 (May), 1963, pp. 3-10.
_____, and B. Batsanov. Vzgliad v zavtra. Moscow: "Mezhdu-
narodnye otnosheniia," 1964.
Jaszunski, Grzegorz. "Poland and Non-Nuclear Zones," Inter-
national Affairs (Moscow), No. 4 (April), 1964, pp. 28-34.
Jensen, Lloyd. "The Postwar Disarmament Negotiations: A
Study of American-Soviet Bargaining Behavior." Ann Arbor,
Mich.: Center for Research on Conflict Resolution, Univer-
sity of Michigan, 1962 (processed).
Kennan, George F. Russia, The Atom and The West. New York:
Harper & Brothers, 1958.
_____. On Dealing With the Communist World. New York:
Harper & Row, 1964.
Khaitsman, Viktor M. Sovetskii Soiuz—razoruzhenie—mir:
sobytiia i fakty 1917-1962. Moscow: Institut Mezhdunarod-
nykh Otnoshenii, 1962.
_____. SSSR i problema razoruzheniia 1917-1939. Moscow:
Akademiia Nauk S.S.S.R., 1959.
Khrushchev, Nikita S. Communism—Peace and Happiness for the
People. 2 vols. Moscow: Foreign Languages Publishing
House, 1963.
_____.For Victory in Peaceful Competition with Capitalism.
Moscow: Foreign Languages Publishing House, 1959.
_____. Let Us Live in Peace and Friendship: The Visit of
N. S. Khrushchev to the U.S.A., September 15-27, 1959.
Moscow: Foreign Languages Publishing House, 1958.

_____ . World Without Arms. World Without Wars. 2 vols. Moscow: Foreign Languages Publishing House, 1959.

Kissinger, Henry. Nuclear Weapons and Foreign Policy. New York: Harper & Brothers, 1957.

Kodachenko, A. "Disarmament and the Underdeveloped Countries," International Affairs (Moscow), No. 7 (July), 1960, pp. 31-35.

Kolkowicz, Roman. "Conflicts in Soviet Party-Military Relations: 1962-1963." Santa Monica, Cal.: The RAND Corporation, 1963 (processed, RM-3760-PR).

Kozlov, Sviatoslav N., Mikhail V. Smirnov, Ivan S. Baz', and Piotr A. Sidorov. O sovetskoi voennoi nauke. 2d rev. ed.; Moscow: Voennoe Izdatel'stvo, 1964.

Kramish, Arnold. Atomic Energy in the Soviet Union. Stanford, Cal.: Stanford University Press, 1959.

Kuusinen, Otto, et al. (eds.). Fundamentals of Marxism-Leninism. Moscow: Foreign Languages Publishing House, 1960. 2d rev. ed.; 1963.

Lambert, Robert W. "Soviet Disarmament Policy, 1922-1931." Washington, D.C.: U.S. Arms Control and Disarmament Agency, 1964 (processed).

Lefever, Ernest W. (ed.). Arms and Arms Control. New York: Frederick A. Praeger, 1961.

Leites, Nathan. "Kremlin Moods." Santa Monica, Cal.: The RAND Corporation, 1964 (processed, RM-3535-ISA).

Leonhard, Wolfgang. The Kremlin Since Stalin. New York: Frederick A. Praeger, 1962.

Levine, Robert A. The Arms Debate. Cambridge, Mass.: Harvard University Press, 1963.

Librach, Jan. The Rise of the Soviet Empire: A Study of Soviet Foreign Policy. New York: Frederick A. Praeger, 1964.
   See in particular Chapter 17.

Lippmann, Walter. The Communist World and Ours. Boston: Little, Brown & Co., 1959.

Long Live Leninism! Peking: Foreign Language Press, 1960.

Lowenthal, Richard. "The End of an Illusion," Problems of Communism, XII, No. 1 (January-February, 1963), 1-10.

_____ . "The World Scene Transformed," Encounter, XXI, No. 10 (October, 1963), 3-10.

Mackintosh, J. Malcolm. Strategy and Tactics of Soviet Foreign Policy. Rev. ed.; New York: Oxford University Press, 1963.

Mahaney, Wilbur L., Jr. The Soviet Union, The League of Nations and Disarmament: 1917-1935. Philadelphia: Privately printed, 1940.

Mehnert, Klaus. Peking and Moscow. New York: G.P. Putnam's Sons, 1963.

Melman, Seymour (ed.). Disarmament: Its Politics and Economics. Boston: The American Academy of Arts and Sciences, 1962.
　　See in particular Herbert Ritvo, "Internal Divisions on Disarmament in the U.S.S.R."

The Military Balance, 1963-1964. London: Institute for Strategic Studies, 1963.

Modelski, George A. Atomic Energy in the Communist Bloc. Cambridge: Cambridge University Press, 1959.

Mosely, Philip E. (ed.). The Soviet Union 1922-1962: A Foreign Affairs Reader. New York: Frederick A. Praeger, 1963.

Nogee, Joseph L. Soviet Policy Toward International Control of Atomic Energy. Notre Dame, Ind.: Notre Dame University Press, 1961.

_____. "The Diplomacy of Disarmament," International Conciliation (New York), No. 526 (January, 1960), pp. 235-303.

Orear, Jay. "Safeguarded Zonal Disarmament," International Affairs (Moscow), No. 3 (March), 1963, pp. 95-98.

People of the World, Unite, for the Complete, Thorough, Total and Resolute Prohibition and Destruction of Nuclear Weapons! Peking: Foreign Language Press, 1963.

Petrov, Vladimir. Razoruzhenie—korennoi vopros. Moscow: Znanie, 1963.

"Razoruzhenie," Diplomaticheskii slovar', Vol. III. Moscow: Izdatel'stvo Politicheskoi Literatury, 1964.

Rock, Vincent P. A Strategy for Interdependence. New York: Charles Scribner's Sons, 1964.

_____."Common Action for the Control of Conflict: An Approach to the Problem of International Tensions and Arms Control." Washington, D.C.: Institute for Defense Analyses, 1963 (processed).

Rotblat, Joseph. History of the Pugwash Conferences. London: Pugwash Continuing Committee, 1962.

Saikowski, Charlotte, and Leo Gruliow (eds.). Current Soviet Policies IV. New York: Columbia University Press, 1962.

Schelling, Thomas C., and Morton H. Halperin. Strategy and Arms Control. New York: Twentieth Century Fund, 1961.

Sheinin, Yulian M. Nauka i militarizm v SShA. Moscow: Akademiia Nauk S.S.S.R., 1963.

_____. "A Soviet Scientist Looks at Disarmament," Bulletin of the Atomic Scientists: A Journal of Science and Public Affairs (Chicago), XX, No. 1 (January, 1964), 19-22.

Shestov, V. "Geneva After the Recess," International Affairs (Moscow), No. 8 (August), 1964, pp. 16-20.

Shulman, Marshall D. Stalin's Foreign Policy Reappraised. Cambridge, Mass.: Harvard University Press, 1963.

_____. "Russia's Gambit on Disarmament," The New York Times Magazine, March 11, 1962, p. 21ff.

_____. "Security in an Era of Conflict"; paper read before the University Seminar on Peace, Columbia University, New York, February 25, 1964 (processed).

Singer, J. David (ed.). Weapons Management in World Politics. Ann Arbor, Mich.: University of Michigan Press, 1963.

Published as a special issue of The Journal of Conflict Resolution, Vol. III, No. 3 (September, 1963); and The Journal of Arms Control (Ann Arbor), Vol. I, No. 4 (October, 1963).

See in particular Russell Bowen, "Soviet Research and Development: Some Implications for Arms Control Inspection"; and Holland Hunter, "The Control of Unknown Arms."

Slusser, Robert M. "Disarmament in Soviet Foreign Policy," World Disarmament, ed. Charles A. Barker. Baltimore: Johns Hopkins University Press, 1963.

Sohn, Louis B. "Zonal Inspection," Disarmament and Arms Control, II, No. 2 (Spring, 1964), 204-6.

Sokolovsky, Vasilii D. (ed.). Voennaia strategiia. Moscow: Voennoe Izdatel'stvo, 1962. 2d ed.; 1963.

First edition translated as Soviet Military Strategy, with Introduction and Supplementary Material by Herbert S. Dinerstein, Leon Gouré, and Thomas W. Wolfe. Englewood Cliffs, N.J.: Prentice-Hall (RAND edition), 1963; and as Military Strategy: Soviet Doctrine and Concepts, with an Introduction by Raymond L. Garthoff, New York: Frederick A. Praeger, 1963.

Sosnovy, Timothy. "The Soviet Military Budget," Foreign Affairs, XLII, No. 3 (April, 1964), 487-94.

The Soviet Stand on Disarmament. New York: Crosscurrents Press, 1962.

A collection of nineteen Soviet documents on disarmament and the relaxation of international tensions.

Starushenko, Gleb B. "The National-Liberation Movement and the Struggle for Peace," International Affairs (Moscow), No. 10 (October), 1963, pp. 3-8.

Stevenson, Adlai E. Friends and Enemies. New York: Harper & Brothers, 1959.

Strachey, John. On the Prevention of War. New York: St. Martin's Press, 1962.

Strausz-Hupé, Robert. "The Disarmament Delusion," Proceedings of the U.S. Naval Institute (Annapolis), LXXXVI, No. 2 (February, 1960), 41-47.

Talensky, Nikolai. "On the Character of Modern Warfare," International Affairs (Moscow), No. 10 (October), 1960, pp. 22-27.

_____."Sincere? Yes. Realistic? No!" International Affairs (Moscow), No. 3 (March), 1963, pp. 98-100.

Tatum, Lawrence B. "An Examination of Soviet Disarmament Policy with Emphasis upon Principles of Disarmament Revealed Therein." Unpublished Ph.D. Dissertation, Syracuse University, 1961.

Tucker, Robert C. The Soviet Political Mind. New York: Frederick A. Praeger, 1963.

_____, Klaus Knorr, Richard A. Falk, and Hedley Bull. Proposal for No First Use of Nuclear Weapons: Pros and Cons (Policy Memorandum No. 28). Princeton, N.J.: Center for International Studies, Princeton University, 1963.

U.S. Arms Control and Disarmament Agency. Documents on Disarmament, 1960. Washington, D.C.: Government Printing Office, 1961.

_____. Documents on Disarmament, 1961. Washington, D.C.: Government Printing Office, 1962.

_____. Documents on Disarmament, 1962. 2 vols. Washington, D.C.: Government Printing Office, 1963.

U.S. Congress, Joint Economic Committee. Annual Economic Indicators for the U.S.S.R., February, 1964 (88th Cong., 2d sess.). Washington, D.C.: Government Printing Office, 1964.

_____. Comparisons of the United States and Soviet Economies (86th Cong., 1st sess.). Parts I, II, and III. Washington, D.C.: Government Printing Office, 1960.

_____. Dimensions of Soviet Economic Power (87th Cong., 2d sess.). Washington, D.C.: Government Printing Office, 1962.

U.S. Department of State. Disarmament: The Intensified Effort—1955-1958. Washington, D.C.: Government Printing Office, 1960.

_____. Documents on Disarmament, 1945-1959. 2 vols. Washington, D.C.: Government Printing Office, 1960.

_____. Geneva Conference for the Discontinuance of Nuclear Weapons Tests: History and Analysis of Negotiations. Washington, D.C.: Government Printing Office, 1961.

U.S. Senate. Khrushchev On the Shifting Balance of World Forces: A Selection of Statements and an Interpretative Analysis (86th Cong., 1st sess.). Washington, D.C.: Government Printing Office, 1959.

   A special study presented by Senator Hubert H. Humphrey; compiled by Joseph Whelan.

_____, Committee on Foreign Relations. Nuclear Test Ban Treaty (Hearings August 12-27, 1963, 88th Cong., 1st sess.). Washington, D.C.: Government Printing Office, 1963.

_____. Nuclear Test Ban Treaty: Report of the Committee on Foreign Relations (88th Cong., 1st sess.). Washington, D.C.: Government Printing Office, 1963.

_____, Subcommittee on Disarmament. Control and Reduction of Armaments (Final Report) (85th Cong., 2d sess.). Washington, D.C.: Government Printing Office, 1958.

Vinnitsky, N., and A. Arkadyev. "Who Stands To Gain from the Splitting Activities of the Albanian Leaders?" International Affairs (Moscow), No. 2 (February), 1962, pp. 57-59.

Volle, Hermann, and Claus-Jürgen Duisberg. Probleme der internationalen Abrüstung: Die Bemühungen der Vereinten Nationen um internationale Abrüstung und Sicherheit 1945-1961. 2 vols. Frankfurt/M.: Alfred Metzner Verlag, 1964.

Wolfe, Thomas W. "A First Reaction to the New Soviet Book 'Military Strategy.'" Santa Monica, Cal.: The RAND Corporation, 1963 (processed, RM-3495-PR).

_____. "Khrushchev's Disarmament Strategy," Orbis, IV, No. 1 (Spring, 1960), 13-27.

_____. "Political Primacy vs. Professional Elan," Problems of Communism, XIII, No. 3 (May-June, 1964), 53-62.

_____. "A Postscript on the Significance of the Book 'Soviet Military Strategy.'" Santa Monica, Cal.: The RAND Corporation, 1963 (processed, RM-3730-PR).

_____. "Shifts in Soviet Strategic Thought," Foreign Affairs, XLII, No. 3 (April, 1964), 475-86.

_____. "Soviet Strategy at the Crossroads." Santa Monica, Cal.: The RAND Corporation, 1964 (processed, RM-4085-PR).

   Forthcoming in book form, Harvard University Press, 1964.

Zagoria, Donald S. The Sino-Soviet Conflict 1956-1961. Prince-
    ton, N.J.: Princeton University Press, 1962.
Zorin, Valerian A. (ed.). Bor'ba Sovetskogo Soiuza za razoru-
    zhenie, 1946-1960 gody. Moscow: Institut Mezhdunarodnykh
    Otnoshenii, 1961.

NEWSPAPERS AND JOURNALS

The Current Digest of the Soviet Press (New York)
Encounter (London)
Foreign Affairs (New York)
Hungch'i (Peking)
International Affairs (London)
International Affairs (Moscow)
Jen-min jih-pao (Peking)
Kommunist (Moscow)
New Times (Moscow)
Peking Review (Peking)
Pravda (Moscow)
Problems of Communism (Washington, D.C.)
World Marxist Review (Toronto)

FOOTNOTES

PART I - THE PROBLEM

CHAPTER 1 - ASSUMPTIONS AND CONCLUSIONS

1. In an informal poll conducted at Airlie House, none of the 21 principal participants subscribed to the statement that the Soviet leadership pursued disarmament talks and proposals only for propaganda purposes. Fourteen indicated their belief that real Soviet interest in arms-control agreements was highly probable; six considered it a medium-range possibility. Virtually all agreed that Soviet disarmament policy has been or can be significantly affected by seemingly extraneous considerations, including United States policy, Soviet elite conflicts, and the Soviet assessment of the strategic balance. Almost all participants indicated that their own replies would have been significantly different five years earlier. (The "participants" cited at various points in this volume refer, unless otherwise indicated, to the same group of 21 principal participants of the Airlie House conference described in the Preface.)

2. "Arms control" is used hereinafter as described, for instance, by Thomas C. Schelling and Morton H. Halperin in their Strategy and Arms Control (New York: Twentieth Century Fund, 1961), p. 2. In their introduction the authors include under arms control

"... all the forms of military cooperation between potential enemies in the interest of reducing the likelihood of war, its scope and violence if it occurs, and the political and economic costs of being prepared for it. The essential feature of arms control is the recognition of the common interest, of the possibility of reciprocation and cooperation even between potential enemies with respect to their military establishments. Whether the most promising areas of arms control involve reductions in certain kinds of military force, increases in certain kinds of military force,

197

qualitative changes in weaponry, different modes of deployment, or arrangements superimposed on existing military systems, we prefer to treat as an open question."

3. Alastair Buchan, "The Age of Insecurity," Encounter, XXI, No. 6 (June, 1963), 3.

4. Richard J. Barnet, "The Soviet Attitude on Disarmament," Problems of Communism, X, No. 3 (May-June, 1961), 33. This is one of the very few published Western analyses of the subject of this Study.

5. For instance, an article advising readers on a model outline for a lecture on disarmament, suggests that speakers dwell on the "fight" of the Soviet Union and its allies for general and complete disarmament. After commenting that "it would be good to remind the listeners that on the initiative of V. I. Lenin the Soviet government for the first time raised the question of general and complete disarmament at the Genoa Conference in April, 1922," the instructions continue: "The account of the Soviet proposals on disarmament which were made in the period between the two world wars and in the first postwar years, must not take up much time in the lecture. One should merely remind the listeners of these proposals...." ("Kak podgotovit' lektsiiu na temu, 'Razoruzhenie—nasushchnaia problema sovremennosti,'" Mezhdunarodnaia zhizn', No. 11, November, 1962, p. 154. The English-language edition of the same journal, International Affairs, did not carry this item.)

6. See Appendix below.

7. Not all participants agreed on the objective significance of economic considerations, whatever their subjective importance in the assessments and expectations of the Soviet leaders. See below, Chapters 5 and 8.

CHAPTER 2 - THE UNCERTAIN BALANCE

1. See the bibliography, above, for some relevant studies.

2. Sovetskoe gosudarstvo i revoliutsiia prava, No. 2, 1930, p. 163.

3. "The Struggle Against Imperialist War and the Tasks of the Communists: Resolution of the Sixth World Congress of the Communist International, July-August, 1928" (New York: Workers Library Publishers, 1932), p. 54.

4. "Statement of the Soviet Government, August 21, 1963"; English translation in Supplement to New Times, No. 35 (September 4), 1963, pp. 36-37; and also in The Current Digest of the Soviet Press, XV, No. 34 (September 18, 1963), 9.

5. N. S. Khrushchev, "For New Victories for the World Communist Movement," speech of January 6, 1961; English translation in World Marxist Review, IV, No. 1 (January, 1961), 18.

6. An authoritative article admonished in October, 1960:

"There is no doubt that in the event of a new war capitalism will succumb completely. But does this mean that the sacrifices of war, however heavy, are justified? This is a harmful, anti-humane point of view. The world population would be reduced by one half as a result of a new global war. Moreover, the most active, capable and civilized portion of mankind would be wiped out. It should also be borne in mind that the material and technological basis for life would be destroyed. Thermonuclear weapons would destroy plants and factories, devastate fields and orchards, destroy means of transportation and communication, almost all buildings, hospitals, etc. Libraries, institutes, and museums would fall into ruin; humanity would be thrown back and its way to Communism would become immensely longer." (Major General Nikolai Talensky, "On the Character of Modern Warfare," International Affairs [Moscow], No. 10, October, 1960, pp. 25-26.)

In January, 1963, Khrushchev reaffirmed:

"Would the socialist countries and the cause of socialism all over the world benefit from a world nuclear disaster? Only people who deliberately shut their eyes to the facts can think that. As for Marxist-Leninists, they cannot propose to establish a Communist civilization on the ruins of the centers of world culture, on land laid waste and contaminated by nuclear fallout.... To use a familiar phrase, blessed is he who talks about war without knowing what he is talking about." (Speech at the Sixth Congress of the Socialist Unity Party of [East] Germany, January 16, 1963; English translation in New Times, No. 4, January 30, 1963, p. 43.)

7. While the Soviet Union has generally refused to recognize the term, "arms control," as anything more than a hoax intended to deceive the advocates of peace and disarmament (since it also permits increase or maintenance of weapons and troops, not only their reduction), a number of agreements—especially in the post-Cuban period—would by U.S. standards qualify as "arms control." In fact, the Soviet argument made to the Chinese Communists, who rejected the test-ban treaty and similar measures of "little means," was couched precisely in terms of limited, step-by-step separable measures as the most realistic procedure toward disarmament. ("Statement of the Soviet Government, August 21, 1963," op. cit.)

Soviet hostility to the term "arms control" may be compounded by a problem of translation. The Russian phrase, kontrol' nad vooruzheniiami, implies a far more sweeping "control over armaments" than does its English equivalent. To the Russian it suggests authority to order or stop the production of weapons, a degree of intrusion clearly intolerable to the sovereignty-conscious and suspicious Soviet bureaucrat. Interestingly enough, some of the more sophisticated Soviet studies now use the phrase, kontrol' za vooruzheniiami—a milder formula that implies "looking after" rather than dictating.

8. Liu Shao-ch'i, speech at Pyongyang, North Korea, September 18, 1963; English translation in Peking Review, VI, No. 39 (September 27, 1963), 12.

9. This hypothesis need not involve the "Machiavellian" formula that the way to "solve" the Soviet problem is for the West to increase the arms and space budgets to such an extent that keeping up would "bankrupt" the Soviet economy. This formula is faulty on various grounds, which need not be discussed here at length. Whatever the moral and practical aspects of the strategy, it would be intellectually respectable only if one were to assume—as we do not—that Soviet operational objectives are immutable.

It is likely that the Soviet assessment of the strain imposed on the economy by further rounds in the arms spiral plays a part in the search for at least a limited détente. One may therefore assume that Moscow fears—second only to war—an intensification of the arms race by the United States, and that it has learned to refrain from certain provocative steps precisely so as to forestall such an American response. To this extent (given the belief in the changeability of Soviet policies), it is cogent to argue for the continued ability of the U.S. to put economic pressure on the U.S.S.R. through the arms race, rather than for the application of such pressure—much in the same way as deterrence is preferable to the use of arms.

10. Speech at Bratsk, Pravda, October 10, 1959; English translation as "Builders Pave the Way to a New Life," in The Current Digest of the Soviet Press, XI, No. 41 (November 11, 1959), 4.

11. Another aspect of economic considerations affecting Soviet interest in disarmament is the extent to which the Soviet leaders might count upon disarmament to cause major economic dislocations in the West. Although occasionally doctrinaire assertions may still be heard that "tottering capitalism" is propped up only by military spending or "militarization" of Western economies, this argument no longer seems to carry much force among the Soviet leaders themselves as a reason for encouraging disarmament. On the contrary, in the course of the disarmament dialogue since 1959, there have been repeated and specific Soviet statements acknowledging that the West would not suffer economic collapse from the process of disarmament. In view of the practical demonstration of (and Soviet references to) U.S. ability to demobilize rapidly and without an economic crisis after World War II, one can suppose that these statements more or less accurately reflect the current Soviet appraisal of Western ability to adjust to the economic consequences of even large-scale disarmament. This evaluation may be taken in either of two mutually contradictory ways. Insofar as it denies any particular American disadvantage in disarmament, it removes one Soviet incentive to disarmament. Insofar as it denies any particular economic disincentive to U.S. participation in disarmament, however, it hints at a Soviet concept that a realistic agreement acceptable to both sides is possible.

12. The CPSU Program of 1961 states,

"General and complete disarmament under strict international control is a radical way of guaranteeing a durable peace. Imperialism has imposed an unprecedented burden of armaments on the people. Socialism sees its duty toward mankind in delivering it from this absurd waste of national wealth. The solution of this problem would have historical significance for mankind. By an active and determined effort the peoples can and must force the imperialists into disarmament."

13. Several participants maintained, going further, that the present "modernist" Soviet orientation has in fact pushed the cooperative element to a new level of acceptance, holding that the U.S. and the U.S.S.R. must develop cooperative relationships in peace-keeping while continuing to compete for international predominance.

14. Khrushchev has on occasion gone even further in limiting the concept of proletarian internationalism. As he declared in April, 1964,

"If it depended only on our desire to make a revolution in any given country, I can assure you that the Central Committee would have done everything to see that the bourgeois world was no more and that the red flag of socialism flew over the entire world. But, comrades, let us not indulge in fantasies. We are people able to think realistically. The wish alone is not enough—even the Party's desire is not enough: if the Party desires a revolution but the people are not ready for it, the Party can [by rising] have its finest elements slaughtered, but the revolution will not be victorious. History shows this. Therefore one cannot play at revolutions.... If we were to listen to the Chinese leaders, one would think we must stop all economic development and start discussing in all Party organizations how and in what countries the revolution can be carried out. But who asks us to do that now? Suppose we want the French working class to win and seize power. Well, then, must we declare war on France for that purpose? This is the logical conclusion from the Chinese argument. And who will die in that war? The French imperialists? No, it will be the French workers and peasants—men just like the Russians, Ukrainians, Poles, and Chinese. This is an erroneous way, and we reject it."

(Pravda, April 16, 1964.)

15. Pravda, February 28, 1963; English translation in The Current Digest of the Soviet Press, XV, No. 9 (March 27, 1963), 12. For a discussion of Soviet policy on inspection and secrecy, see Chapter 10, below.

PART II - THE CONTEXT

CHAPTER 3 - IDEOLOGY AND BEHAVIOR

1. One participant presented an extreme interpretation—that of the complete subordination of Soviet ideology to sheer defense perceptions. In his own words:

"1. The formal ideology is believed in, partly quite genuinely (as English statesmen believe in the Church of England), partly because of its political usefulness. For our purpose it barely matters which [motive is uppermost].

2. Partly for ideological reasons and partly from experience, the Soviet leaders are acutely conscious of a hostile world around them, which it is politically necessary to render less dangerous to themselves. By long tradition, the Communist movement outside Russia is an important means of exercising political influence and diminishing the strength of enemy forces. But it does not follow that the spread of Communism is desired as such in any very active way. For example, a Greek Communist would be preferred to the King of the Hellenes, but primarily because Greece under the King is a hostile base. This point, if correct, is an important element in their attitude to disarmament and to the consequences of a disarmed (or less armed) world, and is certainly consistent with the Chinese accusations. It would follow that the Soviets would 'trade' greater security for themselves against reduced chances of Communist expansion without undue compunction."

Another participant—not himself a specialist on the Soviet Union—saw Marxism as "merely an overlay" over centuries-old traditional Russian thought patterns.

At the opposite end of the spectrum, two or three members stressed the continuing vitality of ideology, including a specific logical sequence of steps in decision-making, which requires a definition of the "nature of the epoch," an assessment of the "relationship of forces," an identification of strategic objectives, tactical opportunities, and then a determination of the various means to be employed for the attainment of the set objectives.

2. Barnet, op. cit., p. 37.

3. Explicit and positive Soviet references to disarmament began to appear in relatively "sacred" documents in 1960, such as Otto Kuusinen's speech on Lenin's 90th birthday (April 22, 1960); the 81-Party Statement (December 5, 1960); and the new CPSU Program (drafted in the first half of 1961).

4. The goal, moreover, provides a justification for partial measures or "separable stages" in the interim.

5. Arnold Horelick, "'Deterrence' and Surprise in Soviet Strategic Thought" (Santa Monica, Cal.: The RAND Corporation, 1962, processed, RM-2618).

6. See, for instance, U.S. Senate, Khrushchev On the Shifting Balance of World Forces: A Selection of Statements and an Interpretative Analysis (Washington, D.C.: Government Printing Office, 1959).

7. It should be added that this process cannot always be measured by the declining use of or reference to doctrinal authorities; in fact, the "erosion" may be accompanied by an increase in lip service, quotation-mongering, and even attempts at more intensive and extensive indoctrination. On the other hand, virtually all participants agreed that the manner in which disarmament is described in the ideological literature, the amount of space devoted to it, the forums in which it is discussed, the authority of the people discussing it, and the words which are used, can all serve as valid though imperfect barometers for understanding the Soviet position on arms control and disarmament. The correspondence between public references and privately-held policy is likely to be considerably higher in areas of ideological innovation (such as disarmament) than in areas of ideological "residue."

8. Zbigniew Brzezinski, Ideology and Power in Soviet Politics (New York: Praeger, 1962), pp. 131-34.

CHAPTER 4 - POLICIES AND POLITICS

1. For surveys of the post-Stalin era, see, for instance, Wolfgang Leonhard, The Kremlin Since Stalin (New York: Praeger, 1962); Merle Fainsod, How Russia is Ruled (rev. ed.; Cambridge, Mass.: Harvard University Press, 1963); and the ten-year appraisals in Survey, No. 47 (April, 1963), and Problems of Communism, Vol. XII, No. 2 (March-April, 1963).

2. Several participants believe that, since the end of 1957, even these limitations on Khrushchev's power no longer obtain and that, in other words, he is (or can be whenever he chooses) an authoritarian despot, much as Stalin had been. Others, on the contrary, see Khrushchev as representing but one of several contending factions, and, according to one participant, a faction which has not always turned out to be in command.

Some participants argue that the Soviet regime has not fundamentally departed from the system evolved under Stalin. Others—also a "minority"—describe the present system as pragmatic and pluralistic, national and non-ideological in outlook and purpose, more "emancipated" (in fact though not in word) from Bolshevik conceptions than the rest of the group would grant.

3. The listing of these labels does not imply agreement on the identification of individual Soviet leaders as die-hards or liberals, or members of any other orientation. Most participants see no evidence to identify any leading officials now in power as principled opponents of Khrushchevian policies; a few participants emphatically disagree. Even those who seek to divide the present leadership by any of the above criteria agree that Khrushchev himself—while often tending toward the "soft" or "modernist" end of the spectrum—has occupied neither an extreme nor a consistent position.

Some participants warn against the use of each of the above sets of terms to describe the dichotomy. In particular, they point out, positions taken by this or that interest group—for instance, some part of the leading military cadres—might be considered "Stalinist" in some regards (e.g., insistence on "vigilance," spending on the military sector and heavy industry, centralization of controls) and "anti-Stalinist" in others (e.g., rehabilitation of victims of the Stalin purges, revision of military doctrine). Indeed a causal connection between "liberal" changes and a proclivity for arms-control agreements must not be taken for granted. On the contrary, the Soviet regime has on several occasions (most recently, in the six-month period following the Cuban crisis) attempted to tighten its ideological controls to offset the pressure of forces stimulated by the détente and encouraged by "cultural exchanges" and other contacts with the West.

4. Our meetings failed to resolve differences among some of the participants regarding the relative weight of ideological

(left-right) differences, differences due to functional differentiation and emerging "interest groups" in Soviet society, and other factors making for elite conflicts. The following represents one "minority" opinion among the participants:

"Khrushchev's revisionism is the result of the (politically and psychologically) necessary effort to accommodate the various group interests in the U.S.S.R. and the Communist commonwealth while maintaining the Party's prerogative of ultimate decision-making; to achieve realism and flexibility while maintaining doctrinal rigidity."

See also Chapter 6, below.

5. For the beginnings of the policy, see Franklyn Griffiths, "Origins of Peaceful Coexistence," Survey, No. 50 (January, 1964), pp. 195-201.

6. One advocate of this view argues not only that the current Soviet usage of the term referred to an indefinite, rather than short-term, period of "coexistence," but that it provided, beyond this, for genuine (rather than merely "tactical") cooperation with the "enemy" in certain fields, and that Soviet leaders and spokesmen were in earnest in using the concept. See also Robert C. Tucker, The Soviet Political Mind (New York: Praeger, 1963), Chapter 10. Others sharply dissented from this interpretation.

7. Whether one should take at face value the "revisionist" interpretation, beginning with the more extensive redefinition of coexistence, or whether this should be considered a rationalization, or else an afterthought generated in the arguments about Communist orthodoxy with the Chinese and others, remained a moot question throughout our deliberations. There was considerable disagreement about the reformulation of coexistence. Some participants argue that the achievement of world Communism, not coexistence, remains the primary Soviet goal, with coexistence merely a momentary condition. Others, while granting the goal of world Communism, still make coexistence an essential conditioning factor and imply that the means may some day become an end as well.

8. Gleb B. Starushenko, "The National-Liberation Movement and the Struggle for Peace," International Affairs (Moscow), No. 10 (October), 1963, pp. 3-4.

9. No attempt is made here to dwell on other, in some cases closely related, facets of Soviet grand strategy which have

undergone serious reconsideration during the past decade. These would include discussion of the "national-liberation movement," of alternative means of struggle, of the place of economic competition in the total effort, the nature of capitalism, the concept of "capitalist encirclement," the adequacy of the "two-camp" thesis, the meaning of "proletarian internationalism," and so forth.

10. Much to the chagrin of Communist China, the Soviet leadership has maintained, since about 1959, that "men of reason" rather than "madmen" are in command in Washington. By implication, the U.S.S.R. has not as a matter of national policy expected U.S. "aggression." On Soviet views of the United States, see Nathan Leites, "Kremlin Moods" (Santa Monica, Cal.: The RAND Corporation, 1964, processed, RM-3535-ISA); and Alexander Dallin, "Russia and China View the United States," The Annals of the American Academy of Political and Social Science, Vol. 349 (September, 1963).

Similarly, with regard to the new nations, Moscow has been obliged to explain the reasons for failure (or, as it prefers to present it, for the delay) in terms of "lack of organization and awareness on the part of the masses... and their inability to grasp fully the objective situation and real possibilities." It now recognizes that "it will naturally take some time before the people get their bearings and learn to distinguish wheat from chaff, sheep from goats.... The path is not smooth and not easy." (K. Ivanov, "The National and Colonial Question Today," International Affairs [Moscow], No. 5, May, 1963, pp. 4, 9.) On the Khrushchev strategy as enunciated in 1955, see Seweryn Bialer, "I Chose Freedom," News From Behind The Iron Curtain, Vol. X, No. 10 (October, 1956). On the Soviet expectations of a "third round," see Richard Lowenthal, "The End of an Illusion," Problems of Communism, Vol. XII, No. 1 (January-February, 1963).

11. Vladimir Petrov, Razoruzhenie—korennoi vopros (Moscow: Znanie, 1963), p. 32.

12. Pravda, February 15, 1964; English translation in The Current Digest of the Soviet Press, XVII, No. 7 (March 11, 1964), 21.

13. It is likely that the Soviet Union will continue to be uninterested in agreements providing for arms embargoes for potential war areas. In most instances the U.S.S.R. would not recognize the warring parties as equally guilty or justified.

Thus arms embargoes might mean the end of "national-liberation wars."

14. A minority of the participants held, on the contrary, that an understanding providing for disengagement of Soviet troops from Eastern Europe or physical international inspection there would require a prior de facto acknowledgment by the U.S. that these areas belong to the Soviet camp. In other words, inspection would, under the circumstances, enforce Soviet control and sanction a divided Europe.

15. One may assume that many East European Communists have favored arms-control measures because they would give them (1) greater security in the absence of war; (2) some status, including the signing of multilateral accords and the possible recognition of parity between NATO and the Warsaw Treaty Organization; (3) greater operational independence from the U.S.S.R., economically and politically.

16. V. M. Khaitsman, SSSR i problema razoruzheniia 1917-1939 (Moscow: Akademiia Nauk S.S.S.R., 1959).

The Institute of International Relations (IMO) in Moscow (not a part of Moscow State University) continues to have close relations with the Soviet Foreign Ministry, for which it acts as a training center. Thus a substantial volume on post-1945 disarmament efforts was produced at the IMO, under the editorship of Valerian Zorin, by a staff which included I. G. Usachev and P. F. Shakhov—both veteran Soviet disarmament experts in the Foreign Ministry (V. A. Zorin, ed., Bor'ba Sovetskogo Soiuza za razoruzhenie, 1946-1960 gody [Moscow: IMO, 1961]). The IMO also published a shorter survey entitled, The Soviet Union—Disarmament—Peace: Events and Facts, 1917-1962 (Sovetskoi Soiuz—razoruzhenie—mir: sobytiia i fakty, 1917-1962 [Moscow: IMO, 1962]) by Viktor Khaitsman; and Oleg Bogdanov's Nuclear Disarmament (Iadernoe razoruzhenie [Moscow: IMO, 1961]).

17. Glagolev, who visited the United States in 1962, is the editor of a volume on the economic aspects of disarmament (Ekonomicheskie problemy razoruzheniia [Moscow: Akademiia Nauk S.S.S.R., 1961]). See also his letter to The New York Times, March 27, 1964.

Sheinin is the author of a volume on science and "militarism" in the United States (Nauka i militarizm v SShA [Moscow: Akademiia Nauk S.S.S.R., 1961]). See also his article, "A Soviet Scientist Looks at Disarmament," Bulletin of Atomic Scientists: A Journal of Science and Public Affairs, XX, No. 1 (January, 1964), 19-22.

18. Novaia i noveishaia istoriia, No. 2, 1964, p. 9. The need for further research is similarly stressed by another author, who writes that "the problem of disarmament is large, complicated and many-faceted. It has its political, economic, legal, technical, and other aspects. They all deserve profound study." (Oleg V. Bogdanov, Vseobshchee i polnoe razoruzhenie [Moscow: "Mezhdunarodnye otnosheniia," 1964], p. 27.)

19. This is not to suggest that Soviet scientists have no political opinions or do not articulate them in certain circles. Men like V. A. Kirillin (formerly chief of the Science Section of the CPSU Central Committee staff, is now Deputy Chief of its Ideological Section, a candidate member of the CPSU Central Committee, and first Vice-President of the Soviet Academy of Sciences) clearly constitute an important link between scientists and policy-makers and themselves have access to the leadership.

20. On the other hand, some analysts have seen the continuing differences

"...reflected in the reporting by the Soviet press of remarks by President Johnson on U.S. policy and the Geneva disarmament talks. Izvestia, which is edited by Khrushchev's son-in-law Adzhubei and usually takes the modernist line, has pointedly included in its Washington coverage those statements by Mr. Johnson that show a conciliatory attitude toward the Soviet Union and an interest in making progress at Geneva; Pravda, in which the conservative orientation has been strongly represented of late, has tended to omit hopeful and positive expressions by the President, and thereby to highlight his anti-Communist militancy. In publishing a Tass cable from Washington on a news conference held at the beginning of February, Izvestia printed— while Pravda deleted—a comment by the President that the U.S. Government is doing all it can to develop fresh initiatives and ideas that might lead to the goal of disarmament. Again, the Tass report on the President's State of the Union message in January included in Izvestia's version, but omitted in Pravda's, a statement of American intention to take new steps and present fresh proposals at Geneva."

(Robert C. Tucker, "Policy Debate in Moscow," The New Republic, May 16, 1964, p. 8.)

On the probable nature of continuing military demurs, see Chapter 7, below.

21. We have no evidence on the opinions represented there. But it may be suggestive to record the entirely impressionistic views of one of our participants—a close student of the Soviet leadership—as reviewed and slightly amended by two other specialists, regarding an entirely hypothetical line-up of the Presidium on the test-ban treaty:

Mikoyan in favor: deduced from general identification with a relatively "soft" line as well as his interest in a détente and East-West trade.

Kosygin likewise; primarily because of decrease of military expenditures and increase in foreign trade likely to result from disarmament agreements.

Ponomarev probably in favor; as successful disarmament would disprove Peking's position further and would strengthen the Soviet line, also giving opportunities to rally other political forces as allies on the disarmament and peace issue.

Suslov likely to oppose the treaty, or at least give it unenthusiastic support; Ilyichev similarly, but to a somewhat lesser degree—in both cases because of their previous political records and present "ideological" functions, which make them receptive to the fear that arms-control measures contribute to ideological erosion and weaken the sense of militancy.

Shvernik (Party Control Commission), Shelepin (Party-State Control), and Semichastny (Security Police) may be assumed to have raised questions and reservations, not because of opposition to the test-ban itself but because of fear that it would be the first step toward measures which would require inspections, increased scientific contact with the West, and other developments likely to weaken Soviet controls at home.

Some members, such as Voronov, Kirilenko, and Grishin, have probably no direct competence or interest in the subject. Where two of the other members stand—Podgorny and Poliansky—is impossible to tell.

The ultimate and collective decision probably depends to a large degree on the position taken by Khrushchev and Brezhnev, who must weigh the different and often conflicting interests on the test ban as on other issues, but tend toward agreement, primarily on political grounds.

CHAPTER 5 - THE SOVIET ECONOMY

1. See also the discussion of economic questions in Chapters 1, 2, 7, and 8 of this Report. See also the series of studies, with extensive statistical evidence, published by the U.S. Congress, Joint Economic Committee, Dimensions of Soviet Economic Power, 87th Cong., 2d sess. (Washington, D.C.: Government Printing Office, 1962); and Annual Economic Indicators for the U.S.S.R., 88th Cong., 2d sess. (Washington, D.C.: Government Printing Office, 1964).

For a survey of trends in the Soviet economy, see, e.g., Gregory Grossman, "The Soviet Economy in the Post-Stalin Decade," in William Petersen, ed., The Realities of World Communism (Englewood Cliffs, N.J.: Prentice-Hall, 1963).

2. According to (uncorrected) official Soviet figures, the industrial growth rate declined as follows (comparing mid-year figures with the preceding year's):

1958-59:	+ 12%
1959-60:	+ 10%
1960-61:	+ 8.4%
1961-62:	"under 10"
1962-63:	8.5%
1963-64:	7.5%

Annual Economic Indicators for the U.S.S.R. (pp. 94-95) asserts, on the basis of certain (plausible but arbitrary) assumptions, that the annual growth rate of the Soviet GNP declined from an aggregate average of 6.8 per cent for 1950-58 to an average of 4.6 per cent for 1958-62.

Other U.S. economists, unlike the participants in our meetings, attribute the slowdown in non-agricultural production and investment growth primarily to the rise in defense spending since 1958.

Obviously the slowdown in 1963-64 is not crucial to an assessment of Soviet motivation if a substantial continuity of Soviet attitudes and intentions since 1955 or at least 1958-59 is assumed.

3. See Chapter 7, below.

4. Another variable is the particular branch of economy affected. Everything else being equal, the more resources are

released, the better, of course, especially where scarce resources are involved (such as certain non-ferrous metals,
chemicals, electronic components, computers, complex machine tools, rubber tires, and foreign exchange).

5. While there was considerable agreement among the participants on the general economic perspective, there was substantial disagreement on the utility and effects of East-West
trade. Fundamentally, one view is that trade with the Soviet
Union is not above politics but rather, as it always has been,
a part of international politics. According to this school,
the East for its economic progress is much more dependent on
imports from the West than the West is dependent on trade
with the East. Hence Western exports represent an asset in
U.S. dealings with the Soviet Union and its allies, which—this
school argues—need not be "given away." They should be used
especially to loosen the ties within the Communist world. The
other view—perhaps a "British" view—charges the former with
an implicit assumption of immutable Soviet hostility. It denies that any strengthening of the Soviet economy is necessarily equivalent to the strengthening of the hostile pressure
which the U.S.S.R. can exert. Instead it believes that trade—
along with other instrumentalities—can help promote the kinds
of changes in the U.S.S.R. which will "denature" its threat
and contribute to some further liberalization. Some observers
would distinguish between trade (especially in "non-strategic"
goods) as a mutually beneficial process, and aid, loans, and
capital investments as asymmetrical in effect.

6. We assume that, out of a military budget of at least
12 billion rubles a year, realistically-feasible arms-control
arrangements (including unilateral steps) might permit a
reallocation of perhaps two billion rubles, at a time when
the Soviet GNP is assumed to be in the general magnitude
of 150 to 200 billion rubles, depending on concepts and methods
(i.e., approximately one per cent of the GNP). Obviously a 50
per cent cut in defense outlays would result in strikingly greater
savings.

Estimates of actual Soviet military spending differ considerably. Specialists are agreed that the overt "Defense"
rubric in the official U.S.S.R. budget does not include all relevant expenditures. While a rather extreme calculation concludes that 1964 military expenditures amount to 31.9 billion
rubles, instead of the announced 13.3 billion (Timothy Sosnovy,
"The Soviet Military Budget," Foreign Affairs, XII, No. 3,

April, 1964, 493), a more cautious and probably more reliable estimate arrives at a "real" range from 14.5 to 23.4
billion for 1962, compared to the announced defense budget
of 12.7 billion rubles (Abraham S. Becker, "Soviet Military
Outlays Since 1955," Santa Monica, Cal.: The RAND Corporation, 1964, processed, RM-3886-PR, p. 36).

7. It is no doubt significant that Soviet writers have repeatedly stressed the cardinal nature of economic problems
connected with disarmament. Thus one Soviet disarmament
specialist writes:

"The greatest practical difficulty of carrying out disarmament lies in the problem of smooth reconversion of the
economic sector.... These problems can be solved. For
example, truly enormous possibilities for the reconversion
of the missile, electronics, and ultimately also of the nu-
cleonics industries are opened by space exploration."
(Yu. Sheinin, "A Soviet Scientist Looks at Disarmament,"
Bulletin of the Atomic Scientists, XX, No. 1, January, 1964,
22.) Another—equally careful in avoiding specificity in stating
whether he refers to Communist or to non-Communist states—
writes:

"It is known that the present means of waging war are not
only the most destructive ever known in history but also
the most expensive. The alienation of a huge share of the
economic resources and energy in order to produce them
has a serious negative influence on the economy."
(Oleg Bogdanov, Vseobshchee i polnoe razoruzhenie, p. 17.)
Finally, a Soviet handbook on militarism and disarmament
declares:

"Disarmament raises various problems for the economy
of socialist states, too. Some of these problems (structural
changes in the economy, conversion of demobilized service-
men to peaceful employment, etc.) are analogous to questions arising in capitalist countries. However... the planned
economy, the absence of unemployment, and other advantages of the socialist system guarantee that the economic
problems of disarmament will be solved in the shortest
time and with the most beneficent results for the people."
(Militarizm — razoruzhenie — spravochnik [Moscow: Gosizdat,
1963], pp. 166-67.)

CHAPTER 6 - SOVIET SOCIETY AND PUBLIC
OPINION

1. For a more adequate discussion of this problem, see George Fischer, Science and Politics: The New Sociology in the Soviet Union (Ithaca, N.Y.: Center for International Studies, Cornell University, 1964). On the Soviet elite, see also the stimulating discussion in Zbigniew Brzezinski and Samuel P. Huntington, Political Power U.S.A./U.S.S.R. (New York: Viking, 1964).

2. Those participants who perceive considerable political flux on the Soviet scene are inclined to foresee greater social changes and to attribute a greater role to social forces. Those who see the Party as still substantially a homogeneous force are inclined to minimize the existence of interest groups and their possible influence on government policy.

3. It should be understood that we speak of social groups, not individuals within them (who are always apt to constitute exceptions to the general trend); and that we speak of long-range social trends, not of political predictions in a finite time span.

Our group was unable to agree on the relative importance of issues and factions (personalities) in explaining alignments within the leadership.

Ethnic origin does not seem to be a pertinent criterion for alignments on these issues.

4. On this score, a regrettable ambiguity remains. One opinion expressed in our group maintains that "the modernist is dissatisfied with pure deterrence, hoping instead to build up a relationship with the West on the basis of relative confidence." Another claims to have empirical evidence that, on various levels, including persons critical of the regime, "fear that the United States, spurred on by West Germany, would soon attack the Soviet Union," was well-nigh universal. No attempt was made to reconcile these two views or indeed to determine whether they are mutually exclusive or ambiguously compatible. Needless to say, it would be important to know whether either or both views are founded in fact.

5. On the other hand, some participants, as well as other Western research, suggest a decrease in the magnitude and in the significance of functional differentiation within the Soviet leadership.

6. For this and the following points, see also George Fischer,

"The Role of Public Opinion in Soviet Politics," Public Opinion Quarterly, Vol. XXVII, No. 4 (Winter, 1963).

7. One participant went so far as to suggest that the formation of public opinion is encouraged only under "modernist" rule, and in turn tends to be given more opportunity for expression when a "modernist" orientation prevails. Others dissented from this view.

CHAPTER 7 - THE SOVIET MILITARY

1. John Erickson, The Soviet High Command: A Military-Political History, 1918-1941 (New York: St. Martin's, 1962), p. 667.

2. The Communist Party

"regards strong political controls over the military as indispensable, since it fears the military as a potential rival in internal struggles for power. This concern stems from the fact that the military establishment possesses a vast power of coercion, is capable of rapid response to orders from its high command, mobilizes as a unit within a short time, and hence may be capable of acting simultaneously at a great many places all over the country."

(Roman Kolkowicz, "Conflicts in Soviet Party-Military Relations: 1962-1963," Santa Monica, Cal.: The RAND Corporation, 1963, processed, RM-3760-PR, pp. 1-2.)

3. After enumerating some of the crimes committed under Stalin, Zhukov went on to assure his Soviet audience that the armed forces stand "firmly on guard over the interests of our country and are always ready to carry out the will of the people, whom they have been serving faithfully for almost forty years." (Pravda, July 15, 1957; English translation in The Current Digest of the Soviet Press, IX, No. 25, July 31, 1957, 4.) He was ousted three months later.

4. V. D. Sokolovsky, Voennaia strategiia (Moscow: Voennoe Izdatel'stvo, 1962; 2d ed., 1963). The first edition is translated into English, with an introduction by Herbert S. Dinerstein, Leon Gouré, and Thomas W. Wolfe, as Soviet Military Strategy (Englewood Cliffs, N.J.: Prentice-Hall, RAND edition, 1963); and, with an introduction by Raymond L. Garthoff, as Military Strategy: Soviet Doctrine and Concepts (New York: Praeger, 1963).

5. For an analysis of the volume and the subsequent commentary on it, see the "U.S. Editors' Analytical Introduction," in Soviet Military Strategy; Thomas W. Wolfe, "A Postscript

on the Significance of the Book, 'Soviet Military Strategy'"
(Santa Monica, Cal.: The RAND Corporation, 1963, processed,
RM-3730-PR); and Leon Gouré, "Notes on the Second Edition
of Marshal V. D. Sokolovsky's 'Military Strategy'" (Santa
Monica, Cal.: The RAND Corporation, 1964, processed, RM-
3972-PR).

6. R. Ya. Malinovsky, "V rukovodstve partii—nasha sila i
nepobedimost'," Krasnaia zvezda, April 17, 1964. The same
article, just as several others in the spring of 1964, spoke of
Khrushchev as Commander-in-Chief of the Armed Forces, a
new designation evidently introduced as a necessity in an age
of nuclear brinkmanship; it betokens the continued control of
ultimate decisions by the Party leadership.

7. See, for instance, Raymond L. Garthoff, Soviet Strategy
in the Nuclear Age (rev. ed.; New York: Praeger, 1962),
Chapter 2; John Erickson, "The 'Military Factor' in Soviet
Policy," International Affairs (London), No. 4 (April), 1963;
and "U.S. Editors' Analytical Introduction," in Soviet Military
Strategy. Thomas W. Wolfe's superb "Soviet Strategy at the
Crossroads" (Santa Monica, Cal.: The RAND Corporation, 1964,
processed, RM-4085-PR; forthcoming in book form, Harvard
University Press) became available after this chapter was
written but should be consulted for a far more adequate discussion of the issues and a richer body of evidence to support
it. On the modernist-traditionalist dichotomy, see Wolfe,
"Soviet Strategy," p. 18ff.; on the balance of civil/military
influences, ibid., p. 106ff.

It is probably proper to speak today of the existence of a
"military-industrial complex" in the U.S.S.R. Its informal
emergence, in recent years, is part of the trend toward a
crystallization of interest groups in the Soviet system. Dmitri
F. Ustinov, appointed First Deputy Chairman of the Supreme
National Economic Council, in March, 1963 (at the peak of one
wave of "conservative" pressures), is representative of the
interests of this complex within the higher leadership.

The references hereinafter to Soviet "marshals" are used
as a form of shorthand, without implying an identity of views
among all marshals or any body of beliefs not shared by their
subordinates.

8. Garthoff, op. cit., p. 19.

9. Whether Khrushchev brought back and promoted Zhukov
from 1953 to 1957, or whether Zhukov was advanced in opposition to Khrushchev, as some writers have alleged, may be

regarded as immaterial in the context of this Report.

10. Kolkowicz, op. cit., p. 3. See also "U.S. Editors' Analytical Introduction," in Soviet Military Strategy.

11. Pravda, January 15, 1960; English translation in Supplement to New Times, No. 4 (January 30), 1960, pp. 13, 14.

12. See, e.g., Wolfe, "A Postscript," pp. 25-30; and Kolkowicz, op. cit., pp. 11, 17, 30, 35.

The replacement of Marshal Zakharov by Marshal Biriuzov as Chief of the General Staff, promptly after the Cuban crisis, may well have been another consequence of the "conservatives'" uneasiness about thermonuclear adventurism.

It has been suggested that the appointment of a "Khrushchev man," General A. A. Epishev (formerly Deputy Minister of State Security) to replace a professional military man, Marshal F. I. Golikov, as head of the Main Political Administration of the high command (and of the Central Committee), in May, 1962, was intended precisely to strengthen political controls and to denature or intimidate possible military opposition to the Khrushchev line.

13. V. Chuikov, "Sovremennye sukhoputnye voiska," Izvestia, December 22, 1963. For further details, see Wolfe, "Soviet Strategy," pp. 187-91.

14. Other lines of division within the military command seem less relevant at this time, though inter-service rivalry no doubt continues in a variety of forms. While the officers who had been associated with Khrushchev on the southern fronts during the war were advanced, in the 1950's, this was clearly due to personal connections rather than to a similarity in policy orientation; in fact, in recent years they have disagreed among themselves on a number of points of military doctrine. Moreover, this generation is being retired and replaced by younger men with vastly different background and training, a process which gained momentum in 1963-64.

15. See, for instance, Garthoff, op. cit.; Herbert S. Dinerstein, War and the Soviet Union (rev. ed.; New York: Praeger, 1963); and "U.S. Editors' Analytical Introduction" in Soviet Military Strategy; Thomas W. Wolfe, "Shifts in Soviet Strategic Thought," Foreign Affairs, Vol. XLII, No. 3 (April, 1964), and his "Soviet Strategy at the Crossroads."

16. Wolfe, "Soviet Strategy," p. 71. Some of the recent debate (involving also Peking) has been couched in terms of the continued validity of Clausewitz's and Lenin's dicta on war as a continuation of politics.

17. A current example of this concern is Soviet preoccupation with United States counterforce doctrine. The military specialists among the participants were agreed that Soviet officials see counterforce strategy not as a system able to destroy Soviet weapons after a first Soviet strike (and therefore requiring superiority in the U.S. military position) but, on the contrary, as a step toward a first-strike capability and, therefore, beyond a certain point, toward a first-strike policy. Soviet analysts evidently perceive it in this way because counterforce involves a large number of weapon carriers—more than would a limited deterrent; and because, as the defending side hardens and disperses its land sites, the size of nuclear warheads needed must increase enormously, too.

It is likely that there are still disagreements about U.S. "aggressive intentions" within the Soviet leadership.

18. Henry Kissinger, Nuclear Weapons and Foreign Policy (New York: Harper's, 1957), p. 392.

19. For further details, see Wolfe, "Soviet Strategy," pp. 143-58. In addressing the military academy graduating class, on July 8, 1964, Khrushchev spoke of local wars in various parts of the world, "which could under certain circumstances develop into a major conflict and even entail a world conflagration." (Pravda, July 9, 1964.)

20. A word should be added about areas which are evidently not a part of Soviet military doctrine. Arms control and disarmament are totally ignored in this context—so much so that Soviet diplomats have jubilantly quoted Western statements to the effect that arms control is an aspect of military strategy, as if they had thereby unveiled unique ulterior motives on the part of those making the statements. Whether other issues are considered too sensitive for inclusion in systematic presentations, such as the Sokolovsky symposium or other Soviet military publications, or whether they have simply not been considered, cannot be ascertained. The contrast is amply apparent from a comparison of the Sokolovsky volume with the writings of American or British theorists, such as Bernard Brodie, Thomas Schelling, Herman Kahn, Hedley Bull, or the contributors to the "arms-control" issue of Daedalus: Journal of the American Academy of Arts and Sciences, Vol. LXXXIX, No. 4 (Fall, 1960).

21. This statement is not meant to explain or justify Soviet control of Eastern Europe in conventional security terms alone.

22. Once again, reference to deterrence as an objective is

not intended to deny or preclude additional considerations affecting Stalin's decision, such as the use of military power for political intimidation of the West, and the availability of such a force if the possibility of offensive action were to be seriously weighed.

23. On the strategy debate and Soviet military policy in the mid-fifties, see, in addition to the Dinerstein and Garthoff volumes cited above, J. Malcolm Mackintosh, Strategy and Tactics of Soviet Foreign Policy (New York: Oxford University Press, 1963), Chapter 8; and his contribution in Louis Henkin, ed., Arms Control: Issues for the Public (Englewood Cliffs, N.J.: Prentice-Hall, 1961), pp. 146-58.

24. This hypothesis is persuasively presented in a detailed examination of the evidence by Arnold Horelick, "The Cuban Missile Crisis: An Analysis of Soviet Calculations," World Politics, Vol. XVI, No. 3 (April, 1964).

25. A lack of evidence makes it necessary to leave unsettled a disagreement over Soviet intentions prior to 1961. According to one reading, the U.S.S.R. opted for a minimum deterrent a number of years ago. Such a choice suggests an analogy with earlier Soviet decisions to bank on technological shortcuts in the future and an assumption that the likelihood of war in the short run was slight. On the other hand, such a posture in 1958-61 is difficult to reconcile with the seemingly genuine euphoria about the shifting balance of forces on the international scene in the aftermath of Soviet sputnik and ICBM launchings.

Others maintain that the Soviet decision to "go for" a moderate or minimal deterrent was not a free choice but the result of deliberate American military policy, which has made it "almost impossible for the Soviet Union to have equal or superior forces." This assertion is rebutted by those who stress the presence, at all times, of choices for the Soviet leadership in budgetary and resource allocation, thus suggesting a rational Soviet decision that an additional expenditure in the military field was not justified in terms of anticipated gains in security, prestige, or bargaining power.

Finally, another view notes the continued Soviet pronouncements in favor of military superiority; only "when their hand was called, as in the Berlin and Cuban situations, did they begin to adjust their policy to what might be described as a minimum deterrent posture."

Another unresolved disagreement concerns the question

whether variations in the magnitude of U.S. military superiority
are likely to result in qualitatively-different Soviet reactions.
Some participants maintain that beyond a certain (undefined)
threshold Soviet response to U.S. superiority may be "rash,"
as if provoked. Others believe, by contrast, that Soviet "adventurism" stems from an exaggeration of their own forces,
not taken from an awareness of military inferiority—an argument that can be taken back to 1918 or earlier in Russian history.

26. This as well as subsequent information on the state of
the armed forces is taken from The Military Balance 1963-
1964 (London: Institute for Strategic Studies, 1963), and sup-
plemented by U.S. Office of the Assistant Secretary of Defense, release, April 19, 1964; President Lyndon B. Johnson, speech of June 3, 1964; and Secretary Robert McNamara,
statement of August 17, 1964.

27. See Wolfe, "Soviet Strategy," Chapter 7.

While Soviet delegates to the Eighteen-Nation Disarmament
Conference in Geneva (ENDC) have continued to claim, in
various formulations, that the Soviet Union is not strate-
gically inferior to the United States, a Czechoslovak delegate
went a step further in the following declaration:

"The opinion prevails in the West that the number of
strategic nuclear weapon delivery vehicles in the possession
of the U.S. is several times greater than the number in
the possession of the Soviet Union. I should like to recall
once again that it does not matter to us what sources these
data are taken from or how far they correspond to the truth.
The important point is that the position of the United States
and the other Western countries in regard to the future
orientation of their arms programs is based upon them."

(Session of July 9, 1964, ENDC/PV. 197, English ed., p. 12.)

CHAPTER 8 - MOTIVES AND "MIX"

1. It is as yet impossible to assess the impact of the Sino-
Soviet dispute on the structure of beliefs and values in the
Soviet elite. Surely the "total victory of Communism" is no
longer a warrant of universal peace if conflicts among Communist states can become, quite literally, explosive. The
Chinese Communist Party, on assuming the mantle of Communist orthodoxy, has already told Moscow: "Time is not on your

side, and you have lost faith in your own future." ("CPC
[Communist Party of China]   Central Committee's Reply to the
CPSU Central Committee's Letter of June 15, 1964," July
28, 1964; English translation in Peking Review, VII, No. 31,
July 31, 1964, 11.)

2. Max Frankel, "Soviet Motives Weighed," The New York
Times, July 12, 1964. The same article illustrates the above
analysis further:

"What to make of a series of appreciable but minor Soviet concessions at the Geneva disarmament talks? What
to make of the newly-phrased but self-servingly designed
Soviet expression of interest in a little more world order
through United Nations peace-keeping? What, indeed, to make
of the now year-long Soviet quiescence on the principal
Cold War fronts? . . .

The Russians are said to have made several modest
concessions in rather quick order, some procedural, some
substantial. Not all of them have yet been revealed, but the
most promising ones have at least raised the possibility of
Soviet-American agreements to toss some obsolete bombers
onto a huge weapons pyre and to issue an appeal for a general
reduction in military spending.

Either agreement would have some symbolic value, keeping aloft the banner of coexistence that has flown since the
signing of the nuclear test-ban treaty last summer and encouraging the cultural contacts and civilized courtesies that
depend so much on a favorable wind.

The Russians might wish an agreement, no matter how
modest, to embarrass and further isolate the Chinese.
They might wish it also to clip the wings of the advocates
of greater military spending inside the Soviet Union.

They might wish it to exacerbate strains in the Western
alliance. They might wish it to sanctify their already natural
reluctance to spread ever more sophisticated families of
weapons to their already overarmed clients, such as Egypt
and Indonesia. They might wish to prepare themselves for
agreement because they suspect that British and American
leaders will want agreements in the midst of their election
campaigns and offer pretty good terms.

In the end, the Russians may wish to make no agreement
at all. . . . Many motives are probably at work at the same
time. It is doubtful that Moscow knows which will prevail."

3. An attempt was made to compare the importance of military and political considerations, by examining the circum-

stances of major Soviet shifts in arms-control policy since Stalin's death. Not too surprisingly, perhaps the retroactive advocates of each position among the participants—political and military—are able to provide arguments which demonstrate to their satisfaction the predominance of "their" motives. Thus, the "political" school can readily point to the three phases in which Soviet interest appears to have been more reasonable, substantial, and immediate: the period following the May 10, 1955, proposal; that which began with the Khrushchev visit to the U.S. in September, 1959; and that ushered in by the test-ban treaty in mid-1963.

The political context of the 1954-55 proposals was the ascendancy of Khrushchev and Bulganin, the reconciliation with Tito, and the "small" Geneva conference. The July, 1955, Central Committee Plenum in effect endorsed the new "co-existence" line. The 1959-60 period followed on a Soviet judgment that the prospects of U.S. aggression against the Soviet Union were nil; that at least a substantial part of Soviet ground forces could be demobilized; and that advocacy of GCD—however utopian—helped establish a desirable frame of mind and image of Soviet objectives.

On the other hand, the "military" see May, 1955, as the time when the future of NATO began to look promising, with West Germany about to join the alliance. Now Moscow was probably interested in slowing the pace of Western military preparations, while Soviet procurement of missiles got under-way.

4. In fact, some experts are prepared to argue that in the Soviet attitude toward arms control the most significant variable—except during a succession crisis—is the Soviet assessment of the strategic balance. On the other hand, it may be surmised that even such manifestly military steps as the nuclear test ban are of interest to the Soviet leaders not so much because of their specific content as because of their symbolic or catalytic political role. Any arms-control measure may be used as a "come-on" for a political easement of tensions; and, just as Soviet agreement to the Austrian peace treaty in 1955 did not represent a sudden Soviet revision of policy for Austria's sake, so the U.S.S.R. may not have been interested in a test ban merely for a test ban's sake.

5. Erickson, International Affairs (London), No. 4 (April), 1963, p. 220.

6. While opinions within the group differed on this score,

most participants concluded with considerable conviction that there still remains a substantial element of "ideology" in the Soviet view of the outside world and the Cold War.

7. A minority of participants argue that this is precisely what has taken place.

8. Investigating the rationality of Soviet policy, Marshall D. Shulman concludes with regard to an earlier but otherwise not entirely dissimilar context: "Given the distinctive framework of analysis which seems to have shaped Soviet perceptions and anticipations,... there is a demonstrably rational relationship between Soviet behavior and changes in the world environment." (His Stalin's Foreign Policy Reappraised [Cambridge, Mass.: Harvard University Press, 1963], p. 3.)

9. It is not possible within the confines of this Report to sketch an adequate picture of the central place which "resource allocation" occupies, year after year, as the single most visible locus at which conflicting priorities within the Soviet elite are expressed and contested. For relevant discussions, see, for instance, John P. Hardt, "Strategic Alternatives in Soviet Resource Allocation Policy," U.S. Congress, Joint Economic Committee, Dimensions of Soviet Economic Power; and Brzezinski and Huntington, op. cit., pp. 272-83.

PART III - THE OUTLOOK

CHAPTER 9 - THE SOVIET RECORD

1. For English-language accounts of the interwar negotiations, not necessarily marked by great political sophistication, see Kathryn W. Davis, The Soviets at Geneva (Geneva: Librairie Kundig, 1934), and Wilbur Lee Mahaney, Jr., The Soviet Union, the League of Nations, and Disarmament, 1917-1935 (Philadelphia: Privately printed, 1940). Three recent studies are Franklyn J. C. Griffiths, "Proposals of Total Disarmament in Soviet Foreign Policy, 1927-1932 and 1959-1960" (Certificate Essay, Russian Institute, Columbia University, 1962); Robert W. Lambert, "Soviet Disarmament Policy 1922-1931" (Washington, D.C.: U.S. Arms Control and Disarmament Agency, 1964, processed, Research Report 64-2); and Walter C. Clemens, Jr., "Soviet Disarmament Proposals and the Cadre-Territorial Army," Orbis, Vol. VII, No. 4

(Winter, 1964). See also Allen W. Dulles, "Disarmament in the Atomic Age," Foreign Affairs, Vol. XXV, No. 2 (January, 1947).

On the period since 1945, see the reliable account by Bernhard Bechhoefer, Postwar Negotiations for Arms Control (Washington, D.C.: Brookings Institution, 1961); the chapters by William R. Frye, J. Malcolm Mackintosh, and Harry Willets, in Louis Henkin, ed., Arms Control: Issues for the Public (Englewood Cliffs, N.J.: Prentice-Hall, 1961); Joseph Nogee, Soviet Policy Toward International Control of Atomic Energy (Notre Dame, Ind.: University of Notre Dame Press, 1961), and his "The Diplomacy of Disarmament," International Conciliation, No. 526 (January, 1960).

2. For further discussion, see Richard J. Barnet, Who Wants Disarmament? (Boston: Beacon, 1960); also Alexander Dallin, The Soviet Union at the United Nations (New York: Praeger, 1962), Chapter VI.

3. For a summary presentation of Soviet proposals, see the chart, "Soviet Disarmament Proposals, 1946-1963," facing p. 283, below.

4. Richard Lowenthal, "The World Scene Transformed," Encounter, XXI, No. 10 (October, 1963), 3.

5. Suffice it to mention the publications of the U.S. Department of State and the U.S. Arms Control and Disarmament Agency; Soviet publications of official documents (in English); United Nations and ENDC records.

6. Barnet, Problems of Communism, X, No. 3 (May-June, 1961), 36.

7. Bernhard G. Bechhoefer, "The Soviet Attitude toward Disarmament," Current History, XVL, No. 266 (October, 1963), 197. This is one of the very few informed and sophisticated discussions of our subject.

8. Soviet propaganda has gone into considerable detail on the benefits to underdeveloped countries (and for that matter, to the U.S. and U.S.S.R., too) which would be likely to result from the reallocation of resources freed as a consequence of GCD. The key reference for Soviet propagandists is still Khrushchev's speech of July 10, 1962, to the World Congress for General Disarmament and Peace in Moscow:

> "If a mere eight to ten per cent of the 120,000 million dollars spent for military purposes throughout the world were turned to [assist the underdeveloped countries], it would be possible to end hunger, disease, and illiteracy in

the distressed areas of the globe within twenty years.

A mere fifth of the amount spent for military purposes would be sufficient to build 96 steel plants the size of the Bhilai works in India, which is to turn out 2.5 million tons of steel a year, or 17 giants like the Aswan Dam in the United Arab Republic. This amount would be enough to set up from 30 to 40 power industry centers of world significance, such as powerful industrial combines in the basins of the Nile, Niger, Congo, and Zambesi in Africa, in the Sahara, in the great basins of the Indus, Ganges, and Mekong in Asia, in the foothills of the Andes, and on the South American rivers.

It is needless to speak of the beneficial effect which these measures would have on the development of the young national states, of the powerful spur they would be to their industrialization and progress. Those countries could within the next 20 to 25 years overcome their economic backwardness to a considerable extent and approach the industrial standards of countries like Britain and France.

Such progress by the newly-established national states would undoubtedly require their close cooperation with the industrially-developed countries. The main condition for this cooperation is genuine equality and mutual benefit. This cooperation would result in expanded production and would provide work for many additional millions of people in all countries.

It has been estimated that with the funds spent for military purposes all over the world during the past ten years, an end could have been put to the housing shortage in all countries. Given general and complete disarmament, the wealth of the world could be more than doubled within 20 to 25 years."

See also Glagolev, ed., op. cit.; A. Kodachenko, "Disarmament and the Underdeveloped Countries," International Affairs (Moscow), No. 7 (July), 1960; and K. Ivanov and B. Batsanov, Vzgliad v zavtra (Moscow: "Mezhdunarodnye otnosheniia," 1964).

9. The standard Soviet text on disarmament policy arranges its chapters in suggestive sequence:

Chapter VI: General and complete disarmament; [presumably, barring this:]
Chapter VII: First step: a test-ban treaty;
Chapter VIII: Partial measures.

(V. A. Zorin, ed., Bor'ba Sovetskogo Soiuza za razoruzhenie: 1946-1960 gody [Moscow: IMO, 1961].)

10. Reprinted as "The East-West Dialogue on Disarmament Continues," War/Peace Report, III, No. 7 (August, 1963), 4.

11. For instance, I. Glagolev and V. Larionov, "Soviet Defense Might and Peaceful Coexistence," International Affairs (Moscow), No. 11 (November), 1963, p. 30; cited in Wolfe, "Soviet Strategy," pp. 40-41. From the Soviet viewpoint, arms-control policies are rich nations' policies, requiring a proliferation of weapons, hardening, and various costly simultaneous steps. There is thus a built-in inhibition against adopting such a course.

12. Cf. Wolfe, "Soviet Strategy," p. 95. As Khrushchev affirmed in his speech of February 27, 1963, "It is necessary to have such [deterrent] strength that the imperialists will know that, if they unleash an atomic war, they themselves will be consumed in the flames." See also his speech of February 14, 1964.

13. Marshall D. Shulman, "Security in an Era of Conflict," paper read before the University Seminar on Peace, Columbia University, New York, February 25, 1964 (processed).

14. The Soviet Union has urged the extension of the nuclear test ban to underground tests. It continues to insist (e.g., in its memorandum of January 28, 1964, to the ENDC) that "the detection of test nuclear explosions under ground...does not require the organization of special international control." The United States has favored the banning of all nuclear weapons tests "under effective verification and control."

15. U.S. State Department Press Release No. 382, August 28, 1964.

16. English translation in The New York Times, January 4, 1964; and Supplement to New Times, No. 2 (January 15), 1964.

17. We cannot determine the extent to which changes in force structure are important and advantageous in this connection. As "hardened" weapons systems decrease the dangers of surprise attack, it may be possible to "wait out" a first alarm, thus reducing the danger of catalytic war with non-recallable missiles. This degree of tolerance may be especially needed as other countries acquire nuclear capability.

18. The U.S.S.R. in 1964 declared itself "prepared to consider" the destruction of all bomber aircraft, as obsolete but still formidable nuclear delivery vehicles. It modified its initial

proposal to the extent of limiting the proposed scrapping of bombers to the major powers, in an apparent effort to enlist the support of other states. It rejected a U.S. proposal that 480 U.S. B-47 bombers and an equal number of Soviet TU-16's be destroyed, labelling it an attempt to use disarmament negotiations as a cover for the modernization of the U.S. Air Force. (The New York Times, April 3, 1964.) France's reliance on aircraft for its nuclear force precludes, in practice, acceptance of the Soviet proposal.

19. The Soviet proposal of January 28, 1964, was "to reduce the military budgets of the nations by ten to fifteen per cent." It was later limited to the major powers. For a discussion of actual Soviet defense expenditures, see above, note 6 in Chapter 5; and especially Becker, op. cit., which addresses itself to some of the difficulties to be contemplated in the context of budgetary limitations.

20. Both the U.S. and the Soviet defense budgets for 1964 were marked by a reduction of about four per cent. In the view of some authorities, such a step-by-step procedure could lead to the reduction of annual defense budgets by a total of perhaps 25 per cent by 1970. (Roswell L. Gilpatric, "Our Defense Needs: The Long View," Foreign Affairs, XLII, No. 3, April, 1964, 374.)

21. For a discussion, see the essays by Robert C. Tucker, Klaus Knorr, Richard A. Falk, and Hedley Bull, Proposal For No First Use of Nuclear Weapons: Pros and Cons (Princeton, N.J.: Center of International Studies, Princeton University, 1963, Policy Memorandum No. 28).

While arguing that major arms-reduction programs must be legally binding on all the powers involved, Soviet international law specialists have also recognized (in the words of one of their spokesmen) "the possibility of separate unilateral disarmament measures as acts of good will and with the aim of creating a favorable atmosphere for broader further measures in this direction." Such moves have already served to "move disarmament off dead center."

Some Soviet international jurists (such as E. A. Korovin, F. I. Kozhevnikov, S. A. Malinin, and O. V. Bogdanov, and with some reservations G. I. Tunkin) have come around to the position that GCD is already a binding principle of international law (an argument which other Soviet law specialists, such as V. A. Romanov, have denied). For a discussion and references to relevant Soviet legal writings, see Bogdanov, Vseobshchee i polnoe razoruzhenie, pp. 132-38.

22. Pravda, August 4, 1964.

23. See Dallin, The Soviet Union at the United Nations, passim.

24. See Joseph I. Coffey, "The Soviet View of a Disarmed World," The Journal of Conflict Resolution, VIII, No. 1 (March, 1964), 1-6. For a Soviet discussion of the problem including a rebuttal of American arguments, see Bogdanov, Vseobshchee i polnoe razoruzhenie, Chapter 5.

25. Bechhoefer, Current History, Vol. XLV, No. 266 (October, 1963).

26. This issue provides an excellent example of the potentially important and rapidly growing role which other East European states can play as (not always impartial) intermediaries between the U.S.S.R. and the Western powers. Whether or not the initial Rapacki Plan was unveiled with Soviet support or at Soviet behest remains in dispute. It is more probable that the Polish proposals contained in Premier Gomulka's speech at Plock on December 28, 1963, and in the Polish Foreign Ministry Memorandum of February 29, 1964, were developed on Warsaw's own initiative, though no doubt "cleared" with Moscow. In essence, Poland has urged a "freeze" on the total stockpiles of nuclear weapons now located in Central Europe, as an entirely separable "first step" (with "an appropriate system of control"). A major obstacle, once again, is the implications of such a "freeze" for the proposed MLF. On the Polish proposal, see for instance, Grzegorz Jaszunski, "Poland and Non-Nuclear Zones," International Affairs (Moscow), No. 4 (April), 1964; and V. Shestov, "Geneva After the Recess," International Affairs (Moscow), No. 8 (August), 1964, p. 19, for a Soviet comment that prompt implementation of the Polish proposal "would ease tension and strengthen security."

One may assume that various East European representatives have privately gone further on various issues relating to arms control and national security.

CHAPTER 10 - SECRECY AND INSPECTION

1. The following interpretation differs from the most thorough discussion of the problem, an article by Walter F. Hahn, "The Mainsprings of Soviet Secrecy," Orbis, VII, No. 4 (Winter, 1964), 719-47.

2. George F. Kennan, Russia, The Atom and The West (New York: Harper's, 1958), p. 20.

3. On this, as on other related points, see also U.S. Congress, Senate Subcommittee on Disarmament, Control and Reduction of Armaments, 85th Cong. 2d sess. (Washington, D.C.: Government Printing Office, 1958).

4. In fact, it can be argued that secrecy may be an integral part of Soviet strategic doctrine, which in simplest terms would amount to the formula, "minimum deterrent plus secrecy":

"If the 1961 American estimates of the relatively modest scale of Russian strategic capacity are correct, we have a ready explanation of the Russians' unwillingness to allow their territory to be inspected to this degree [required by the West]. For it is undeniably likely that teams of inspectors visiting several times a year any part of Russia in which a shock wave has been recorded, might locate one or more of the Russian ICBM sites. And if there are indeed less than fifty of these missiles in existence—grouped probably in sites containing several missiles—the discovery of even a few of these sites would begin to destroy the invulnerability of the main Russian strategic deterrent. Such are the awkward consequences of the Russians' having adopted a policy of the 'minimum deterrent' dependent for its invulnerability upon secrecy."

(John Strachey, On the Prevention of War [New York: St. Martin's, 1963], p. 171.)

5. This perspective needs to be taken seriously even if one judges the basic Soviet approach as affective. As two leading analysts of arms-control problems put it,

"One of the difficulties in any inspection scheme is that it is bound to yield information beyond its intended purposes. This is partly because the personnel and techniques of surveillance will simply 'see' a lot of things other than the particular objects and activities that they are intended to monitor. It is partly because some of the very knowledge required in order to verify compliance, or in order to safeguard against dangerous military preparations outside the agreement, will itself be 'sensitive' information. That is, it will be information that can be misused by the inspecting country, or that is conducive to military instability. The obvious example, and one that is alleged to underlie the Soviet depreciation of inspection and control, is the acquisi-

tion of targeting information for a strategic attack as a by-product of an inspection system intended to reduce vulnerability."
(Schelling and Halperin, op. cit., p. 103.)

6. On this prospect, see also Holland Hunter, "The Control of Unknown Arms," in J. David Singer, ed., Weapons Management in World Politics (Ann Arbor, Mich.: University of Michigan Press, 1963), pp. 419-20.

7. This is the opinion shared by most Soviet-affairs specialists among the participants.

8. Newspaper dispatches in 1963-64 indicated that the United States apparently was successfully perfecting detection systems precluding the possibility of "cheating" on the nuclear test ban. While the Cuban missile crisis indicated that reliance on external unilateral inspection was risky at best, an informed military-affairs writer states that the United States, "with its high-flying aircraft, reconnaissance satellites and all kinds of electronic, infra-red, radar, and other sensing devices, can obtain a great deal of important military information about major military developments and concentrations in the Communist countries." (Hanson W. Baldwin, in The New York Times, April 26, 1964.)

9. Khrushchev made these comments in a conversation with William H. Benton, on May 28, 1964. He urged the U.S. to shift from aircraft (U-2) to the more "non-intrusive" space satellite surveillance over Cuba. (The New York Times, May 30, 1964.)

10. In the view of several specialists, it is likely that—unless the Soviet system changes radically—such schemes would not actually be productive of reliable information. To begin with, there would be a great asymmetry, since more U.S. than Soviet citizens would feel that they were doing their moral duty by informing on their government to a supranational authority or to a foreign power. More basically, the very situation seems highly unreal. As one seasoned observer of the Soviet scene puts it,

"If the Soviet government in its wisdom decides that certain things should not be done or certain information should or should not be kept secret, then almost any Soviet citizen would assume that his government had at its disposal adequate means for carrying out its decisions. To imply that this was not so would be a most damaging admission for Soviet authorities to make. The calling in of a currency issue might perhaps need an appeal to the cooperation of the public; the disclosure of a limited number of facts about nuclear defense does not need this."

See also Holland Hunter (op. cit.), who argues cogently that "Soviet people, especially those dealing with foreigners, have had long experience in stating official views when they are called for, regardless of personal views. No training or practice would be required to enable Soviet personnel to maintain an official facade around arms-control evasions." Moreover, "Soviet people have had long experience, in a situation of chronic shortages, with 'hood-winking,' report manipulation, embezzlement, and many other devices for fooling the authorities."

11. The following chart is based on "Verification and Response in Disarmament Agreements," a study conducted by the Institute for Defense Analyses, (Washington, D.C., 1962, processed).

It should be understood that these are broad and over-simplified gradations. Thus, no effort is made to differentiate between the degree of inspection needed to ascertain reduction of forces and that required to verify total destruction of weapons, stockpiles, or materials. Similarly, no attempt is made here to differentiate between the adequacy of national, bilateral, or international inspection machinery in every given case.

12. While there has been considerable Soviet interest in zonal arms control, some of the most sophisticated Soviet rebuttals have come precisely in response to such proposals. See, for instance, General Talensky's article, "Sincere? Yes. Realistic? No!" which "disposes" of Professor Jay Orear's plan for zonal disarmament combined with selective control ("Safeguarded Zonal Disarmament"; both articles in International Affairs [Moscow], No. 3, March, 1963, pp. 95-100). Here Talensky insists on the "practical impossibility of creating a system of zones which would have equal strategic value without exposing every detail of the defense system of the state concerned." In addition to geographic, organizational, and other objections, he raises the likelihood of "fundamental violation of strategic equality in favor of one side" in the course of such zonal disarmament, either by chance or by taking advantage of the disclosures required by the American "Outline of Basic Provisions of a Treaty."

For a recent restatement of a zonal proposal which has

aroused Soviet interest, see Louis B. Sohn, "Zonal Inspection," Disarmament and Arms Control, II, No. 2 (Spring, 1964), 204-6.

13. This view was shared by many participants, but a few dissented vigorously.

CHAPTER 11 - THE CHANGING CALCULUS

1. Soviet military policy appears to have responded far more slowly, more selectively, or not at all, to American action, though not necessarily because of any failure of communication. On the contrary, Moscow's failure to demobilize at the same rate as the United States did in 1945-46 served its political ends in Eastern Europe and East Asia. More recently, Soviet force reductions have been related primarily to the modernization of the military establishment or to explicit economic or political purposes, rather than to force levels maintained by the United States. With some specific exceptions (such as the air defense system), Soviet force posture has been characterized by considerable sluggishness in reacting to quantitative changes in other military establishments. On the other hand, American failure to develop new weapons systems at great speed and expense has probably been decisive in restraining the U.S.S.R. from similar programs (such as the ABM) once it concluded that a gross equilibrium existed or that "keeping up" was more expensive than worthwhile. There is room for a study of Soviet-American political and military interaction.

2. While the term, "containment," provides a suggestive parallel, no political or moral equivalence with Western policy is implied.

3. This statement should not conceal the fact that there was serious disagreement among the participants regarding the relative risks and advantages of alternative military postures—notably, parity versus superiority.

4. Walter Lippmann, describing the policy of the Kennedy Administration. (The Washington Post, December 3, 1963.)

5. A comparison of the first and second editions of Fundamentals of Marxism-Leninism, the official textbook used for political indoctrination, carefully composed as a vessel of orthodoxy, reveals significant changes in the treatment of

disarmament. The first edition (1960) merely mentions disarmament in an enumeration of many Soviet foreign-policy objectives and techniques, in a section intended to demonstrate the "peace-loving policy" of the Communist Bloc. The second edition (1963) includes a new subsection entitled, "General and complete disarmament is a reliable guarantee of lasting peace." The revised version omits some of the earlier text on the general danger of imperialism and world wars, and stresses instead (with appropriate references to the CPSU Program of 1961) that "the main thing is to ward off a thermonuclear war, to prevent it from breaking out." The general tone of expectations is more modest and the treatment of the United States somewhat more realistic in the second edition (Chapter 19). For the English-language editions, see Otto Kuusinen et al., eds., Fundamentals of Marxism-Leninism (Moscow: Foreign Languages Publishing House, 1960; 2d rev. ed., 1963).

6. Shulman, "Security in an Era of Conflict," p. 14.

7. The term and the concept were introduced by Thomas C. Schelling. See, in particular, his contribution to the "arms-control" issue of Daedalus, op. cit., pp. 892-914.

8. Pravda, December 31, 1963. Other Soviet spokesmen refer to it as the policy of "parallel steps."

9. In this section we are leaving aside Soviet views, as these are dealt with in the bulk of our Report. For an astute analysis of American thinking on military and arms-control policy, see Robert A. Levine, The Arms Debate (Cambridge, Mass.: Harvard University Press, 1963). This book includes an extensive analysis of various current views of Communism and the Soviet Union in particular.

10. On the recent "convergence" debate, see especially Brzezinski and Huntington, op. cit.

11. For a clear presentation of this point of view, see Robert Strausz-Hupé, "The Disarmament Delusion," Proceedings of the U.S. Naval Institute, LXXXVI, No. 2 (February, 1960), 41-47.

12. A somewhat more sophisticated argument, based on a static conception—not of Communism, but of disarmament—is a variant of the old dictum that arms control becomes possible only once it is no longer necessary. It maintains that since "disarmament follows peace," it is not possible to make serious progress until "crucial political settlements are made with the Soviet Union—the most important being the future of Germany." Disarmament, which is here identified as "a favorite of world

Communist propaganda," becomes "foremost among...false bypasses." (Arthur Krock, "Wrong Turning on the Road to Peace," The New York Times, December 26, 1963.)

13. For the fullest development of this approach, see Vincent P. Rock, "Common Action for the Control of Conflict: An Approach to the Problem of International Tensions and Arms Control" (Washington, D.C.: Institute for Defense Analyses, 1963, processed).

14. A thorough investigation concludes even that tension reduction is distinctly not conducive to disarmament. Judging from the record of postwar negotiations, that monograph reports, agreements are more likely to be negotiated at a time of political tension. (Lloyd Jensen, "The Postwar Disarmament Negotiations: A Study in American-Soviet Bargaining Behavior" [Ann Arbor, Mich.: Center for Research on Conflict Resolution, University of Michigan, 1962, processed].) The experience of the Cuban crisis of 1962 seems to lend support to this rather disturbing notion of the utility of shocks.

15. Strachey, op. cit., p. 36.

16. On the succession problem, see Wolfgang Leonhard, "Das Problem der Nachfolge Chruschtschows," Aus Politik und Geschichte (Bonn), No. 21 (May 20), 1964; and Myron Rush, "Succession and Institutions in the Soviet Union," Journal of International Affairs, Vol. XVIII, No. 1 (Spring, 1964).

17. Merle Fainsod, "Khrushchev's Russia," The Australian Outlook, XVII, No. 3 (December, 1963), 233-59.

18. With literally two or three exceptions, our group was uniquely incompetent in scientific and technological matters. The expert opinions we heard were by no means unanimous but (surprisingly, to many of those present) most scientists and specialists in weapons technology appear to believe that the coming decade is unlikely to see any technological breakthrough by the Soviet Union of a magnitude or uniqueness sufficient to jeopardize U.S. predominance. True, past predictions of similar groups have proved to be disastrously imperfect. Still, our group accepted this opinion as a guideline for its deliberations.

19. Hoc Tap (Hanoi), January, 1964; English translation in Peking Review, VII, No. 15 (April 10, 1964), 15.

20. See, for instance, Adlai E. Stevenson, Friends and Enemies (New York: Harper's, 1959), pp. 10-11, and Walter Lippmann, The Communist World and Ours (Boston: Little, Brown, 1959), p. 13.

21. Wolfe, "Soviet Strategy," p. 296.

22. Sheinin, Bulletin of the Atomic Scientists, XX, No. 1 (January, 1964), 22.

23. Wolfe, "Soviet Strategy," p. 296.

APPENDIX

THE DISARMAMENT ISSUE IN THE SINO-SOVIET DISPUTE:

A CHRONOLOGICAL DOCUMENTATION

To many observers, one of the most persuasive sources of evidence regarding Soviet attitudes toward disarmament has been the record of exchanges and debates within the international Communist movement. While most of the available materials are overt communications between parties and governments—notably the Soviet, Chinese, and Albanian—some internal Communist sources not originally intended for dissemination fully bear out the rest of the evidence.[1]

The following compilation is based on all available types of communications, from 1959 to 1964. As this record is limited to explicit arguments relating to one major problem area only, no claim is made that it presents a rounded or complete picture of the Sino-Soviet conflict or its causes. Nor can all the claims and charges be accepted at face value. The purpose here is not to reconstruct the evolution of intra-Communist strife but rather to indicate the recurring references to disarmament and their context, as an additional tool in the search for enlightenment on Communist attitudes. A chronological rather than a thematic presentation of the evidence was chosen, in the hope that this approach would provide a better perspective and some sense of the flow of developments.

I. ROOTS OF THE DISARMAMENT DISPUTE

At the Twentieth Congress of the Communist Party of the Soviet Union (CPSU), in February, 1956, N. S. Khrushchev declared that war was no longer "fatalistically" inevitable. At the Twenty-first Congress, three years later, he went further and sanctioned the view that even the final world-wide victory

---

1. There is no doubt about the authenticity of the documents. The suggestion that they were fabricated to deceive the West is no longer seriously tenable.

of Communism over capitalism could be achieved without war. Soviet views on war and peace had apparently changed with Soviet mastery of thermonuclear weapons production (1953) and, a few years later, the successful firing of the first ICBM and space satellite (1957). Khrushchev came around to a view he had earlier opposed: the destructive power of nuclear weapons was such that general war was bound to mean mutual annihilation. Hence, given a gross balance of mutual deterrence among the major powers, the initiation of nuclear war was tantamount to suicide.

The Chinese Communists, it is now clear, disagreed with the Khrushchev line, as announced at the Twentieth CPSU Congress, particularly the re-evaluation of Stalin and the thesis of the non-inevitability of war. While a careful reading of key documents might have led foreign observers to detect clues to Sino-Soviet divergencies at the time, Peking made an effort to keep the differences from the public. A more systematic exchange of Soviet and Chinese views on the prospects and the nature of thermonuclear war took place during Mao Tse-tung's visit to Moscow for the 40th anniversary of the October Revolution (November, 1957). In the wake of Soviet successes in science, space, diplomacy, and economics, Mao confidently predicted that the "East wind" was prevailing over the "West wind." Mao was to conclude from this meteorological phenomenon that the Communist Bloc could with impunity exert increasing military and other pressure on the "imperialists," especially in supporting so-called national-liberation movements in colonial and formerly colonial countries. The imperialists would resist, of course, since they never give up without a struggle, but because of the strength of the Socialist camp, the imperialists would not dare to raise wars of national liberation to the level of general world wars. A Chinese codicil added that in the unlikely event of a general (nuclear) war, the net result would be the destruction of capitalism and the eventual triumph of world Communism. As has become known more recently, it was at the November, 1957, gathering of Communists that Mao made the oft-rumored comment that in the event of thermonuclear war, China might lose 300 million men, but the remaining 300 million would emerge as victors to go on to build a Communist society. [2]

2. "Statement of the Soviet Government, September 21, 1963," New Times (Moscow), No. 39 (October 2), 1963, p. 43. See also "The Origin and Development of the Differences Between the Leadership of the CPSU and Ourselves," September 6, 1963, by the Editorial Departments of Jen-min jih-pao [People's Daily] and Hungch'i [Red Flag]; English translation in Peking Review, VI, No. 37 (September 13, 1963), 6.

This whole complex of assumptions and reasoning obviously ran counter to the developing Soviet attitudes on war and revolution.

In 1958, Communist China proceeded to launch a sharply stepped-up campaign of economic and social reorganization, appropriately termed the Great Leap Forward. Its industrial aspects earned some Soviet scorn and skepticism because of what Moscow considered Peking's primitive notions. The agricultural plans—and above all, the system of people's communes, with the Chinese claim that they were a short-cut to the achievement of a Communist society—contributed to the distinct cooling of Sino-Soviet relations in 1958 and early 1959.

The Khrushchev regime gained in strength in the two years following the November, 1957, meeting. If Chinese allegations are correct (as they appear to be), by June, 1959, Khrushchev chose to renege on a secret commitment made in 1957 (at a time of greater Soviet weakness) to share with Communist China thermonuclear "know-how" and a "sample bomb." [3]

Having in 1958 withheld support from Peking in its endeavors to strike at the Nationalist-held islands off mainland China and perhaps at Taiwan, Moscow also refused to support Peking in its border clashes with India. The Chinese Communists point to the Tass communiqué of September 9, 1959, as the first instance in which a "socialist state" failed to abide by its treaty obligations and by the dictates of "proletarian internationalism," assuming instead publicly a pose of neutrality and even regret at the action of a "fraternal" government. Thus, by the time Khrushchev visited the United States, Peking already had cause for considerable alarm over the new and suspiciously "revisionist" Soviet policy.

By 1959 Khrushchev was ready to seek a détente with the United States from what he assumed or pretended to be a position of strength. Keynoting his trip to the United States was the Soviet Premier's article, "On Peaceful Coexistence," in the October, 1959, issue of Foreign Affairs. In a tone that was notable for its lack of belligerence, Khrushchev expounded the

3. This revelation appeared in the "Statement by the Spokesman of the Chinese Government" of August 15, 1963:
"As far back as June 20, 1959, when the   was not yet the slightest sign of a treaty on stopping nuclear tests, the Soviet gover ..ent unilaterally tore up the agreement on new technology for national defense concluded between China and the Soviet Union on October 15, 1957, and refused to provide China with a sample of an atomic bomb and technical data concerning its manufacture. This was done as a presentation gift at the time the Soviet leader went to the United States for talks with Eisenhower in September [1959]."
(English translation in Peking Review, VI, No. 33, August 16, 1963, 14.)

virtues of peaceful coexistence in general, and complete disarmament in particular. He highlighted Soviet moves toward disarmament and emphasized the benefit to mankind of a "world without arms":

> Is it not yet clear to everybody that consistent adherence to the policy of peaceful coexistence would make it possible to improve the international situation, to bring about a drastic cut in military expenditures and to release vast material resources for wiser purposes?
>
> The well-known British scientist, J. Bernal, recently cited figures to show that average annual expenditures for military purposes throughout the world between 1950 and the end of 1957 were expressed in the huge sum of about 90 billion dollars. How many factories, apartment houses, schools, hospitals, and libraries could have been built everywhere with the funds now spent on the preparation of another war! And how fast could economic progress have been advanced in the underdeveloped countries if we had converted to these purposes at least some of the means which are now being spent on war purposes! [4]

In his talks with President Eisenhower and Mr. Adlai Stevenson, and in his address before the United Nations (September 18, 1959), Khrushchev presented grandiose schemes, culminating in his comprehensive proposal for general and complete disarmament. He tried to persuade American interlocutors that the U.S. could afford to disarm. (This position represented a remarkable abandonment of the long-standing Marxist-Leninist tenet that a capitalist economy needs armaments as a safety valve to avoid economic and hence political crises.) Whatever the motives, the public posture was unmistakable.

After leaving the United States, the Soviet premier traveled to Peking and, with some disregard for Chinese sensibilities, there also emphasized the necessity and the possibility of a détente with the West. "The question stands thus:" he declared, "Either peaceful coexistence or war with its catastrophic consequences." [5]   En route from Peking to Moscow, Khrushchev repeatedly discussed the benefits of disarmament in a series of "whistle-stop" speeches across Siberia.

4. Reprinted in Philip E. Mosely, ed., The Soviet Union 1922-1962: A Foreign Affairs Reader (New York: Praeger, 1963), p. 413.
5. G. F. Hudson, Richard Lowenthal, and Roderick MacFarquhar, eds., The Sino-Soviet Dispute (New York: Praeger, 1961), p. 62.

II.   1960

Khrushchev's major report to the Supreme Soviet on January 14, 1960, was titled, significantly, "Disarmament—The Road to Durable Peace and Friendship among the Nations." In this speech he announced the unilateral reduction of Soviet conventional forces by 1.2 million men and the reorganization of the armed forces due to increased reliance on missiles and nuclear weapons. While exuding confidence about the Soviet Union's increasing reliance on nuclear weapons, Khrushchev also stressed the need for disarmament to prevent a nuclear catastrophe:

It goes without saying that after we have reduced our armed forces, we shall continue our efforts as before to reach agreement with the Western countries on general and complete disarmament. We are anxious to rid ourselves and others of the threat of war, to rule out the possibility of accidents that might involve mankind in war, for, any war in the present conditions would inevitably be global. [6]

In this speech Khrushchev also tried to allay Chinese suspicions about Soviet-American negotiations which excluded Communist China:

True, there have been isolated pronouncements, notably in certain small countries, expressing apprehension lest the Great Powers, in agreeing among themselves jettison the interests of small nations and disregard the views of states not represented at the conference. Permit me to state that these apprehensions are absolutely unfounded. As far as the Soviet government is concerned, now as in the past, it has no intention of reaching agreement behind the backs of other states on questions in which their interests are directly involved. We believe that any attempt to attain unilateral advantages at the expense of other states is in general contrary to the objectives of the forthcoming meeting, the results of which must benefit universal peace and, consequently, all nations, big and small. [7]

6. N. S. Khrushchev, "Report to the Supreme Soviet of the U.S.S.R.," Pravda (Moscow), January 15, 1960; English translation in Supplement to New Times No. 4 (January 30), 1960, p. 21.

7. Ibid., p. 7.

Khrushchev expressed his confidence in the West's willingness to abide by any nuclear test-ban agreement it would sign:

> If any country violated its obligations [not to test], the initiators of such violation would be stigmatized by all the nations. I have already said that there have been no nuclear explosions for over a year now. That is the result of voluntary commitments in the absence of an international agreement. Evidently, if there were such an agreement, it would be even more binding, obligating all the signatory powers scrupulously to observe it. [8]

The same speech also contained an affirmation that there need be no economic barriers to disarmament in the United States and that, furthermore, economic benefits from disarmament would be world-wide:

> It is argued in the West that disarmament is fraught with severe economic consequences for the capitalist countries. . . .
>
> The most charitable thing that can be said about these views is that there is not a shred of evidence to support them. I had occasion to talk with many representatives of the American business world, and they did not share these gloomy views. They felt certain that American industry was fully in a position to cope with the task of converting the entire economy to peace production.
>
> Indeed, are we not justified in believing that conversion to peace production would make it possible drastically to reduce taxation of the population, increase home market capacity and, at the same time, spend more on education, public health, and social welfare? And is it not true to say that there would be immensely better opportunities for foreign trade? . . .
>
> With the reduction in armed forces, which means less expenditure on armaments, we shall have even greater opportunities to develop our economy and consequently to increase our assistance to the so-called underdeveloped countries.
>
> As we have said on more than one occasion, if agreement on general and complete disarmament is reached, enormous funds would be released, thus making it possible to render

8. Ibid., p. 10.

much more assistance to all economically-underdeveloped countries. [9]

At the meeting of the Warsaw Treaty Organization powers, in February, 1960, the Chinese "observer," K'ang Sheng, in a tone that contrasted strikingly with the Soviet mood, attributed the progress made on "procedural matters" in disarmament talks to the growing strength of the Socialist camp and the national-revolutionary forces. Since the United States was now "far behind" in science and weapons technology,

> . . .and particularly under pressure of the strong desire for peace of the people everywhere, the U.S. ruling circles were obliged to make some peace gestures. Of course, it is better to talk peace than to talk war. Nevertheless, even the U.S. ruling circles themselves do not try to hide the fact that the change in their way of doing things is aimed at numbing the fighting spirit of the people of the world by means of the "strategy to win victory by peace," wrecking the unity of the peace forces of the world and disintegrating the Socialist camp; . . .these wild ambitions of the U.S. ruling circles will, of course, not be realized. While being obliged to make certain peace gestures, the U.S. ruling circles are still pushing ahead vigorously with their arms expansion and war preparations, making a strenuous effort to develop inter-continental ballistic missiles, setting up and expanding missile bases in various places, claiming to be ready at any time to resume nuclear weapons tests, and actively trying to strengthen and patch up military blocs in an attempt to gain time to improve their inferior military position.

The United States, said K'ang, does not openly oppose disarmament, but has in the negotiations "sabotaged universal disarmament" by retreating from its own former proposals after the Soviet Union had accepted them. He predicted that the road to disarmament led through "a long-term and complicated struggle between us and imperialism." Perhaps with the forthcoming Paris summit meeting in mind, K'ang warned:

> . . .the Chinese Government has to declare to the world that any international disarmament agreement and all other

9. Ibid., pp. 12, 21. The above version, carried in English by New Times, corresponded to the Pravda text of January 15, 1960. On the same date, Izvestia's text of the Khrushchev address read at this point (in lieu of "they") "the most sensible among them."

international agreements which are arrived at without the formal participation of the Chinese People's Republic and the signature of its delegate cannot, of course, have any binding force on China. [10]

In April, 1960, the Chinese Communists launched a bitter attack on Soviet policy positions in a series of three articles aimed at the "modern revisionists" who try to "paint an utterly distorted picture of the world." While the articles explicitly condemned Tito, it was obvious that it was Khrushchev who was being accused of "revising, emasculating, and betraying" the basic tenets of Leninism.

In the article, "Long Live Leninism!" (in the Chinese Party's theoretical journal, Hungch'i, of April 16, 1960) the section on "War and Peace" begins by attacking the contention that the Soviet deterrent and the "peace forces" of the world are adequate to prevent the imperialists from launching a war. It points out that "since the Second World War there has been continuous and unbroken warfare."

A long passage denies the qualitative impact of weapons technology on world politics and condemns Soviet warnings about the destructive power of nuclear weapons as part of the "U.S. imperialist refrain to spread terror of atomic warfare among the masses." The Chinese deny that "weapons mean everything":

> Marxist-Leninists have always maintained that in world history it is not technique [i.e., technology] but man, the masses of people, that determine the fate of mankind. . . . Comrade Mao Tse-tung pointed out that the most abundant source of strength in war lay in the masses, and that a people's army organized by awakened and united masses of people would be invincible throughout the world. . . .After the Second World War, the triumph of the Korean and Chinese peoples in the Korean war over the U.S. aggressors, far superior in weapons and equipment, once again bore out this Marxist-Leninist thesis.

However, the Chinese continued:

> Of course, whether or not the imperialists will unleash a war is not determined by us; we are, after all, not their

10. English translation in Hudson et al., op. cit., pp. 73-74.

chief-of-staff. As long as the people of all countries enhance their awareness and are fully prepared, with the Socialist camp also possessing modern weapons, it is certain that if the U.S. or other imperialists refuse to reach an agreement on the banning of atomic and nuclear weapons and should dare to fly in the face of the will of all the peoples by launching a war using atomic and nuclear weapons, the result will be the very speedy destruction of these monsters themselves encircled by the peoples of the world, and certainly not the so-called annihilation of mankind....But should the imperialists impose such sacrifices on the peoples of various countries, we believe that, just as the experience of the Russian Revolution and the Chinese Revolution shows, those sacrifices would be rewarded. On the debris of imperialism, the victorious people would create very swiftly a civilization thousands of times higher than the capitalist system and a truly beautiful future for themselves.

The conclusion can only be this: Whichever way you look at it, none of the new techniques like atomic energy, rocketry, and so on, has changed, as alleged by the modern revisionists, the basic characteristics of the epoch of imperialism and proletarian revolution, as pointed out by Lenin. The capitalist-imperialist system definitely will not crumble of itself. It will be overthrown by the proletarian revolution within the imperialist country concerned, and by the national revolution in the colonies and semi-colonies. Contemporary technological progress cannot save the capitalist-imperialist system from its doom but only rings a new death knell for it. [11]

The editorial proceeded to deny that peace and disarmament must have priority over "liberation."

To attain its aim of plunder and oppression, imperialism always has two tactics: the tactics of war and the tactics of "peace"; therefore the proletariat and the people of all countries must also use two tactics to deal with imperialism: the tactics of thoroughly exposing imperialism's peace fraud and striving energetically for a genuine world peace, and the tactics of being prepared to use a just war to end the imperialist unjust war if and when imperialism should unleash it. [12]

11. Long Live Leninism! (Peking: Foreign Languages Press, 1960), pp. 20-22.
12. Ibid., p. 31.

Peking accused the Soviet Union of concentrating on the visions of peace and disarmament to the extent of abandoning the national-liberation movement and neglecting the goal of the world-wide triumph of socialism:

> The struggle for peace and the struggle for socialism are two different kinds of struggle. It is a mistake not to make a proper distinction between these two kinds of struggle....
>
> "Peace" in the mouths of modern revisionists is intended to whitewash the war preparations of imperialism . . . and to distort the policy of us Communists concerning peaceful coexistence of countries with two different systems into elimination of the people's revolution in various countries.
>
> Naturally, we must continue to explain to the masses Lenin's thesis that the capitalist-imperialist system is the source of modern war; we must continue to explain to the masses the Marxist-Leninist thesis that the replacement of capitalism-imperialism by socialism and Communism is the final goal of our struggle. We must not conceal our principles from the masses. [13]

The reply to Peking's public blast came promptly, in a speech by Otto Kuusinen, veteran member of the CPSU leadership, on April 22, 1960. Praising Soviet flexibility in foreign policy, Kuusinen emphasized the radical nature of the new weapons technology, which made war "inconceivable":

> To be true to Marxism-Leninism today . . . it is not enough to repeat the old truth that imperialism is aggressive. The problem is to take full advantage of the new factors operating in favor of peace and for sparing mankind from the catastrophe of a new war. The dogmatic position is a backward position....
>
> The change in the correlation of forces in the international arena, the growth of the Socialist camp's might, and the obviousness of the catastrophic consequences of a new war—all these have been making for a division in the ruling circles of the imperialist states. Alongside the die-hard opponents of peace are appearing sober-minded statesmen who are aware that a war involving the use of the new means of mass obliteration would be madness.

13. Ibid., pp. 51-52.

Such are the dialectics of progress in military technology —a new weapon created for war begins to exert pressure in favor of peace. For Marxists, there is nothing enigmatic in this. The classical Marxist writers never denied that new types of arms not only produce a revolution in military affairs but may also have an effect on politics. Engels, for example, wrote this in "Anti-Duehring," and Lenin, according to N.K. Krupskaya's account, foresaw that "there will be a time when war comes to be so devastating that it is altogether impossible." . . .

The gains made in the struggle for peace create a good basis for moving ahead. The main task now is to bring about disarmament. It is highly symptomatic that it should have been our socialist state, possessing acknowledged superiority in the military field, that put forward the proposal for general and complete disarmament, placing this task at the focus of world politics. [14]

The Sino-Soviet conflict rapidly grew more bitter and more public. The General Council of the World Federation of Trade Unions (WFTU), meeting in Peking in June, 1960, was the scene of a blunt Chinese attack on Soviet strategy toward the West and the underdeveloped nations. With the recent U-2 incident as a trump, Liu Chang-sheng condemned the thesis that war could be eliminated before the end of imperialism as a dangerous "illusion" leading to "evil consequences." He recognized a "possibility" of avoiding world wars, but stressed the "danger of imperialism launching a war." Local wars, particularly wars of national liberation, are "unavoidable," and the idea that they can be avoided harms the people in colonial countries and keeps them "forever in the state of enslavement." According to the official Chinese account,

Liu Chang-sheng said: We support the disarmament proposals put forward by the Soviet Union. It is of course inconceivable that imperialism will accept proposals for general and complete disarmament. The purpose of putting forward such proposals is to arouse the people throughout the world to unite and oppose the imperialist scheme for arms drive and war preparations, to unmask the aggressive and bellicose nature of imperialism before the peoples of the world

14. English translation in The Current Digest of the Soviet Press (New York), XII, No. 17 (May 25, 1960), 10.

in order to isolate the imperialist bloc headed by the United States to the greatest extent, so that they will not dare unleash a war lightly. But there are people who believe that such proposals can be realized when imperialism still exists and that the "danger of war can be eliminated" by relying on such proposals. This is an unrealistic illusion.

As to the view that after disarmament, imperialism would use the funds earmarked for war purposes for "the welfare of the laboring masses" and for "assisting under-developed countries," and that this would "bring general progress to people as a whole without exception"—this is downright whitewashing and embellishing imperialism, and indeed this is helping imperialism headed by the United States to dupe the people throughout the world.

Liu Chang-sheng pointed out that only when the socialist revolution is victorious throughout the world can there be a world free from war, a world without arms. Such a world is inconceivable while imperialism still exists. This is not a question of whether we want it or not; the question is that the imperialists will never lay down their arms of their own accord. . . .

We hold that the utmost efforts must be made to reach agreement on the banning of nuclear weapons and to prevent the outbreak of a nuclear war in the world, Liu Chang-sheng said: . . . But even if agreement is reached, imperialism can still tear it to pieces. And even if in their own interests the imperialists dare not unleash a large-scale nuclear war, they still can wage war with the so-called conventional weapons. . . .

Liu Chang-sheng pointed out: To win world peace, the struggle of the world's peoples and diplomatic negotiations carried out by the socialist countries should go hand in hand. It should not be supposed that since diplomatic negotiations are needed, the struggle of the peoples can thus be dispensed with. On the contrary, diplomatic negotiations must be backed up by the united struggle of the world's peoples. To win world peace, we should mainly rely on the struggles waged by the peoples of various countries. [15]

At the impromptu conference of Communist Party delegates attending the Rumanian Party Congress in Bucharest in late

15. Liu Chang-sheng, Speech at the WFTU General Council Meeting, June 7, 1960; English report in Peking Review, III, No. 24 (June 14, 1960), 10-13.

June, 1960, the Soviet delegation launched an offensive against the Chinese positions and revealed to the other Communist leaders present the extent and seriousness of Sino-Soviet differences. According to Edward Crankshaw, CPSU Secretary Boris Ponomarev circulated to the other Communist Parties an eighty-page letter explaining Soviet policy. This letter contained a novel defense of the Soviet position on disarmament. Crankshaw paraphrases this letter in his report on the conference:

> As for disarmament, the Chinese objections to the call for disarmament, namely that it encouraged "illusions" among the masses, was based on a failure to appreciate the real meaning of the Soviet proposals. This was that by concentrating on disarmament the creation of broad popular fronts and mass movements in favor of peace would be facilitated, thus embarrassing "bellicose circles" in their efforts to intensify the arms race. One of the major Soviet aims in the disarmament campaign was to get rid of U.S. overseas bases. The Chinese line could lead only to a continuation of the Cold War and of the arms race. It would, moreover, obstruct the peace policies of the Soviet Union by appearing to give substance to the claims of the imperialists that Communists believe in war and want it. [16]

Reports of the private talks revealed bitter accusations and harsh arguments. Khrushchev accused Mao of knowing little of the realities of the modern world or of the dangers of thermonuclear war. P'eng Chen, the head of the Chinese delegation, is said to have answered that the Chinese did not trust Khrushchev's analysis of the world situation. He denounced Khrushchev's usurping the right to speak for China on disarmament matters. [17]

Throughout the summer of 1960 articles appeared in the Soviet press, condemning the "dogmatist position" on disarmament, along with other issues on which there was growing disagreement.

> We can only call erroneous, dogmatic, and left-sectarian all kinds of attempts to interpret the policy aiming at peaceful

---

16. Edward Crankshaw, The New Cold War: Moscow v. Pekin (Baltimore, Md.: Penguin, 1963), p. 102.

17. Donald S. Zagoria, The Sino-Soviet Conflict 1956-61 (Princeton: Princeton University Press, 1962), p. 327. See also Crankshaw, op. cit., pp. 97-110.

coexistence and the struggle for disarmament as a departure
from Marxist-Leninist positions in the class struggle of the
proletariat, [and all] efforts to cast doubt on the correct-
ness of the decisions of the Twentieth and Twenty-first
CPSU Congresses regarding the possibility of averting a new
world war under present-day conditions. [18]

Other articles indirectly accused the Chinese of believing that
it is impossible to achieve disarmament:

From what premises do they [the countries of the Socialist
camp] proceed in calling for the destruction of military
weapons? . . . From the scientifically-grounded conclusion
of the Twentieth CPSU Congress that today war is not
fatally inevitable, that it can be avoided. . . . They are
becoming more and more convinced each day of the fact that
war can and must be banished from the life of human society.
Only near-sighted people who have lost contact with reality,
can fail to recognize the urgent necessity for full disarmament of all states, can fail to believe in the possibility of
achieving this goal. [19]

Yuri Frantsev, Director of the Academy of Social Sciences
attached to the Central Committee of the CPSU, writing in
Pravda of August 7, 1960, accused the (still unnamed) Chinese
of wanting to give a military "push" to revolutions, which "would
merely play into the hands of the imperialists by helping them
to spread false stories about the 'aggressiveness of Communism.' " He likewise attacked the hope of building a great new
civilization on the nuclear ruins of the old:

Nor can one fail to see that the result of a modern war would
do great damage to productive forces, including the chief
productive force—the working people—and that mankind
would experience great difficulties in rebuilding a new social
system on the ruins remaining after the catastrophe of war.
Destructive war would only make the process of building a
new society more difficult. [20]

18. Major General N. Pukhovsky, writing in Pravda, July 24, 1960. See also D. Bekasov, in
Trud (Moscow), August 30, 1960.
19. Pravda, June 13, 1960. See also F.K. Konstantinov and Kh. Momdzhian, "Dialektika i sov-
remennost'," Kommunist (Moscow), No. 10 (July), 1960; and A. Butenko and V. Pchelin, "Sov-
remennaia epokha i tvorcheskoe razvitie marksizma-leninizma," Kommunist, No. 12 (August), 1960.
20. English translation in The Current Digest of the Soviet Press, XII, No. 32 (September 7,
1960), 5. See also General Nikolai Talensky, "On the Character of Modern Warefare," International Affairs (Moscow), No. 10 (October), 1960, pp. 22-27, on the destructiveness of nuclear
weapons and the escalation of lim' ed wars.

While the Soviet and Chinese Parties' Central Committees were circulating extensive documents in preparation for a major international Communist conference called to reconcile the conflicting positions, Chinese Communist concern over Khrushchev's "belief in" disarmament was shown in another document which became available in 1963 by the sheerest accident. [21] It consists of excerpts from the stenographic record of a conversation between Mao Tse-tung and Lawrence L. Sharkey, Secretary-General of the Communist Party of Australia, on September 25, 1960. It was obviously not intended for publication. At a time when the Chinese position was distinctly a minority view and anti-Soviet charges were still voiced with the greatest caution, the two explored common ground, for instance, in disputing the British Communist view of "peaceful transition" to socialism. Then the record reads:

SHARKEY: The CPSU was the initiator of the proposal for general and complete disarmament.

MAO TSE-TUNG: I still do not understand what is meant by general and complete disarmament.

SHARKEY: Nor do I. It was when the Soviet Party raised this slogan that we came to realize the serious nature of the question. . . .

This was evidently as far as the two were prepared to confide in each other at that time.

Both sides had made their positions clear by the time the Conference of 81 Communist and Workers' Parties met in Moscow in November, 1960. The Conference witnessed weeks of acrimonious debate. Several authoritative reports speak of repeated references to disarmament among the numerous issues in dispute. In what is admittedly a hostile summary, the Politburo of the Belgian Communist Party later described the Chinese objections to the Khrushchev "line" on peaceful coexistence. According to the Belgian paraphrase, Teng Hsiao-p'ing supported the thesis that

. . . the struggle for peaceful coexistence can be considered a mere tactical maneuver, a means of morally disarming

---

21. It was among papers taken with him and later published by the leader of a dissident pro-Chinese group, E.H. Hill, who was ousted from the Communist Party of Australia (CPA) in 1963. Hill used the transcript to demonstrate—as was indeed true—that the Secretary-General of the CPA, L.L. Sharkey, had himself been on the side of the Chinese Communists in 1960 and had returned to the pro-Moscow orientation only after the Twenty-second CPSU Congress, late in 1961.

the peoples of the capitalist countries and of materially disarming the same countries. World-wide disarmament and true peaceful coexistence will be possible only when there are only socialist countries throughout the world. . . . . [22]

Edward Crankshaw (who apparently had the opportunity to read a transcript or summary of the proceedings) also reported that in his two main speeches Teng charged that "the Soviet Party was opportunist and revisionist; it lacked any deep knowledge of Marxism; its ideas about disarmament were absurd; . . . peaceful coexistence could mean nothing, except as a tactical weapon to deceive the enemy. . . ." In reply, Khrushchev reportedly "gave an impassioned evocation of nuclear war and insisted that he was absolutely sincere about disarmament ('the only true humanism')." [23]

Speeches by Italian and French delegates, made behind closed doors but published later, contained criticism of the Chinese view of disarmament. Thus Maurice Thorez declared:

The fight for general and complete disarmament and, at the same time, for partial measures to reduce armaments has come into focus. To achieve disarmament is to eliminate the material possibilities for starting a war. . . .

To tell the peoples that, by their struggles, they can impose effective measures toward partial disarmament and even achieve general disarmament is not to show bourgeois pacifism or nourish an illusion; on the contrary, it means grasping an incomparable lever for the mobilization of the masses against the threat of war. [24]

Luigi Longo, the Italian delegate, criticized the Chinese assessment of the likelihood of war in these words:

It is in the mobilization of the people in defense of the peace that . . . a clear-cut stand on the possibility or impossibility of war, under today's conditions, becomes so important.

22. "Statement of the Politburo of the Belgian Communist Party," in Le Drapeau Rouge (Brussels), February 22, 1962; English translation in Alexander Dallin et al., eds., Diversity in International Communism (New York: Columbia University Press, 1963), p. 524.

23. The Observer (London), February 12, 1961; William E. Griffith, "The November 1960 Moscow Meeting," The China Quarterly (London), No. 11 (July-September, 1962), p. 42. For detailed accounts of the 81-Party conference, see also Zagoria, op. cit., pp. 343ff; Crankshaw, op. cit., pp. 122-36; and David Floyd, Mao against Khrushchev (New York: Praeger, 1963), pp. 110-29.

24. English translation in Dallin et al., op. cit., pp. 834-35.

This mobilization will be successful insofar as we reject any notion of inevitability of an imperialist war. Such an idea would quickly dampen any enthusiasm or vigor in mass action. You cannot get the masses to fight for goals that can't be won, particularly if it is you yourself who have said that they can't be won. . . . A thermonuclear war would practically destroy the foundations of modern civilization. This destructive nature of war broadens the possibility of mobilization in defense of peace, and of attracting strata and groups who are determined not to place the life of their nation in danger. . . .

In this way, we can create a situation in which it will be possible to force the capitalist governments to take practical measures to ease tensions and to further disarmament, and to create a situation in which, thanks to the steady strengthening of the Socialist camp, the spread of the national-liberation movement, the struggle of the masses of the people, and the action of the other forces interested in peace, war will become impossible in human society, even though socialism has not yet conquered everywhere. [25]

The Statement which the 81-Party Conference produced after some five weeks of argument was, in the words of one observer, "an ambiguous compromise." Among other issues, it failed to resolve the argument over the Chinese complaint that Moscow expected too much from negotiations with the West. Nor did it endorse the Chinese belief that agreements can be reached only after the enemy camp has been severely weakened. This passage in the final statement managed to combine a call to anti-imperialist struggle with the prospect of successful disarmament negotiations:

Hence it is essential to wage an active and determined struggle against the aggressive imperialist forces, with the aim of carrying this program [general and complete disarmament] into practice. It is necessary to wage this struggle on an increasing scale and to strive perseveringly to achieve tangible results—the banning of the testing and manufacture of nuclear weapons, the abolition of military blocs and war bases on foreign soil, and a substantial reduction of armed forces and armaments, all of which should pave the way to general disarmament. [26]

25. Ibid., pp. 852-54.
26. Hudson et al., op. cit., pp. 191-92.

Speculation that at the conference the major parties disagreed on the possibility of reaching agreement with the West on partial disarmament measures, such as a nuclear test ban or nuclear-free zones,[27] is supported by an article in the Peking Hungch'i, which chose to select for special comment the necessity of "imposing" agreement on the imperialists since they "would not easily accept even partial disarmament."

III.   1961

The different Communist interpretations of the 81-Party Statement have been widely cited. The most significant was Khrushchev's speech of January 6, 1961. Disarmament was one of its many subjects:

> Comrades, if prevention of a new war is the question of questions, then disarmament is the best way to do it. The meeting of representatives of the Marxist-Leninist parties declared that the realization of the Soviet program for general and complete disarmament would be an act of historic importance.
>
> Our struggle for disarmament is not a tactical move. We sincerely want disarmament. In this we stand squarely on Marxist-Leninist ground. Engels pointed out as far back as the end of the last century that disarmament, which he described as the "guarantee of peace," was possible. In our times, disarmament was first advanced as a practical goal by Lenin, and the first Soviet proposals for complete disarmament—or, for partial disarmament—were made at the Genoa Conference.
>
> The struggle for disarmament is a most important factor for the prevention of war. It is an effective factor in the fight against imperialism. In this fight the Socialist camp has most of mankind on its side. [28]

After a spring and summer of relative quiescence in Sino-Soviet polemics, Khrushchev, at the Twenty-second Congress of the CPSU in October, 1961, openly attacked the leadership

27. See Zagoria, op. cit., p. 359.
28. "For New Victories for the World Communist Movement," World Marxist Review (Toronto), IV, No. 1 (January, 1961), 17.

of the Albanian Party, a Chinese protegé.[29] In addition to adopting a new Party Program, the Congress heard Khrushchev resume the "de-Stalinization" campaign and launch a new attack on followers of the so-called "anti-Party" group in the CPSU. Former Premier Viacheslav Molotov, "a hopeless dogmatist," was now assailed for his views on war and revolution:

> He especially dislikes the way the [new CPSU] Program poses the question of the winning over of new hundreds upon hundreds of millions of people to the side of Communism "not through war with other countries but by the example of a more perfect organization of society." It turns out, according to Molotov, that it is precisely through war that we must win over hundreds of millions of people to the side of Communism! But this is precisely what our enemies want to impute to us; it is the same "big lie" about the Soviet Union's supposed intentions of promoting the spread of Communism to other countries by means of war, rather than by force of example, that is spread by imperialist propaganda.[30]

One indication of the importance which the Soviet leaders attached to disarmament is the direct reference to it in the CPSU Party Program, adopted at the Twenty-second Congress. The Program—criticized by the Chinese as a "revisionist"

29. For a detailed analysis, see William E. Griffith, Albania and the Sino-Soviet Rift (Cambridge: The Massachusetts Institute of Technology Press, 1963).

30. Piotr Pospelov, Director of the CPSU Institute of Marxism-Leninism, Speech at the Twenty-second CPSU Congress; English translation in Charlotte Saikowski and Leo Gruliow, eds., Current Soviet Policies IV (New York: Columbia University Press, 1962), p. 183.

Some uncertainty remains on the question whether disarmament figured, as part of an entire foreign policy "package" of disagreements, in the arguments between the Khrushchev leadership and the so-called "anti-Party group" (above all, former Foreign Minister Molotov). Charges against the Molotov grouping at the time of their ouster in 1957 did not include references to disarmament; but subsequent evidence indicates that a number of other actual issues were not then publicly listed. Subsequent Soviet references (since 1959 and especially after the Twenty-second CPSU Congress in 1961) did on several occasions identify the anti-Party group with opposition to disarmament agreements. These charges have not been very explicit and may have been part of a post facto effort to blacken the reputations of the losers. However, there is little doubt that (1) Molotov and his associates looked with considerable skepticism (and probably active impatience and hostility) on efforts to arrive at negotiated agreements with the West on such matters as arms control, control of atomic energy, and reduction of nuclear stockpiles; (2) such a position was entirely in harmony with their views on negotiations in general and on a number of moves undertaken precisely in the months between February, 1955 (when the Khrushchev-Bulganin combination emerged triumphant), and July, 1955 (when the Central Committee Plenum in Moscow in effect approved the new line in foreign policy pioneered by Khrushchev). Analogous disagreements existed on issues including the Austrian State Treaty (May, 1955), Khrushchev's approaches to Tito (culminating in his trip to Belgrade, in June, 1955), the revision of border agreements with Finland, the establishment of diplomatic relations with the Bonn government, and a variety of other moves made in approximately the same period as the Soviet note on disarmament of May 10, 1955. On the other hand, there is no firm evidence that Khrushchev "took disarmament seriously" then or prior to that time.

document—defines in the most authoritative and comprehensive form the outlook and future goals of the Soviet Communist Party. It declares disarmament to be both necessary and possible:

> General and complete disarmament under strict international control is a radical way of ensuring lasting peace. Imperialism has imposed an unprecedented burden of armaments on the people. Socialism sees its duty to humanity in delivering it from this senseless waste of national wealth. Accomplishment of this task would have historic significance for mankind. An active and determined struggle by the peoples can and must force the imperialists into disarmament. [31]

During the following months the debate became increasingly public. At the December, 1961, meeting of the World Peace Council in Stockholm, the Chinese delegation repudiated the Soviet approach on two grounds. It refused to leave the settlement of disputes to the superpowers (at least, so long as Communist China was excluded):

> The settlement of international disputes through peaceful negotiations by no means implies that major international problems can be solved by relying only on negotiations among a few big powers. . . . The idea of a few big countries straightening out international problems without respecting the opinion of small countries is also wrong and can never be realized. Every nation, be it big or small, strong or weak, is independent and enjoys equal rights. The days when a few big powers could control the destiny of the world are gone. [32]

And, second, Liu Ning-i joined battle with those who gave the "struggle for disarmament" priority over the "struggle for national liberation."

He pointed out that there are some who hold that general and complete disarmament is the only road to peace, that it is the basic task of the movement for the defense of world peace at the present time, and that it is the key to the solu-

31. Saikowski and Gruliow, eds., op. cit., p. 14.
32. Liao Ch'eng-chih, "The Way to Defend Peace," Speech at Stockholm Session of World Peace Council, December 16, 1961; English translation in Peking Review, IV, No. 51 (December 22, 1961), 13.

tion of all the pressing problems of our time. They hold that the national independence movement should be subordinated to the movement for general and complete disarmament, and that if general and complete disarmament is achieved, all the important problems of the world will be solved. He said he could not agree with this erroneous and harmful view. . . . He emphatically pointed out that when it comes to the question of defending peace, discussion should not be confined to the question of disarmament alone, still less to discussion of this question in vague and general terms. One of the primary and major tasks of the peace movement is to tell the people truthfully who is the most ferocious enemy of peace.[33]

A leading Italian Communist official, interviewed in December, 1961, on his return from the Stockholm meeting, identified disarmament as one of the issues in the bitter Sino-Soviet exchange which had taken place at that meeting:

. . . a fundamental contrast was manifested between the positions of those who firmly believe in the possibility of averting war, in the existence of genuine conditions which today render possible the realization of general disarmament, bringing it down from the plane of the ideal to the plane of political reality, who . . . are convinced that in every country the struggle for peace ought to have its own particular line of development, and on the other hand those who have less faith in peaceful coexistence and disarmament and, therefore, place the accent on the basic struggle against imperialism, making their objectives for peace coincide with those for the liquidation of imperialism and colonialism in all its forms.
It was soon evident . . . that any attempt at reconciliation would be quite useless. . . . [34]

IV.   1962-63

Since the Albanian leadership had been publicly denounced at the Twenty-second CPSU Congress, Albania and the Soviet Union could attack each other with a frankness and vehemence

33. English report in Peking Review, IV, No. 52 (December 29, 1961), 13-14.
34. Interview with Velio Spano, in L'Unita (Rome), December 23, 1961; English translation in Griffith, op. cit., p. 129.

that was still avoided in the direct Sino-Soviet exchanges. Among other charges, Moscow accused the Albanians of not believing in disarmament:

> The Albanian leaders have shown by their deeds that, while recognizing in words the importance of general and complete disarmament, they have no faith in the possibility of disarmament; and more, they have resorted to the falsification of the Soviet proposals on this question. One must sink to the full depths of moral degradation in order to allege, as Hoxha is doing, that the Soviet Union has urged unilateral disarmament on the socialist countries![35]

The Albanians fought back by accusing Khrushchev personally of whitewashing imperialism, placing excessive faith in disarmament, and harming the national-liberation movement:

> N. Khrushchev and his group are making a great clamor, accusing the Albanian Party of Labor of being against total and complete disarmament. This is nothing but a smoke screen to hide the distorted pacifist-bourgeois views of N. Khrushchev on general and complete disarmament.
>
>   What are, in fact, the dangerous views which N. Khrushchev tries to impose on the international Communist and workers' movement concerning general and total disarmament?
>
>   First, that general and complete disarmament is the only real way to ensure peace; that it represents the primary and most urgent task of the hour, on which depend all other tasks and all other problems of the international Communist movement and contemporary world development. According to N. Khrushchev and his followers, all the fundamental questions that preoccupy the peoples today, such as national liberation and others, can be settled only as a result of general and complete disarmament, and the creation of a world without arms, armies, and wars. . . .
>
>   Secondly, N. Khrushchev hopes to achieve universal and total disarmament solely by issuing a general appeal for disarmament and has intentionally ignored the necessity of struggling to unmask the warmongering activities of imperialism, especially of American imperialism, which not only prevents disarmament by every means possible, but

---

35. N. Vinnitsky and A. Arkadyev, "Who Stands to Gain from the Splitting Activities of the Albanian Leaders?" International Affairs (Moscow), No. 2 (February), 1962, p. 57.

actually intensifies the unbridled arms race daily. Experience has shown, however, that the beautiful words of Kennedy and the other imperialist leaders about "peace" and their "desire for negotiations" are completely false and demagogic. [36]

In a later article, the Albanians objected vehemently to what they considered to be Khrushchev's specious reasoning in saying that the cause of national-liberation movements would be advanced by disarmament and negotiation with the imperialists: Khrushchev's position, they alleged, amounted to nothing less than the subordination of the goal of national liberation to that of disarmament. Under the existing conditions, the Albanians concluded,

. . . it is a crime to put a brake on the struggle of the oppressed peoples for their national liberation from the colonial yoke of imperialism, to condemn them to live in untold suffering and misery, while awaiting with folded arms the achievement of general and complete disarmament. [37]

One of the Soviet replies to the Chinese and Albanian accusations came in a speech by Anastas Mikoyan:

The experience of the struggle for disarmament, said the speaker, indicates that this task is not an easy one. There are great difficulties which must be overcome in order to achieve this goal because of the many overt and covert opponents of disarmament and partisans of the arms race. All peace-loving forces of the world are waging a persistent and lengthy struggle against them. . . .
  It is not accidental that the violent opponents of disarmament well understand that a world without arms, a world without war, would mean the worst conditions for the imperialists' opposition to the revolutionary movement of the proletariat and the peasantry, and deprivation of their opportunities to suppress the people's national-liberation struggle.
  And if the reactionaries and colonialists understand this well, then it is all the more amazing to hear criticism supposedly made from "leftist" positions, that peaceful coex-

---

36. "Deeper and Deeper into the Mire of Anti-Marxism," Zeri i Popullit (Tirana), January 9, 1962; English translation in Griffith, op. cit., pp. 308-9.
  37. "Modern Revisionism to the Aid of the Basic Strategy of American Imperialism," Zeri i Popullit, September 19-20, 1962; English translation in Griffith, op. cit., p. 371.

istence and the demand for complete and general disarmament allegedly impede the national-liberation struggle of
the peoples of the colonial and dependent nations. . . .

Of course, in our proposals for disarmament, there is no
question of weakening the defense of the newly-formed states
which defend their independence, struggle against the
schemes of imperialism and colonialism. And what is more,
the Soviet Union and the other socialist countries are helping these states create national armed forces to defend their
independence.

The struggle for peaceful coexistence and for general
disarmament is class struggle on a world scale. . . . How
then can one oppose the slogan of disarmament to the tasks
of the national-liberation struggle? [38]

Khrushchev's speech at the World Congress for General
Disarmament and Peace, in Moscow in July, 1962, reiterated
Mikoyan's arguments and painted again an enticing picture of
the potential economic benefits of disarmament to underdeveloped countries:

The underdeveloped countries are now spending approximately $5 billion to $6 billion a year on military requirements. . . . There can be no doubt that under conditions of
peace and deliverance from the burden of military expenditures, the underdeveloped countries could develop their
economies   faster   and   gain   economic   independence
sooner. . . .[39]

On a related issue, the Chinese Communists in October,
1962, attacked the Soviet contention that armaments and the arms
race can in themselves be a cause of tensions leading to war:

These "theories" of the modern revisionists are utterly pre-
posterous. Arms are only tools of war, not the source of war.
In circulating the fallacy that arms engender war, the aim of
the modern revisionists is simply to divert the main thrust
of the world's popular struggles away from U.S. imperialism

38. Pravda, March 15, 1962; English translation in Dallin et al., op. cit., pp. 638-39. See
also the article by the French Communist, Jean Kanapa, "General and Complete Disarmament
is the Urgent Need of our Time," World Marxist Review, V, No. 5 (May, 1962), 21-27, which
accused the "dogmatists of the type of the Albanian leaders" of being opposed to the struggle
for disarmament.

39. Pravda, July 11, 1962; English translation in The Current Digest of the Soviet Press, XIV,
No. 28 (August 8, 1962), 9.

and the Kennedy Administration at which the peoples now point their accusing fingers, and to make them oppose indiscriminately the arms of any country, of any people. In other words, one need not distinguish between arms in the hands of U.S. imperialists for its policy of aggression and its preparations for a new world war, and arms in the hands of the socialist countries to defend their motherlands and world peace; nor between arms used by imperialism to stamp out the national and democratic revolutions, and arms used by the oppressed nations and peoples to fight for freedom, independence and liberation. [40]

In September, 1962, Marshal Tito stated explicitly that there were differences between the Chinese and Soviet positions on disarmament. In reply to a question by Drew Pearson, Tito declared:

As we understand these differences between China and the Soviet Union, we consider that the Soviet foreign policy is not properly understood by the Chinese leaders. China has great internal requirements—which is one of the reasons. The other is that China has slightly different views from the Soviet Union in regard to foreign policy, the question of disarmament, and so on. [41]

The Cuban crisis of October, 1962, and the simultaneous Sino-Indian conflict brought about a critical escalation of Soviet-Chinese enmity. By the end of the year, the differences could no longer be contained, and a series of long editorials began to restate the Chinese position and to provide a point-by-point criticism of the Soviet view. The Chinese again accused the Soviet leadership of putting too much faith in negotiated agreements:

To achieve world peace it is necessary to rely mainly on the strength of the masses of the people of the world and on their struggles. In the course of the struggle to defend world peace, it is necessary to enter into negotiations on one issue or another with the governments of the imperialist countries, including the Government of the United States, for the pur-

40. Jen Ku-ping, "The Tito Group," Peking Review, V, No. 41 (October 12, 1962), 12.
41. "President Tito's Answers to the Questions of the American Journalist, Mr. Drew Pearson," Review of International Affairs (Belgrade), XIII, No. 298 (September 1, 1962), 32.

pose of easing international tension, reaching some kind of compromise and arriving at certain agreements, subject to the principle that such compromises and agreements must not damage the fundamental interests of the people. However, world peace can never be achieved by negotiations alone, and in no circumstances must we pin our hopes on imperialism and divorce ourselves from the struggles of the masses. Those who attack the Communist Party of China misrepresent this correct viewpoint of ours as showing lack of faith in the possibility of averting a world war.... They want the people of the world to believe in the "sensibleness," the "assurances," and the "good intentions" of imperialism and to place their hopes for world peace on "mutual conciliation," "mutual concessions," "mutual accommodation," and "sensible compromises" with imperialism. To beg imperialism for peace, these persons do not scruple to impair the fundamental interests of the people of various countries, throw overboard the revolutionary principles, and even demand that others also sacrifice the revolutionary principles. [42]

The Chinese accused the Soviet leadership of making a "fetish" of nuclear weapons, because Soviet statements had emphasized the revolutionary impact of the new weapons in qualitatively changing the nature of war. Peking once more denied that nuclear weapons had influenced the designs of the imperialists to any significant degree, and they accused Moscow of "prettifying" the nature of imperialism.

A fortnight later, Khrushchev, in his speech at the Sixth Congress of the Socialist Unity Party of [East] Germany, dwelt on the horrors of nuclear war. He warned that "the effects of a nuclear war would continue to tell through the life time of many generations, causing disease, death, and hideous deformities." As for the consequences of such a war,

There can be no doubt that a world nuclear war, if the imperialist maniacs were to start it, would inevitably result in the downfall of the capitalist system, a system breeding wars. But would the socialist countries and the cause of socialism all over the world benefit from a world nuclear

42. "The Differences Between Comrade Togliatti and Us," editorial in Jen-min jih-pao, December 31, 1962; English translation in Peking Review, VI, No. 1 (January 3, 1963), 11.

disaster? Only people who deliberately shut their eyes to the facts can think that. As for Marxist-Leninists, they cannot propose to establish a Communist civilization on the ruins of the centers of world culture, on land laid waste and contaminated by nuclear fallout. And this quite apart from the fact that for many peoples the question of socialism would no longer arise at all, because they would have disappeared bodily from the face of the earth. . . . [43]

Khrushchev went on to contrast the allegedly irresponsible, warlike stand of the Chinese with the soundness of the Soviet position on disarmament:

The Soviet Union, which has rockets and nuclear arms, is well aware of the potentialities of these weapons. We have made them to defend our country and the other socialist countries. We therefore take a responsible attitude toward the problems of war and peace. We do not want war, but neither are we afraid of it. Should war be forced on us, we shall be able to repel the aggressors in no uncertain fashion, and the aggressors know it.

To use a familiar phrase, blessed is he who talks about war without knowing what he is talking about. The Albanian [read: Chinese] leaders talk a lot about rocket and nuclear war, but nobody is worried by their talk. Everybody knows that they have nothing to their name but idle talk, that they command no practical potentialities. (Animation.) As you see, our positions and our responsibilities in these matters are different. . . . [44]

The Chinese denied that their stand was "warlike." Their counter-attack identified Khrushchev with earlier traitors to the cause.

That old-line opportunist Kautsky held that "war is a product of the arms drive," and that "if there is a will to reach agreement on disarmament," it will "eliminate one of the most serious causes of war." (Kautsky, The National State, the Imperialist State, and the League of States.) Lenin sharply criticized these anti-Marxist views of Kautsky and other old-line opportunists who examined the causes of war

43. Pravda, January 17, 1963; English translation in Dallin et al., op. cit., pp. 754-55.
44. Ibid., p. 755.

without reference to the social system and the system of exploitation. . . .

Being incapable of explaining the question of war and peace from the historical and class angle, the modern revisionists always talk about peace and about war in general terms without making any distinction between just and unjust wars. Some people are trying to persuade others that the people's liberation would be "incomparably easier" after general and complete disarmament, when the oppressors would have no weapons in their hands. In our opinion this is nonsensical and totally unrealistic and is putting the cart before the horse. [45]

Once more, in its letter to the Chinese Party, on March 30, 1963, the CPSU Central Committee refuted the accusation that Soviet policies had betrayed the international revolutionary movement. While the polemics showed the two positions to be increasingly irreconcilable, the door remained open for a bilateral Sino-Soviet discussion of differences. Prior to the scheduled meeting (postponed until July 5), the Chinese Party on June 14 restated its outlook in its famous "25 Points." Only the total victory of Communism, it hammered home, could abolish arms and banish the threat of war. It continued:

However, certain persons now actually hold that it is possible to bring about "a world without weapons, without armed forces and without wars" through "general and complete disarmament" while the system of imperialism and of the exploitation of man by man still exists. This is sheer illusion.

An elementary knowledge of Marxism-Leninism tells us that the armed forces are the principal part of the state machine and that a so-called world without weapons and without armed forces can only be a world without states.

Lenin said: "Only after the proletariat has disarmed the bourgeoisie will it be able, without betraying its world historical mission, to throw all armaments on the scrap heap; and the proletariat will undoubtedly do this, but only when this condition has been fulfilled, certainly not before" (Lenin, "The War Program of the Proletarian Revolution," Selected

---

45. "More on the Differences Between Comrade Togliatti and Us," by the Editorial Department of Hungch'i, No. 3/4 (March 4), 1963; English translation in Peking Review, VI, No. 10/11 (March 15, 1963), 25.

Works [Moscow: Foreign Languages Publishing House, 1952], I, Part II, 574).

What are the facts in the world today? Is there a shadow of evidence that the imperialist countries headed by the United States are ready to carry out general and complete disarmament? Are they not each and all engaged in general and complete arms expansion?

If one regards general and complete disarmament as the fundamental road to world peace, spreads the illusion that imperialism will automatically lay down its arms, and tries to liquidate the revolutionary struggles of the oppressed peoples and nations on the pretext of disarmament, then this is deliberately to deceive the people of the world and help the imperialists in their policies of aggression and war. . . .

In recent years, certain persons have been spreading the argument that a single spark from a war of national liberation or from a revolutionary people's war will lead to a world conflagration destroying the whole of mankind. What are the facts? Contrary to what these persons say, the wars of national liberation and the revolutionary people's wars that have occurred since World War II have not led to world war. The victory of these revolutionary wars has directly weakened the forces of imperialism and greatly strengthened the forces which prevent the imperialists from launching a world war and which defend world peace. [46]

V.   The Test Ban and After

On July 15, 1963, negotiations for a test-ban treaty with the United States and the United Kingdom reopened in Moscow, precipitating an inevitable "recess" in the Sino-Soviet talks. On the eve of the negotiations the Central Committee of the CPSU published an unprecedented "Open Letter" to all CPSU Party organizations and all Party members, in effect answering the Chinese pronouncement of June 14. In this extensive indictment Moscow emphasized Peking's alleged willingness to court thermonuclear war. Moscow was now prepared to recognize

---

46. "A Proposal Concerning the General Line of the International Communist Movement: The Letter of the Central Committee of the Communist Party of China in Reply to the Letter of the Central Committee of the Communist Party of the Soviet Union of March 30, 1963," June 14, 1963; English translation in Peking Review, VI, No. 30 (July 26, 1963), 18.

explicitly that "the atomic bomb does not adhere to the class principle—it destroys everybody within the range of its devastating force." A long passage in the letter describing the impact of nuclear weapons on the nature of war, questioned the ability of the Chinese to make authoritative statements on nuclear weapons. It asserted:

> Clearly those people who call thermonuclear weapons a "paper tiger" are not fully aware of the destructive force of these weapons.
>
> We take this soberly into account. We ourselves make thermonuclear weapons and have manufactured a sufficient quantity of them. We are well aware of their destructive force. [47]

Accusing the CPC (Communist Party of China) leadership of "ignoring the struggle for disarmament," the CPSU reasserted: "We sincerely want disarmament." Now Moscow suggested that the Chinese evidently believed it was in their interest to keep international tension at a high level.

When the test-ban treaty was concluded, Peking promptly launched a major attack on Soviet policy. Numerous Chinese articles condemned the treaty, charging that it was "the result of open capitulation by the Soviet leaders to U.S. imperialism." The Soviet government, they claimed, had accepted a "reproduction" of a British-American draft treaty that the Soviet delegate in Geneva had rejected in August, 1962. According to Peking, Khrushchev had reversed his former "correct line" on three major aspects of disarmament: he had now accepted a partial test-ban agreement, had divorced the test ban from further commitments to general and complete disarmament, and had yielded on the issue of international controls. The test-ban treaty, the Chinese argued, creates only an "illusion of peace," provides a screen behind which the U.S. can manufacture, develop, and proliferate nuclear weapons so as to gain nuclear superiority, and legalizes underground tests, which favor the development of tactical weapons by the United States. The Soviet leaders had, in capitulating to the demands of the imperialists, sold out the true interests of the people of the world. The "Statement of the Chinese Government," on July 31, 1963, made

---

47. Pravda, July 14, 1963; English translation in The Current Digest of the Soviet Press, XV, No. 28 (August 7, 1963), 20; and in New Times, No. 29 (July 24), 1963, pp. 32-56.

clear its refusal to sign the treaty and called instead for a meeting of all nations of the world to discuss Chinese proposals for the complete prohibition of nuclear weapons and the prompt establishment of a series of nuclear-free zones as first steps toward truly general and complete disarmament. As Moscow sarcastically replied, "Fine standard-bearers they turn out to be, with their policy of obstructing even the first step toward a complete ban on nuclear weapons!" [48]

The Soviet government, in a statement on August 3, insisted that the test-ban treaty serves the vital interests of humanity and that "a real step has been taken and a good beginning made in solving international problems in the spirit of the principles of peaceful coexistence." [49]

Moscow argued there had been no "capitulation." The test-ban treaty did not unilaterally disarm the Soviet Union, which was after all free to manufacture and stockpile arms, and even to use nuclear weapons if hostile action required it. One must always be prepared to negotiate and settle for the possible:

> It is clear to every sober-minded politician or diplomat that the desire of each party in negotiations with other parties is to achieve the maximum. We fought for this maximum, i.e., for a ban on all nuclear weapon tests, including underground tests. But at this stage it proved impossible. So under these conditions the Soviet Union agreed to a ban on nuclear testing in three environments. [50]

Peking in turn has made clear its view that the test-ban treaty was directed against China. In fact, it has alleged that the pact was the result of a plot between the Soviet Union and the imperialists to preserve a three-nation monopoly of nuclear weapons and to "contain" Communist China:

---

48. "Statement of the Soviet Government, August 21, 1963"; English translation in Supplement to New Times, No. 35 (September 4), 1963, p. 44; and in The Current Digest of the Soviet Press, XV, No. 34 (September 18, 1963), 13.

49. "Statement of the Soviet Government, August 3, 1963"; English translation in The Current Digest of the Soviet Press, XV, No. 31 (August 28, 1963), 4.

When, by the middle of September, more than ninety nations had signed the test-ban treaty, the Soviet leaders gloated that this represented a "world-wide referendum, which swept all the continents after the conclusion of the treaty, [and] demonstrated that the Chinese leaders, having come out against the banning of tests, suffered a serious moral and political defeat." Four other "socialist" states did not sign the treaty: North Korea, North Vietnam, Albania, and Cuba.

50. "Statement of the Soviet Government, August 21, 1963"; loc. cit., p. 10.

The Soviet leaders see only the U.S. imperialists. They believe that everything would be plain sailing if only the U.S. imperialists would give a nod and pat them on the shoulder. In their eyes, the other socialist countries and all other peace-loving countries are nothing. The Chairman of the Council of Ministers of the U.S.S.R., Nikita S. Khrushchev, has publicly stated: "If peaceful, friendly relations were established between the United States and the U.S.S.R., it is doubtful whether anyone could complicate the international situation, as he would have to reckon with the position of our two countries."... Now they have cooked up this treaty in Moscow with the United States and its partner, Britain; they want the more than 130 other countries to put their signatures to it. What is more, they have said that this is "a good start," which means that they intend to proceed along this path of U.S.-Soviet cooperation to dominate the world.

It is most obvious that the tripartite treaty is aimed at tying China's hands. The U.S. representative to the Moscow talks has said publicly that the United States, Britain, and the Soviet Union were able to arrive at an agreement because "we could work together to prevent China from getting a nuclear capability." Recently, while fraternizing with U.S. imperialism on the most intimate terms, the Soviet leaders and the Soviet press have been gnashing their teeth in their bitter hatred towards socialist China. In abusing China they use the same language as U.S. imperialism. This is a U.S.-Soviet alliance against China, pure and simple. [51]

The Soviet leaders charged that the Chinese stand on disarmament was prompted above all by China's desire to obtain nuclear weapons; they continued to dramatize the perils of nuclear proliferation and obliquely defended their determination not to share nuclear weapons with their allies. In turn, the Chinese leaders denied that the danger of war would increase if more socialist countries possessed the bomb. On the contrary, "the only effective way to avert the threat of a nuclear war is for more socialist and other peace-loving countries to possess nuclear self-defense capability." [52]

51. "This Is Betrayal of the Soviet People!" editorial in Jen-min jih-pao, August 3, 1963; English translation in Peking Review, VI, No. 32 (August 9, 1963), 11.

52. Liao Ch'eng-chih, "Thoroughly Expose the Reactionary Nature of the Tripartite Treaty," August 1, 1963; English translation in Peking Review, VI, No. 32 (August 9, 1963), 14.

Two months before the test-ban treaty was concluded, Liu Shao-ch'i issued a joint statement with Ho Chi Minh, who until then had carefully avoided taking sides in an unmistakable

With regard to preventing nuclear proliferation, the Chinese Government has always maintained that the arguments of the U.S. imperialists must not be echoed, but that a class analysis must be made. Whether or not nuclear weapons help peace depends on who possesses them. It is detrimental to peace if they are in the hands of imperialist countries; it helps peace if they are in the hands of socialist countries. It must not be said undiscriminatingly that the danger of nuclear war increases along with the increase in the number of nuclear powers. Nuclear weapons were first the monopoly of the United States. Later, the Soviet Union also came to possess them. Did the danger of nuclear war become greater or less when the number of nuclear powers increased from one to two? We say it became less, not greater.

Nuclear weapons in the possession of a socialist country are always a means of defense against nuclear blackmail and nuclear war. So long as the imperialists refuse to ban nuclear weapons, the greater the number of socialist countries possessing them, the better the guarantee of world peace. [53]

The Soviet reply implied hope for at least a tacit agreement against proliferation of nuclear weapons:

An increase in the number of socialist countries possessing nuclear weapons would immediately set off a chain reaction in the imperialist camp and the nuclear sarcoma would spread over the whole globe. This would immensely increase the menace of nuclear war. The authors of the Chinese statement hint that the Soviet Union could, if it

fashion. In contrast with the Soviet insistence that the forces of Communism were steadily gaining on those of its enemies, the Liu-Ho statement claimed that "the forces of socialism have surpassed those of imperialism." It went on to press, in somewhat guarded terms, the demand for nuclear sharing by the Soviet Union: "In the circumstances in which imperialism rejects disarmament and continues preparations for nuclear war, it is highly necessary to strengthen the national defense might of the countries in the Socialist camp, including the development of nuclear superiority of the socialist countries...." ("Liu Shao-ch'i and Ho Chi Minh Issue Joint Statement," May 16, 1963, New China News Agency.)

53. "Statement of the Spokesman of the Chinese Government, August 15, 1963"; English translation in Peking Review, VI, No. 33 (August 16, 1963), 12. See also "Statement of the Spokesman of the Chinese Government, September 1, 1963"; English translation in Peking Review, VI, No. 36 (September 6, 1963), 13; and Liu Shao-ch'i's speech at Pyongyang, September 19, 1963; English translation in Peking Review, VI, No. 39 (September 27, 1963), 12.

According to the Chinese Statement of August 15, 1963, Moscow had notified Peking on August 25, 1962, of the Soviet acceptance of the U.S. proposal of an agreement on nuclear non-proliferation. Peking claimed to have notified Moscow three times (on September 3, 1962, on October 20, 1962, and on June 6, 1963) that, while the Soviet Union was free to do what it wished, the Chinese People's Republic (CPR) hoped that the Soviet Union would not violate Chinese sovereignty by assuming on its behalf an obligation to refrain from the manufacture of nuclear weapons.

so wished, give China nuclear weapons and at the same time oppose the United States giving nuclear weapons to West Germany. But such formulae have a foul smell, so to speak.

For, what would happen if the Soviet Union began supplying nuclear weapons to its allies and, at the same time, issuing one protest after another against the United States doing the same? What consequences would this have? The most deleterious. [54]

An important article in the CPSU's theoretical journal, Kommunist, summed up the Soviet case against the Chinese. According to it, disarmament must be achieved step by step; two important steps in this process are non-proliferation of nuclear weapons and the campaign to warn the people of the world of the extent of the "ruins" that a nuclear war would leave behind it. Here Moscow hinted that China would like to see the United States and the Soviet Union destroy each other:

Were the estimates on the death of 300 million Chinese perhaps only sensational talk? Can it be that what [Mao Tse-tung] meant was that a thermonuclear war would be a conflict between the U.S.S.R. and the United States only?...

Why is it precisely that normalization of relations between the two great nuclear powers—the U.S.S.R. and the United States—always arouses such a sharply negative reaction among the Chinese leaders? Are they really interested in bringing about a head-on clash between these two powers in the world arena? One is involuntarily prompted to the conclusion that the Chinese leaders, invariably opposing the many practical steps being taken by the socialist countries in the struggle for peaceful coexistence, are guided exclusively by benefits to China, as they understand them. Further evidence of this is their position on the question of disarmament, on the nuclear weapons test ban. . . . [55]

After the recognition of the fundamental nature of the Sino-Soviet rift, in the summer of 1963, with the test-ban

54. "Statement of the Soviet Government, September 21, 1963"; English translation in New Times, No. 39 (October 2), 1963, p. 37.

55. "Za general'nuiu liniiu mirovogo kommunisticheskogo dvizheniia, protiv levogo opportunizma, natsionalizma i avantiurizma," Kommunist, No. 14 (signed to press September 30), 1963, pp. 19-20.

treaty as a major catalyst, the public debate on disarmament subsided. In the following year Peking restated its views in a sequence of lengthy pronouncements "by the Editorial Departments of Jen-min jih-pao and Hungch'i." Moscow's major reformulation came in Mikhail Suslov's report to the CPSU Central Committee on February 14, 1964 (not published until April 3, 1964).[56]

Suslov reviewed at length the Chinese arguments and vigorously rebuffed once again the charge that the CPSU had abandoned revolution for the sake of peace:

> For Marxist-Leninists there neither is nor can be the dilemma: "either the struggle for peace, or the revolutionary struggle." They are interrelated and are, in the final analysis, spearheaded against imperialism. The struggle for peace is one of the main forms of the struggle of the peoples against imperialism, against the new wars being prepared by it, against the aggressive acts of the imperialists in the colonial countries, against the military bases of the imperialists on the territory of other countries, against the arms race, and so on. [57]

Suslov reiterated the counter-charges that "the CPC leaders even contend that war is an acceptable and, in fact, the only means of settling the contradictions between capitalism and socialism," and that the Chinese were callous to the sacrifices which a world war would require:

> When in a conversation with Tao Chu, member of the CC CPC [Central Committee of the Communist Party of China], a Czechoslovak journalist remarked that in the event of a thermonuclear war the whole of Czechoslovakia, with a population of fourteen million, might be destroyed, the answer he received was: "In the event of a war of annihilation the small countries in the Socialist camp will have to subordinate their interests to the common interests of the camp as a whole." Another high-ranking CPR [Chinese People's Republic] official told Soviet representatives that Comrade Togliatti, General Secretary of the Italian Commu-

56. Pravda, April 3, 1964; English translation in Supplement to New Times, No. 15 (April 15), 1964; and in The Current Digest of the Soviet Press, Vol. XVI, No. 13 (April 22, 1964). See also "Za splochennost' mezhdunarodnogo kommunisticheskogo dvizheniia na printsipakh marksizma-leninizma," Kommunist, No. 5 (March), 1964, pp. 13-52.
57. English translation in Supplement to New Times, No. 15 (April 15), 1964, p. 52.

nist Party, was wrong when, expressing anxiety for the fate of his people, he said that the whole of Italy would be destroyed in a thermonuclear war. "Other people will remain," declared this official, "and imperialism will be wiped out. . . ." [58]

It had of course not escaped Suslov's attention that since the summer of 1963, Chinese tactics had become more circumspect and "reasonable," especially in dealing with non-Communist states. Moscow hardly missed any opportunity to disparage the Chinese "peace offensive" and its new diplomatic endeavors, highlighted by Premier Chou En-lai's travels in Asia and Africa.

Yesterday [Suslov proceeded] they abused peaceful coexistence; today they are posing as practically its only and most zealous supporters. Yesterday they declared that disarmament was a deception of the peoples; today they sign statements in which they undertake to work for disarmament.

This volte-face could only be welcomed if there had been evidence that the CPC leadership really perceives its mistakes and is taking a correct stand. Unfortunately, all the evidence indicates that the aims and objectives of the Chinese leaders have not changed. Their "love of peace" is nothing but an ostentatious screen masking their real intentions, which have received a rebuff and have been censured by world public opinion.

The true Chinese attitude, he continued, is revealed in the fact that

. . . they are out to put their hands on nuclear weapons at all costs. Highly indicative in this respect is the interview given to Japanese journalists in October, 1963, by Chen Yi, member of the Politbureau of the CC CPC and Deputy Premier of the CPR. Referring to China's intention to create her own nuclear weapon, whatever the price, he declared, as was reported in the Japanese press, that possibly it would take

58. Ibid., pp. 47-48. The French Communist official responsible for relations with other Communist Parties, Raymond Guyot, was later to question Peking's belief in its own assertions of "men over weapons": "What Mao Tse-tung said about the atom bomb during a meeting with the Gaullist MP's visiting China echoes de Gaulle's own claims: 'I know, you are ahead of us, but we shall have our own bomb. This is the way to be strong.'" (Raymond Guyot, "Report to the Central Committee of the French Communist Party, March 25-26, 1964"; English translation in Information Bulletin No. 9, Supplement to World Marxist Review, VII, No. 4, April, 1964, 78.)

China several years and perhaps even longer to begin mass production of bombs. But China, he said, would produce the most modern weapon, even if it would cost them their last shirt. And several days later a statement by a Chinese Government spokesman, published in Jen-min jih-pao, said that China would adhere to this line "even if it takes the Chinese people more than a hundred years to create the atomic bomb. . . ."

It thus turns out that possession of the atomic bomb, which the Chinese leaders call a "paper tiger," is their cherished goal. [59]

Suslov could thus conclude that the "discrepancy between the words and deeds" of the Chinese leaders invalidated their attacks on Soviet policy and once again vindicated the Soviet position that "peace helps to strengthen socialism." [60]

Thus, while the Soviet leadership attempted to demonstrate that its "peace policy" was radical, the Chinese sought to prove that its radical posture was peaceful.

Peking's sensitivity to the image of China's bellicosity in the outside world is mirrored in the following interview which Chou En-lai granted a French journalist during his travels in Africa.

59. Supplement to New Times, loc. cit., pp. 50-51. Suslov's reference to China's novel professions of support for disarmament relates to the series of communiqués signed by Premier Chou En-lai during his trip through Africa, in late 1963 and early 1964. The usual formula was similar to that used in the Sino-Sudanese communiqué of January 30, 1964:
"Both parties expressed their readiness to fight together with all countries and peoples for the realization of general disarmament, the total prohibition of nuclear weapons and complete destruction of nuclear stockpiles. In this connection both parties made particular reference to the resolution of the Summit Conference of African States in declaring Africa a nuclear-free zone."
(English translation in Peking Review, VI, No. 6, February 7, 1964, 31.) Ghana went further, endorsing part of the Chinese "line" in agreeing to state:
"The two parties considered that a world conference of heads of governments would be beneficial if it could be convened for the purpose of signing an international convention of the prohibition of the development and use of all nuclear weapons and their stockpiles."
(Signed in Accra, January 16, 1964; English translation in Peking Review, VII, No. 4, January 24, 1964, 14.)
60. Supplement to New Times, loc. cit., p. 52. See also the attacks on Chinese "maneuvers" on the disarmament question, by V. A. Zorin, in Izvestia, June 30, 1964, and by Yuri Zhukov, in Pravda, June 21, 1964. Zhukov, an authoritative spokesman for the Soviet leadership, warned the CPR that China's "dangerous political game, aimed at undermining the very foundations of Sino-Soviet friendship," might jeopardize future military cooperation between the two states, and in effect served public notice that Peking could not drag Moscow into military adventures of its own choosing. Deputy Foreign Minister Zorin wrote that, in opposing Soviet disarmament proposals, "the Chinese leaders have actually found themselves in the company of the most aggressive imperialist circles that are hindering the entire process of easing international tensions and consolidating general peace."

QUESTION: Is it true that in the event of a nuclear war China feels she is less vulnerable than any other country on the globe and that she would hope to emerge victorious from such a war which might destroy the rest of the world? ANSWER: This is fabrication, pure and simple. There is one Chinese out of every four persons in the world. If a nuclear war breaks out, China would lose more people than would other countries. The Chinese people, like the French people and the other peoples of the world, resolutely oppose nuclear war. It is with ulterior motives that the imperialists and certain other persons unscrupulously have distorted China's position and made widespread propaganda about it. The Chinese Government has consistently stood for the complete prohibition and thorough destruction of nuclear weapons and has proposed that a conference of heads of government of all countries be convened to discuss this problem. We are deeply convinced that so long as all peace-loving countries and peoples in the world unite and wage an unremitting struggle against the imperialist policies of aggression and war, nuclear weapons can be prohibited and nuclear war can be prevented. If imperialism should dare to defy world opinion by imposing a nuclear war on the people of the world, it will only destroy itself. [61]

The Chinese Communists compensated in part for this posture of "reasonableness" by giving greater publicity to statements from other Communist Parties that sided with the CPC against the CPSU. Thus Victor Wilcox, Secretary-General of the Communist Party of New Zealand, related in China how the previous September, Suslov had complained that the Chinese and their allies denied Moscow's argument that "the fight for peace is not just a tactical matter but one of the bases of strategy of the international Communist movement." Wilcox warned, in reply, that the imperialists see in this Soviet approach "a sign of weakness in our world movement." Since "the imperialist lions will never lie down with the socialist lambs . . . we must build bigger, stronger, fiercer lions ourselves." [62]

61. Chou En-lai, Interview with Bernard Tesselin, Editor-in-Chief of Agence France Presse, in Mogadishu, Somalia, February 3, 1964; English translation in Peking Review, VII, No. 7 (February 14, 1964), 16.

62. Speech by Victor G. Wilcox at the [Chinese Communist] Party School in Canton, February 18, 1964; reprinted in Peking Review, VII, No. 12 (March 20, 1964), 20.

Similarly, Peking publicized the fact that the Indonesian Communist Party Central Committee resolved, after debating the test-ban treaty, that "it would have been much better had there been no such treaty. Events have also proved that since the signing of the treaty the world peace movement has been paralyzed. The ceaseless underground nuclear tests of the United States meet with no opposition because they have the approval of the treaty." [63]

Perhaps the most radical formulation publicized by Peking came in an article reprinted from Hoc Tap, the theoretical journal of the Vietnamese Workers' Party (January, 1964):

Today the struggle for world peace helps to prevent a new world war. But this does not mean that it removes all dangers of war. The hotbed for wars of aggression of all types remains so long as imperialism exists. To rule out the possibility of war, revolutions must be carried out so as to eradicate the source of war—imperialism, first piecemeal and then completely. The social and national sources of war can be uprooted only when socialism triumphs throughout the world.

General disarmament is a concrete slogan to mobilize the world's people in the struggle to oppose the imperialist policy of the arms race, prevent war and safeguard world peace. With the world balance of forces now in favor of revolution as against counterrevolution, it is possible for the peoples to force the imperialists through struggles to agree to gradual disarmament. . . .

General disarmament can be realized and the source of war removed only when imperialism is wiped out by revolution. [64]

The lines have been essentially drawn for some time, and neither side appears to be prepared to yield or retract. Peking alleges that

. . . the heart and soul of the general line of peaceful

---

63. "Resolution of the Second Plenum of the Central Committee of the Indonesian Communist Party Approving the Political Report of D.N. Aidit," Harian Rakjat (Jakarta), January 15, 1964; English report in Peking Review, VII, No. 13 (March 27, 1964), 17.

64. English translation as "The Correct Way to Defend World Peace," in Peking Review, VII, No. 15 (April 10, 1964), 15.

coexistence pursued by the leaders of the CPSU is Soviet-U.S. collaboration for the domination of the world. [65]

Moscow meanwhile charges the Chinese with promoting

. . . international tension, which is regarded as a favorable atmosphere for implementing hegemonistic plans, masked in the slogan of "world revolution." If one follows the course that is being imposed from Peking concerning a world thermonuclear war that might be provoked, it seems that this is not a hindrance but, on the contrary, a good thing for the revolution. [66]

Thus continues the Sino-Soviet dispute, with thermonuclear war, peaceful coexistence, and disarmament among the major bones of contention.

65. "Peaceful Coexistence—Two Diametrically Opposed Policies: Comment on the Open Letter of the Central Committee of the CPSU," by the Editorial Departments of Jen-min jih-pao and Hungch'i; English translation in Peking Review, VI, No. 51 (December 20, 1963), 16.
66. "Marksizm-leninizm—osnova edinstva kommunisticheskogo dvizheniia," Kommunist, No. 15 (October), 1963, p. 14; English translation in The Current Digest of the Soviet Press, XV, No. 43 (November 26, 1963), 3.

ABBREVIATIONS

ABM	Anti-ballistic missile
ACDA	United States Arms Control and Disarmament Agency
AICBM	Anti-intercontinental ballistic missile
BBC	British Broadcasting Company
CC	Central Committee
CPC	Communist Party of China
CPR	Chinese People's Republic
CPSU	Communist Party of the Soviet Union
ENDC	Eighteen-Nation Disarmament Conference
GCD	General and complete disarmament
GNP	Gross national product
ICBM	Intercontinental ballistic missile
IMEMO	Institut mirovoi ekonomiki i mezhdunarodnykh otnoshenii (Institute of World Economy and International Relations), of the Academy of Sciences of the U.S.S.R.
IMO	Institut mezhdunarodnykh otnoshenii (Institute of International Relations), Moscow
IRBM	Intermediate-range ballistic missile
MLF	Multilateral nuclear force
MRBM	Medium-range ballistic missile
NATO	North Atlantic Treaty Organization
R&D	Research and development
SAC	United States Strategic Air Command
WFTU	World Federation of Trade Unions
WTO	Warsaw Treaty Organization

INDEX

279

Stevenson, Adlai E., 240
Stockholm Appeal, 118
Strachey, John, 171
Strausz-Hupé, Robert, 169
Suslov, Mikhail A., 210, 271–74

Taiwan, 94, 239
Talensky, General Nikolai, 102, 231
Tao Chu, 271
Teng Hsiao-p'ing, 251–52
Thorez, Maurice, 252
Tito, Josip, 58, 87, 171, 222, 244, 255, 261
Togliatti, Palmiro, 271–72
Truman Doctrine, 161
Tsarapkin, Semion K., 61
Tunkin, Grigori I., 227

U.S.S.R., Academy of Sciences, 61ff., 209; Armed Forces, 48, 82, 90, 97, 122, 136; Ministry of Defense, 61, 98; Ministry of Foreign Affairs, 63; Scientific Group for Disarmament, 61; Security Police, 201; State Committee on Questions of Disarmament, 62; State Secrets Act, 144; Supreme National Economic Council, 216; Supreme Soviet, 89, 241
United Kingdom, 66, 129
United Nations, 89, 112, 137ff., 140, 164, 221, 224, 240
United States, military doctrine and policy, 18ff., 25, 66, 95, 97, 131, 136ff., 147, 162, 167ff., 218, 220, 227, 230; Soviet image of, 41, 86, 89, 93, 102, 143, 166, 201, 207, 218, 233, 242

U.S.-U.S.S.R. relations, 12, 15, 65, 68, 94, 128ff., 133, 141, 150, 157, 159, 164, 167, 170 177, 180ff., 202, 232; strategic balance, 23, 32, 67, 86, 92ff., 101 (chart), 102ff., 118, 122ff., 127, 131, 162, 175, 181ff., 200ff., 214, 220, 226, 229, 232, 243
Universal Postal Union, 181
Usachev, I. G., 61, 208
Ustinov, Dmitri F., 216

Vietnam, 94, 134, 275
Voice of America, 120, 149, 167
Voronov, Gennadii I., 210

Warsaw Treaty Organization, Warsaw Pact, 85, 97, 102, 133ff., 141, 156, 208, 243
West Germany. See Germany
World Congress for General Disarmament and Peace, 224, 260
World Federation of Trade Unions, 247
World Peace Council, 256
World War II, 17, 66, 82, 83, 96, 118, 146, 244, 265

Yemen, 58
Yugoslavia, 8, 110

Zakharov, Marshal Matvei V., 217
Zanzibar, 58
Zhukov, Marshal Georgii K., 83, 87ff., 95, 127, 215ff., 273
Zorin, Valerian A., 208, 273